AF522362

Rural Development and Rural Employment

Rural Development and Rural Employment

Anand Roy

RANDOM PUBLICATIONS
NEW DELHI (INDIA)

Rural Development and Rural Employment

ISBN 978-93-5111-485-7

Published in 2015 in India by

RANDOM PUBLICATIONS

4376-A/4B, Gali Murari Lal, Ansari Road
New Delhi-110 002
Phone : +9111-43580356, 011-23289044, 011-43142548
e-mail: sales@randompublications.com,
info@randompublications.com, randomexports@gmail.com

Reprinted 2025

Type Setting by : Friends Media, Delhi-110089
Digitally Printed at : Replika Press Pvt. Ltd.

Preface

Rural areas are home and workplace to half the world's population, 75 per cent of the poor and a majority of the jobless and underemployed. Contexts are complex: modern, productive and high-return agriculture and industries coexist with widespread small-sized, traditional, survival-type rural activities. Some developing countries, mainly in Asia and in Latin America, have achieved rapid poverty reduction through increased agricultural productivity, improved local processing, storage, transportation, and access to global markets, as well as better-enabled human resources.

Rural policies need to be context-specific and integrated – reflecting local features and potential as well as addressing important deficits. They also need to be interconnected as regards investment, incentives, infrastructure, labour market institutions, skills, entrepreneurship, working conditions, social protection, labour rights and workers' and employers' representation, to defend local interests and guide national strategy and resources towards rural areas.

Today's sharp revaluation of rural development is linked to pressing concerns such as the poverty reduction drive of the Millennium Development Goals, food security, the environment and climate change, economic growth, youth employment, women's empowerment, the management of migration flows, and socio-economic stability, that push to unleash rural potential for sustainable growth, employment, wealth creation and resilience to crisis.

Rural development is a key research and policy issue in many industrialised countries. Central to this is the subject of rural employment. This book presents an international perspective on rural development and rural employment. It gives a timely review of an important subject that will interest a wide range of academics and policy makers in rural studies.

Author

Contents

1

Characteristics of Rural Labour Markets

The world faces the "urgent challenge" of creating 600 million productive jobs over the next decade in order to generate sustainable growth and maintain social cohesion, according to the annual report on global employment by the International Labour Organization (ILO). "After three years of continuous crisis conditions in global labour markets and against the prospect of a further deterioration of economic activity, there is a backlog of global unemployment of 200 million," says the report. Moreover, the report says more than 400 million new jobs will be needed over the next decade to absorb the estimated 40 million growth of the labour force each year.

The world faces the additional challenge of creating decent jobs for the estimated 900 million workers living with their families below the US$ 2 a day poverty line, mostly in developing countries. Despite strenuous government efforts, the jobs crisis continues unabated, with one in three workers worldwide – or an estimated 1.1 billion people – either unemployed or living in poverty. What is needed is that job creation in the real economy must become our number one priority.

The recovery that started in 2009 has been short-lived and that there are still 27 million more unemployed workers than at the start of the crisis. The fact that economies are not generating enough employment is reflected in the employment-to-population ratio (the proportion of the working-age population in employment), which suffered the largest decline on record between 2007 (61.2 per cent) and 2010 (60.2 per cent). At the same time, there are nearly 29 million fewer people in the labour force now than would be expected based on pre-crisis trends. If these discouraged workers1 were counted as unemployed, then global unemployment would swell from the current 197 million to 225 million, and the unemployment rate would rise from 6 per cent to 6.9 per cent.

The rural economy is mostly agriculture based and it is of tremendous importance because it has vital supply and demand links with the other Indian industries. Agriculture is the main stay of the rural economy, as it constitutes the backbone of rural India which inhabitants more than 70% of total population. Rural economy has been playing an important role towards the overall economic growth and social growth.

Today, the rural economy and its subsequent productivity growth is predicated to a large extent upon the development of the rural population. The rural section of population is primarily engaged with agriculture, directly or indirectly.

Contributions of Productive Rural Employment

Productive employment provides a pathway out of poverty. In rural areas, the challenge is great due to the many decent work deficits faced by rural workers. These include low pay, poor-quality jobs that are unrecognized and unprotected by law, widespread underemployment, the absence of rights at work, inadequate social protection, and the lack of a representative voice. Efficient labour markets can contribute to raising the quantity and quality of employment; nonetheless, improving the functioning of rural labour markets remains a major challenge. While badly neglected in many countries, new approaches have been developed in others that show that improvements are within grasp, if the political will is there.

Rural Poverty Reduction

The argument for developing and implementing strategies to reduce poverty by increasing productive employment opportunities in rural areas is compelling. About 75 per cent of the world's poor reside in rural areas and in most developing countries the likelihood of being poor and the severity of poverty are greater in rural than in urban areas.

Approximately 3.4 billion people, slightly under half of the world's population now live in rural areas. Some 97 per cent of the world's rural population live in developing countries. In most countries, poverty levels are higher in rural areas than in urban areas and in some cases the differences are considerable, most typically in the poorest countries. Because the extent and severity of poverty are greater in rural than in urban areas, providing opportunities for productive employment and decent work for rural workers is a major development challenge. From 1961 to 2000, the world's rural population increased by 1.2 billion and it will continue to grow for at least another decade. It is only as a portion of total population that gradual decline has begun.

Table 1: Rural population in figures and as a percentage of total population: World and regional estimates

	1991	*2007*	*2015*	*1991*	*2007*	*2015*
World	3,047 727	3,371 403	3,442 118	56.7	50.6	47.2
Developed economies and European Union	255 371	242 210	228 960	27.7	24.1	22.1
Central and South-Eastern Europe (non-EU) and CIS	133 618	135 128	132 413	36.6	35.9	34.8
East Asia	856 126	786 528	723 056	69.3	55.7	49.1
South-East Asia and the Pacific	308 117	317 247	309 280	67.9	54.7	48.6
South Asia	868 7,641	111 741	1,197 034	74.8	70.9	67.9
Latin America and the Caribbean	128 923	124 836	121 333	28.6	21.9	19.4
Middle East	54 732	67 456	74 123	40.4	35.0	32.9
Sub-Saharan Africa	361 575	492 266	557 648	71.3	64.1	60.3
Northern Africa	80 501	93 991	98 271	54.8	48.0	44.2

Source: ILO calculation based on United Nations Population Division: *World population prospects: The 2006 revision*, Population database, 2007

Africa and Asia, each with over 60 per cent of their populations in rural areas in 2007, are experiencing very rapid rates of urban growth due to natural increase, the influx of migrants from the countryside as well as the aggregation of population in small towns. Nonetheless, their rural populations are continuing to rise as well, most strongly in Africa.

Urbanization is part of a healthy economic development process, but its unguided shape and speed have often outpaced the capacity of policies, institutions and markets to cope. Urban poverty is increasing rapidly: by 2002 the urban share of the poor had increased to almost 25 per cent from around 19 per cent in 1993. Thus, there is a heightened challenge to design policies that address both rural stagnation and urban impoverishment, rather than to treat them in isolation. Investment, infrastructure and market and non-market institutions are needed to facilitate interaction between populations, businesses, services and economic sectors in rural and urban areas, to spread development along the continuum that links the remote farm to the megacity.

Rural areas tend to get short shrift in terms of investment in enterprise creation, infrastructure development, and the provision of basic services, such as health care and education. Public policy generally fails to correct this urban bias. Lack of access to capital, technology, markets or public goods and a strong reliance on the natural resource base restrict opportunities for diversified economic growth.

The OECD distinguishes five rural "worlds" that require different menus of policy responses. These are the world of large-scale commercial agricultural households and enterprises; the world of traditional landholders and enterprises, that are not internationally competitive; the world of subsistence agricultural households and micro-enterprises; the world of landless rural households and micro-enterprises and, finally, chronically poor rural households. Similarly, the World Bank suggests that there are three distinct groups of countries – the first, where the economy is based on agriculture; the second, transforming; the third, urbanized – and suggests that the agenda for sustainable growth and poverty reduction differs for each. The obvious implication of such typologies is that policies to address rural poverty and to increase employment opportunities in rural areas must be context specific if they are to have any chance of success. They also need to recognize the heterogeneous nature of the rural poor – those who live from the land (smallholder farmers, the landless, waged workers, cultural and ethnic minorities working on plantations, indigenous peoples, artisanal fisher folk, nomadic pastoralists) as well as members of female-headed households, the elderly and the disabled.

A broad body of evidence suggests that rapid poverty reduction in developing countries can be achieved through agricultural and rural development. This is because increased per capita agricultural output and value added tend to have a disproportionately positive impact on the incomes of the poorest, making agriculture and rural development key to pro-poor growth. Strong agricultural growth has been a feature of countries that have successfully reduced poverty, such as those parts of Asia where agricultural productivity improvements played an important role in combating poverty. In contrast, in much of Africa, per capita food production and yields have largely stagnated, slowing overall growth, impeding structural transformation and increasing hunger and poverty.

Attention has recently focused on the rural–urban continuum and its economic implications for rural areas. Agricultural growth is seen to benefit farm households directly by raising incomes and food security, but also to benefit both urban and rural households by promoting higher wages, lowering food prices, increasing the demand for consumer and intermediate goods and services, encouraging the development of agro-and rural-based businesses, raising the returns to labour and capital and improving the overall efficiency of markets. That, at least, is the theory. In reality, many countries are experiencing a widening gap between urban and rural livelihoods, with the positive effects mentioned above mainly felt in sub-urban perimeter areas and along main trunk roads. Often, however, increases in commodity prices fail to reach the very small producer, who faces rising costs for inputs, but receives an ever-shrinking portion of the market value of his or her crops.

In early stages of development, when the agricultural population is numerous and moving to other types of employment, the impact of increased farm incomes and wages on the rest of the economy can be particularly important: labour market transmission mechanisms raise wages in other sectors, while business opportunities improve through the impact of higher incomes on demand. Conversely, if increasing wealth fails to make its way back to the farm, and farm incomes fail to rise, a stagnating rural economy can hold back overall economic performance. Increasing total agricultural productivity through technical progress and investment is central to poverty reduction, but for this to happen, agricultural support services need to be tailored to serve the needs of small-scale farms that engage the bulk of the rural population and account for most food production in developing countries.

Productivity improvement can result from the introduction of labour-enhancing innovations which allow the same amount of agricultural labour to cultivate more land, or through the introduction of better seed varieties, improved soil fertility and irrigation that raise land productivity. Technical progress is not just a question of mechanization, but rather the application of good agricultural practice with a view to raising the productivity of land through the selection of crops and livestock suitable to the soil quality, terrain and weather conditions, the judicious choice of inputs, and the use of appropriate technology, tillage and crop rotation practices. In that sense, technical progress relies heavily on the skills and education of the agricultural workforce as well as on the availability of information, credit and markets. Technical progress in agriculture may be labour displacing or labour augmenting. Hence, the employment impact of various approaches to increasing productivity needs to be considered.

Distinguishing Features of Rural Labour Markets

Labour markets can be said to function well if they achieve two primary objectives concerning efficiency and fairness. In an efficient labour market, all workers willing to work at the going wage rates are likely to quickly find suitable jobs that match their skills, education and experience. Fairness is most typically measured in terms of whether a worker is paid according to the value of his or her work. A well-functioning labour market is also characterized by adequate protection of workers against the risk of income loss by enabling workers to quickly find a new job or through the provision of suitable social protection. According to all these criteria, rural labour markets tend to function poorly.

In fact, the term "labour market" suggests a unity that is absent in practice. Rather, there are multiple markets for labour, demarcated by industry, crop, occupation or geographical area. Rural economies are generally mixed, with the rural farming and non-farming populations earning their living from interdependent agricultural and non-agricultural activities and with employers competing with each other for available labour supply, especially during peak periods of the farming season.

Strong economic, social and political power imbalances between employers and workers tend to be more prevalent in rural society than in urban areas and can undermine the fair and effective functioning of rural labour markets. Often employers own and control not only agricultural land, but also other assets needed by workers, such as housing, access to water, access to forest resources, animals, convenience stores, credit, and, in some cases, schools and health-care facilities. Complex interlocking relationships that can involve wages, barter and other types of exchanges between employers and workers can reinforce workers' dependence. For instance, when workers can only obtain loans from their employer or can only hire oxen from the landlord they work for, negotiations on wage rates may be tied to outcomes in those other areas as well. Bonded or forced labour exchange often originates in the interlocking of the labour and credit markets whereby the labourer, who is in debt to the employer, has the obligation of working for the employer until the debt has been repaid. Such types of labour exchange constitute a denial of basic human rights.

Labour organization tends to be weak in rural areas, where traditional, even feudal labour relations persist, where rural workers enjoy lesser legal rights than other workers as well as in areas where seasonal and casual employment on small farms predominates. Labour organization is much stronger when farms are large, employment is more permanent, and labour relations more formalized, as in plantations.

Serious barriers to employment associated with factors such as gender, ethnicity, or caste can severely restrict labour mobility. Such discrimination contributes to labour market dysfunction. Improving the functioning of rural labour markets is essential to the success of policies intended to promote pro-poor growth. Labour is often the only asset of the poor, and it is through the labour market that the poor participate in economic activity.

Rural labour markets are largely markets for unskilled labour where supply comes from workers with little formal education or training. The prevalence of casual labour and child labour contributes to low productivity, low wages and weak bargaining capacity. Where small family farms predominate, much of the supply of labour is from small farmers and their families who need to supplement the income obtained from their own holdings by hiring out their labour. The supply of labour is largely determined by how they value the returns to labour on their own farms compared to the wages they could earn by working for others. Where labour is abundant and population pressure on land is high, there is often involuntary unemployment, with workers being unable to find employment at the going wage rate. The prevalence of child labour in agriculture perpetuates a cycle where household income for both farmers and waged workers is insufficient to meet their economic needs.

Agriculture is subject to risks of weather and price volatility that tend to reduce the overall demand for labour and to influence the contractual arrangements under which farm production is carried out. Major oscillations in labour demand and labour productivity throughout the agricultural cycle result in seasonal employment patterns, seasonal migration, intra-year wage variations, widespread underemployment and the dominance of casual over permanent employment. Waged agricultural workers typically find employment for only half the year and have little income to sustain them between seasons. The employment relationships in rural labour markets are often complex and difficult to regulate, especially where much labour is supplied through labour contractors, subcontractors and gang masters.

Rural migration has a strong seasonal component. People are "pulled" into other rural areas during agricultural peak times when demand for labour is strong, whereas during the low season farmers may become temporary migrants to urban areas to take advantage of job opportunities there, often in the informal economy. Seasonal migration can be welfare enhancing. For instance, a recent study in Viet Nam found that seasonal migration resulted in an annual increase of about 5 per cent of household expenditure, and a 3 percentage point decrease in the poverty headcount. Nonetheless, seasonal migration comes at a cost. Migrant workers in agriculture often experience discriminatory treatment on the job and face strong disadvantages in terms of pay, social protection, housing and medical care. When families migrate for agricultural work, it is often only the male head of household who appears on the employer's payroll, despite the involvement of the spouse and children in the actual work. When parents migrate alone, families are broken up for months at a time with children left in the care of others.

The structure of the agricultural production system strongly affects the amount of labour engaged on a farm or plantation and the conditions of employment and work. Outgrower schemes are one variant of contract farming, which has become a growing feature of agricultural commodity production. Typically, a large plantation company augments its own production by buying in agricultural commodities of a specified quality at a guaranteed price from local farmers, who in turn employ agricultural workers to carry out the production. Increasingly, the main company helps the farmers to set up and run outgrower associations, often with their own labour hiring departments which bring in seasonal and casual labour to work on the small-scale farms of their members.

The IUF, supported by the International Land Coalition, analysed the changing patterns of agricultural work in the Ugandan sugar industry, which was shifting from production based on large company-owned plantations to a system through which much cane was produced by outgrowers working under contract to the sugar company. The resulting report found the following social and labour outcomes: ongoing downsizing of the permanent waged workforce on plantations directly managed by the sugar company (i.e. the nucleus plantation); an increase in the number of waged workers on short-term contracts on the nucleus plantation; increased use of casual waged workers on nucleus plantations; increased hiring of casual waged workers by self-employed farmers, producing sugar under contract as "outgrowers" to the sugar plantation companies; outgrower associations acting as labour contractors, hiring casual waged labour to work on the farms of its members; and an overall increase in the casualization of employment. The combined effects of these changes for waged workers were growing job insecurity, lower rates of pay, poorer working conditions, increasing food insecurity and growing levels of poverty.

A competitive business environment need not lead to declining conditions of employment and work. The Kenya Flower Council, whose members include more than 50 floriculture companies that represent more than 70 per cent of Kenya's flower exports, has developed a code of practice, backed by regular audits, that includes social and environmental standards as well as statutory and international requirements. The basic social requirements include workers' health and safety (provision of a safe working environment, provision of personal protective equipment, working instructions and supervision); general worker welfare (work contracts, job descriptions, wages, housing, safe transportation, medical provision, annual leave, maternity leave, pro-rata leave and other terms and conditions of employment); and social accountability issues, including freedom of association and collective bargaining, child labour, gender and equity committees, mechanisms of harassment prevention, equal pay for equal work, and worker grievance handling procedures among others. The Council intends to broaden its membership to more small and medium flower growers, and from 2001 to 2004 provided training for smallholders.

Farmapine Ghana Limited (FGL), which is a pineapple marketing cooperative that processes and exports its members' produce, offers a contrasting example. It is owned by members of five farmers' cooperatives and two former pineapple producer–exporters. The arrangement is guided by formal contracts signed between FGL, the cooperatives and cooperative members. Farmapine outgrowers in the cooperatives make higher profits and face lower risks than outgrowers not affiliated with FGL. The arrangement has been successful in increasing farmers' income, generating employment, and stemming migration to the cities in search of jobs. In addition, the cooperative members have been active in their communities, funding the building of schools and providing other basic amenities.

The majority of cooperatives are found in rural areas where they are often a significant source of employment. Furthermore, cooperatives also maintain farmers' ability to be self-employed given that for many farmers the fact that they are members of a cooperative and derive income from the services, allows them to continue to farm and contribute to the rural community. Cooperatives of all types are found in the rural context: in agriculture (production, processing, marketing, purchasing and sales) but also in financial services, energy, housing, tourism and handicrafts.

Globalization and Rural Economy

Globalization has had a far-reaching impact on the structure of the world economy, creating uneven patterns of growth in a new economic landscape. The costs and benefits of globalization are not equitably distributed either between countries or within them. For some, abundant capital, high skills levels and technological excellence have led to unprecedented opportunities to benefit from the expansion of trade, the growth of foreign direct investment and the integration of financial markets. Some developing countries have become major exporters, achieving dynamic growth by looking outward for investment and for marketing opportunities. Yet for many countries, notably the 50 least developed countries (LDCs), exclusion from the benefits of globalization remains a stubborn reality. World poverty has declined in aggregate in the past two decades, but most of that change has been seen in a few dynamic Asian economies, whereas stagnation or even rising poverty rates are seen elsewhere. Nor is globalization neutral with respect to the income distribution within countries, as many countries are experiencing rising inequality. One of the major challenges for public policy is to create the conditions that will enable the poor, both in urban and rural areas, to benefit from globalization instead of being bypassed by it.

Today, for the first time in human history, the majority of the world's population lives in cities. In most developed countries, with close to 80 per cent of the population now living in towns and cities, the process of urbanization is largely complete. In much of the developing world, however, a massive population shift is taking place and many cities are struggling to cope with the influx of rural migrants. Urbanization progressed at an unprecedented pace in the period 2000–05, averaging 2.7 per cent per annum in developing countries generally, but over 4 per cent in the LDCs. Most of the growth in towns and cities is occurring in Asia and Africa. In 2005, 71 per cent of the world's rural population lived in Asia; by 2030 Asia is expected to rank first in terms of total urban population, and Africa second. The economic hardship of rural life, the lack of employment opportunities and the limited prospects of working one's way out of poverty are all major "push" factors driving the process of urbanization. Tens of millions of firstgeneration city dwellers live in urban and peri-urban slums, swelling the ranks of the informal economy. An additional 250 to 310 million people are expected to become urban dwellers by 2015. Clearly, the employment challenges of today's burgeoning cities cannot be met without addressing the need for full and productive employment in rural areas. Much of today's urban poverty is simply yesterday's rural poverty displaced.

Adoption of the Millennium Development Goals

The adoption of the MDGs as a global goal in 2000 marked an important turning point in UN attention to development and poverty reduction in a number of ways. It signalled unambiguously a new consensus around the multifaceted nature of poverty and the need for integrated responses. Poverty is not simply a question of income, but also of access to health care, education, potable water, improved sanitation, roads, markets and opportunities for productive employment. In all of these areas, data show that rural populations fare worse than the urban. Economic growth, while necessary, is now recognized as insufficient to reduce the gap between rich and poor, between men and women or between those in the cities and those in the countryside. Growth alone would not provide stable incomes for the poor, insure vulnerable households against livelihood risks, remove child labourers from workplaces, combat discrimination, or widen opportunities for voice and representation. Indeed, the phenomenon of jobless growth and widening income disparities in many countries has highlighted the need for pro-poor growth policies with employment at their centre. The eight MDGs and their 18 targets are seen as interrelated and mutually reinforcing in their contribution to social well-being. They represent a partnership between the developed countries and the developing countries "to create an environment, at the national and global levels alike, which is conducive to development and to the elimination of poverty".

The Decent Work Agenda, with its integrated approach to rights, employment, social protection and social dialogue, is increasingly recognized as offering a complement to and an enrichment of these goals. Indeed, the 2005 World Summit of the United Nations General Assembly confirmed the importance of the Decent Work Agenda for attainment of the MDGs. Its outcome statement declared: "We strongly support fair globalization and resolve to make the goals of full and productive employment and decent work for all, including women and young people, a central objective of our relevant national and international policies as well as our national development strategies, including poverty reduction strategies, as part of our efforts to achieve the Millennium Development Goals."In May 2006, the European Commission reiterated its commitment to promoting decent work for all, pledging to "harness its external policies, its development aid and its trade policy for this purpose".

The adoption of the MDGs placed poverty reduction at the heart of a common development agenda. With this common focus came renewed attention to the rural sector in general and to agriculture in particular. Historically, agriculture has been an engine of economic development, providing the food, feed, fibre and fuel with which to create more diversified products and services in other sectors. In many countries, agriculture continues to be the mainstay of rural livelihoods, a major contributor to GDP and an important source of export earnings. For the past four decades world food production has constantly outstripped population growth; rising agricultural productivity has lifted hundreds of millions out of poverty. The recent experience of countries in East and South-East Asia has demonstrated that rising labour productivity in agriculture along with the absorption of surplus rural labour in non-agricultural jobs in rural and urban areas can dramatically reduce rural poverty, and that strong and labour-intensive agricultural growth can be sustained. Such pro-poor growth contributes to food security, reduces food costs, and stimulates non-farm economic activity through its forward and backward linkages with the industrial and service sectors.

Agriculture cannot play this dynamic, wealth-creating role without an enabling policy environment, adequate institutions, and sufficient, well-targeted public and private investment. The experience of recent decades has been disappointing in this regard in a number of countries, particularly the LDCs, where investment has declined, rural poverty remains widespread and a very large share of the labour force is engaged in low-return agricultural work. Cuts in health and education budgets and in other public services, as well as the dismantling of publicly funded agricultural extension services during the structural adjustment processes of the 1980s and 1990s, undermined the foundation for bottom-up development for a generation. The effects are being felt today with a large number of poorly educated rural youth with few skills and poor job prospects and a smallholder agricultural sector that cannot thrive due to lack of support in terms of policy, infrastructure, inputs and investment. Clearly, to be successful, development of the rural sector must be part of a much larger process of social, economic and political development. Peace, good governance and political stability are among the prerequisites for job-rich, pro-poor sustainable growth to occur.

The MDGs incorporated the principle of environmental sustainability as an inherent aspect of poverty reduction. This principle is of particular importance to the rural poor, who through their work in agriculture, forestry and fishing, depend closely on the natural environment for their livelihoods and are highly vulnerable to environmental stress. In turn, research shows that poverty is associated with unsustainable practices and damage to the environment, so reducing poverty is important to improving the environment in poor countries. In addition, the early effects of climate change are already making themselves felt in terms of extreme weather events, increased incidence of droughts and floods, variability in rainfall patterns and degradation of marginal lands. Cereal production, which is particularly sensitive to changes in temperature and precipitation, could falter in areas where low-input, low-technology agriculture is practised, leading to increased hunger and poverty. The LDCs, sub-Saharan Africa, many poor island States and other food-insecure countries are particularly at risk from the effects of climate change. The question of environmental sustainability will necessarily underpin any in-depth discussion of rural employment and the changing nature of agriculture will be at the heart of this debate. Sustainable agriculture and rural development (SARD) seeks to balance the social, economic and environmental aspects of development while providing durable employment, sufficient income and decent living and working conditions for all those engaged in agricultural production.

The MDGs also called for greater coherence in national and international policies. Commitments made within the framework of the global partnership for development (MDG 8) focus on the need to create an environment that will enable poor countries to grow. This will require improved governance at both national and international levels as well as the active support of the international community to improve market access, provide debt relief and increase official development assistance (ODA) to the LDCs. The development of an "open, rule-based, predictable, non-discriminatory trading and financial system" and the comprehensive handling of the debt problems of developing countries are key targets that require concerted multilateral effort in order to create an environment conducive to development and the elimination of poverty. The Doha Development Round, initiated by the WTO in 2001, has yet to achieve the required consensus, with divergences on agriculture being the most difficult to bridge. While the international financial institutions have set in place mechanisms to enable heavily indebted poor countries (HIPC) to redirect the resources earmarked for debt service toward social expenditure, much remains to be done in terms of increasing resource flows from donors to match agreed targets and actual commitments in terms of ODA. Concurrently, the reform process being undertaken within the United Nations system aims at achieving greater policy coherence among UN agencies as well as a strengthened capacity to work together at national level to assist member States in their efforts to achieve the MDGs. UN agencies are being challenged to "Deliver as One" on the multisectoral development policies defined within national development frameworks.

Improving Rural Labour Markets

Rural labour markets tend not to function well because labour market governance and institutions are usually weak and have little capacity to directly address factors determining supply or demand for labour.

Where effective labour market institutions are absent, social and cultural factors tend to play a significant role in the functioning of rural labour markets. Family connections and informal networks provide information on jobseekers and job opportunities, and influence the allocation of certain types of work to certain categories of workers, as well as the terms and conditions of the labour contract. Cultural norms may prevent some types of workers from accessing certain jobs and may determine levels of hiring and wages according to social distinctions based on sex, age, caste, religion, nationality, ethnicity, among others.

To counter this, governments and the social partners can work together to improve rural labour market function in order to increase equity and reduce the incidence of poverty. However, labour market reforms and/or regulations tend, for a variety of reasons, to be controversial. In rural areas, a significant measure of this controversy may rest in the effect on power structures and, in particular, the politics of agrarian change and the threat to vested interests posed by reforms. To be successful, labour market reforms need to be coordinated with other public policies, such as those in the fields of education, agriculture or public works. However, the provision of public services in rural areas tends to be poor and policy coordination and coherence are usually a major challenge in such resource- and capacity-constrained environments.

Stimulating growth of farms and rural businesses is essential to enhance rural labour market performance and governments have a key role in creating an enabling environment for business and investment in rural areas. The basic requirements for rural growth are well known – investment, physical infrastructure, education and health services and institutions that support smallholder agriculture and small business development, notably by providing access to credit, markets and technical information and assistance. In many rural areas, agriculture is the chief driver of the economy and enterprises of all types and sizes provide agricultural inputs and purchase and process outputs, typically along value chains running from the farm gate through to the retailer's shelf. They are important for realizing the potential of agriculture. A supportive environment for agriculture would create a more level playing field by avoiding macro, trade and fiscal policies harmful to the sector and by redressing the serious under-investment in agriculture by both the public and private sectors. Adequate investment levels could encourage greater productivity, stimulate linkages with the wider economy and, through the resulting multiplier effects, induce improved social and labour outcomes in the rural sector.

Governments establish laws, regulations and policies which have a direct bearing on the supply and demand for rural labour. Labour codes provide the legislative framework governing the employment relationship, conditions of work, including minimum wages, and prohibitions on certain types of employment and employment practices. Although labour codes are ubiquitous, their implementation in rural areas is usually limited, given that the bulk of work is self-employed or hired under informal arrangements that lie beyond the reach of most governments. Policies on minimum wages and conditions of work and prohibitions on discrimination and on the use of child labour all tend to be underdeveloped or poorly implemented in rural areas.

Government regulations and programmes that garner tripartite support can reduce the discrimination that men and women migrant workers typically face and protect them from abusive hiring practices. For example, the UK Gangmasters (Licensing) Act 2004, aims to curb the exploitative activities of gangmasters supplying labour to the agricultural, horticultural and shellfish industries by requiring them to register with the Gangmasters Licensing Authority.

In some countries, the social partners have worked together with government and the private sector to improve implementation of the law down the supply chain. For example, the Ghana Employers' Association and five commercial oil palm and rubber plantations in western Ghana have developed a code of conduct on the elimination of child labour. The code of conduct enables the plantation companies to establish principles for responsible farming and labour practices among contractors, subcontractors, smallholders, outgrowers and agents in relation to child labour. The Association and the companies have developed voluntary inspection teams made up of representatives from: the Ministry of Labour's Child Labour Unit, and Factory Inspectorate; the Association; oil palm and rubber companies; Ghana General Agricultural Workers Union; smallholder, outgrower and contractor associations; and ILO–IPEC.

In others, the focus has been on extending protection to agricultural workers previously excluded from coverage. In 1991, when the National Employment Fund was created in Argentina, agricultural workers found themselves excluded from unemployment insurance. In response to this situation, trade unions pushed for a registration scheme for agricultural workers, which led to the creation of RENATRE, the National Registry of Rural Workers and Employers. RENATRE registers rural workers and gives them access to social security benefits. The scheme covers all agricultural workers, whether local or migrants and whether engaged on a permanent, temporary or transitory basis. Employers are obliged to register their workers and to assist them in obtaining an employment record card from local registry offices within five days. Failure to do so results in penalty. Rural employers contribute 1.5 per cent of the worker's total monthly salary to the RENATRE fund. The employment record card serves as proof of employment and entitles rural workers to unemployment insurance, family allowance payments, access to health insurance and from age 65 onwards to a pension. Over a recent five-year period, RENATRE registered 400,000 workers, including migrant workers from Bolivia, Chile, Paraguay and Uruguay who account for approximately per cent of those registered. RENATRE is instituted under public law, but its board of directors is independent of government. The board is composed of four directors from the Argentine Union of Rural Workers and Stevedores (UATRE) and four directors from the Agricultural Inter-cooperative Confederation Limited Cooperative (CONINAGRO), the Argentine Agrarian Federation (FAA), the Argentine Rural Confederation (CRA), and the Argentine Rural Society (SRA). Two auditors from the Department of Labour are also included.

Governments and the social partners have also sought to improve labour mobility, particularly the seasonal migration of casual labourers, by providing information on opportunities, ensuring that entitlements to state services are portable and by facilitating remittances. In the United Kingdom, for example, the Seasonal Agricultural Workers Scheme ensures that workers recruited abroad receive information on the type of work that awaits them, pay and deductions; hours of work, breaks and overtime; holiday pay, sick pay and bad weather pay entitlements; employment rights, including rights to written terms and pay details; the worker's rights and responsibilities under health and safety laws; minimum standards of accommodation; immigration status and the consequences of overstaying; and how and where to complain if something goes wrong. A bilateral agreement between the Governments of Kazakhstan and Kyrgyzstan sets out the legal framework through which migrant workers' rights are protected. Non-discrimination, the minimum age for recruitment set at 18 years, the prohibition of recruitment by unlicensed intermediaries and the provision of access to social insurance were among the key provisions. Collaboration between agricultural trade unions in the two countries led to improved information for potential migrants on their rights at work.

Among poor households, there may be limited capacity to take up employment opportunities in the modern sector, even through migration, due to inadequate opportunities for education and training and the high incidence of self-employment and informality. Nonetheless, there is a need to diversify household income sources. In such cases, government can intervene directly to provide employment with a degree of social protection, as is the case in

India under the National Rural Employment Guarantee Act, 2005. The Act provides a legal guarantee of 100 days of employment in every financial year to adult members of rural households willing to do unskilled manual work at the statutory minimum wage. Adult members of rural households register and are issued a job card, containing the details and photo of the enrolled adult. Employment is usually provided within a 5 km radius of the household, but if the distance is greater, additional wages are paid. If employment under the scheme is not provided within 15 days of receipt of the application, daily unemployment allowance is paid to the applicant. Central and state governments together cover the wage bill, unemployment insurance and administrative costs. The scheme has been operating since February 2006 in 200 districts, and aims to cover all 593 districts within five years.

Membership organizations, including employers' and workers' organizations, cooperatives, business, farmer and producer groups and other civil society organizations, can work with local government authorities to structure and strengthen rural labour markets. The number of associations and organizations representing rural farms and enterprises appears to be growing. Between 1992 and 2002, the percentage of villages in Senegal with producer organizations rose from 8 to 65 per cent, and in Burkina Faso from 21 to 91 per cent. Rural workers' unions are more often of a territorial than a subsectoral type and frequently include small producers alongside pure wageworkers. The social partners provide a certain structure to an otherwise fluid rural labour market and serve, inter alia, to carry out wage and other negotiations relative to labour issues. Governance reforms that ensure freedom of association and thereby enable workers, employers, farmers and other rural producers, to form representative organizations that can work for the interests of their members, are essential to tripartite efforts to improve rural labour market function.

Towards a Comprehensive Strategy to Promote Rural Employment

A major change in the response of the development community to poverty and inequality since the last ILC general discussion on rural employment promotion is the potential of the concept of decent work to shed new light on development issues, including issues of agricultural development and rural employment. The Decent Work Agenda provides a framework for shaping policies and actions to reduce poverty by generating more and better jobs. It calls for the integration of economic and social objectives and for a well-orchestrated combination of measures in the areas of employment promotion, rights at work, social protection and social dialogue. Addressing decent work deficits offers pathways out of poverty. The Global Employment Agenda (GEA), which addresses both the quantitative and qualitative aspects of employment, provides the analytical framework for promoting both productive employment and decent work in a mutually reinforcing manner. The pursuit of fundamental workers' rights is an ethical imperative that can also lead to more productive job matches and higher productivity. Social protection offers a degree of security to workers and their families, but can also improve labour market functioning. Social dialogue can contribute to durable solutions to problems and can also increase commitment and transparency, and speed adjustment to change. Decent work is thus a productive factor, and social policies based on decent work have a dynamic role to play in promoting a healthy economy and a just society. The relevance of the Decent Work Agenda for reducing poverty and social exclusion is now widely accepted.

Since the Millennium Summit, and particularly following the work of the World Commission on the Social Dimension of Globalization, wide consensus has emerged that full and productive employment and decent work for all are indispensable for economic growth, social cohesion and poverty eradication. The ILO, through its Decent Work Country Programmes (DWCPs), has already initiated the process of strategic prioritysetting on social and labour issues with its tripartite constituents at the national level. It can therefore bring to the inter-agency table a clear nationally agreed policy framework within which to carry out its mandate. The ILO can also offer a comprehensive body of international labour standards, internationally agreed policy instruments, such as the GEA, and practical tools, such as the *Toolkit for mainstreaming employment and decent work*, which can benefit both national and international development partners. Finally, the ILO brings a philosophy and working method imbued with the spirit and practice of tripartism and social dialogue, which is unique among international agencies.

The relevance of the GEA to the discussion of the promotion of rural employment for poverty reduction cannot be overstated. The insight that employment is the missing link between growth and poverty reduction and the recognition that sustainable poverty reduction requires simultaneously social policy transfers, investments in social and physical infrastructure and good labour market performance, constitute key policy orientations for any country to succeed in reducing poverty in rural areas. The GEA emphasizes the need to create the conditions for productive investment and enterprise development, to raise skill levels in the workforce and to promote technological change. Efforts need to be specifically targeted on agriculture and the rural economy, where most of the world's poor are found. The GEA considers decent work to be a productive factor which contributes to job creation, development and poverty reduction and emphasizes the role of trade and market access, and a sound and stable macroeconomic environment. Taken together, the ten core elements of the GEA aim to promote employment, economic development and social justice, by addressing the economic, social, environmental and labour market issues in an integrated way.

The GEA provides an agreed framework through which such strategies can be explored and developed. Globally, the GEA constitutes an "invitation to governments, the social partners, the multilateral system of the United Nations agencies, the Bretton Woods institutions and the regional development banks to review, rethink and reorient the policies of the past". Clearly, in today's integrated world economy, the challenge of reducing poverty by providing full, productive and freely chosen employment cannot be fully addressed at the national level alone.

Since the adoption of the Decent Work Agenda in 1999, the International Labour Conference has considered a range of social and labour issues not limited to, but of great relevance to, the rural sector. The Director-General's Reports *Reducing the decent work deficit: A global challenge* (2001) and *Working out of poverty* (2003) were of particular significance. A series of general discussions resulted in the adoption of conclusions in the areas of human resources training and development (2000), social security (2001); decent work and the informal economy (2002); migrant workers (2004); youth employment (2005); the role of the ILO in technical cooperation (2006) and the promotion of sustainable enterprises (2007). In terms of standard setting, the Conference adopted the Occupational Safety and Health in Agriculture Convention, 2001 (No. 184), and its accompanying Recommendation (No. 192), as well as the Promotion of Cooperatives Recommendation, 2002 (No. 193), the Human Resources Development

Recommendation, 2004 (No. 195), and the Employment Relationship Recommendation, 2006 (No. 198). In addition, the Office has convened three international tripartite sectoral meetings on agriculture (1994, 1996, 2000), the Bureau for Workers' Activities has organized two major international workers' symposia on decent work in agriculture (2003) and the role of trade unions in the global economy and the fight against poverty (2005) and both headquarters and field offices have collaborated on technical cooperation projects in the rural sector in many member States.

References

Hirschman, Albert O. (1958). *The Strategy of Economic Development*, Yale University Press, New Haven, Connecticut.

Perroux, Francois (1950), "Economic Space: Theory and Applications," *Quarterly Journal of Economics* 64: 89-104

Porter, Michael E. (2000). "Location, Competition, and Economic Development: Local Clusters in a Global Economy," *Economic Development Quarterly*, 14(1): 15-34.

Reardon, Thomas, Kostas G. Stamoulis and Prabhu Pingali (2007), "Rural Nonfarm Employment in Developing Countries in the Era of Globalization", *Agricultural Economics*.

World Bank (1997), *Rural Development: From Vision to Action*, ESD Studies and Monographs Series. Washington DC.

2

Trends in Rural Employment

The World of Work Report 2012: Better Jobs for a Better Economy published by the UN International Labour Organization (ILO) – says that around 50 million jobs are still missing compared to the situation that existed before the global economic crisis. It also warns that the global jobs crisis is likely to get worse due to several factors, including the fact that many governments, especially in advanced economies, have shifted their priority to a combination of fiscal austerity and tough labour market reforms. Such measures are having "devastating" consequences on labour markets in general and job creation in particular, ILO stated in a news release.

The narrow focus of many Eurozone countries on fiscal austerity is deepening the jobs crisis and could even lead to another recession in Europe. Countries that have chosen job-centred macroeconomic policies have achieved better economic and social outcomes. Many of them have also become more competitive and have weathered the crisis better than those that followed the austerity path. We can look carefully at the experience of those countries and draw lessons

Another factor leading to a worsening jobs crisis is that many jobseekers in advanced economies are demoralized and are losing skills, something which is affecting their chances of finding a new job. In addition, small companies have limited access to credit, which in turn is depressing investment and preventing employment creation.

In most advanced economies, many of the new jobs are precarious and there exists the possibility of increased social unrest in many parts of the world. According to the report's Social Unrest Index, 57 out of 106 countries with available information showed a risk of increased social unrest in 2011 compared to 2010. The regions with the largest increases are sub-Saharan Africa and the Middle East and North Africa.

If a job-friendly policy-mix of taxation and increased expenditure in public investment and social benefits is put in place, approximately two million jobs could be created over the next year in advanced economies.

Employment rates have only increased in six of the 36 advanced economies since 2007 – Austria, Germany, Israel, Luxembourg, Malta and Poland – and that youth unemployment rates have increased in about 80 per cent of advanced countries and two-thirds of developing countries.

Decent Work

Decent work is about opportunities for women and men to obtain productive employment in conditions of freedom, equity, security and human dignity. Decent work deficits are evident when labour is forced, rather than freely chosen, when opportunities for remunerative work are limited to certain groups at the expense of others, when social and labour conditions increase workers' exposure to risk rather than protect them from it, and when lack of productive work keeps workers and their families in a cycle of poverty and powerlessness.

Dysfunctional labour markets contribute to decent work deficits in rural areas. The Decent Work Agenda, with its focus on rights, employment, social protection and social dialogue, provides a framework for addressing these deficits through policies and programmes that integrate economic and social objectives. Because most poverty is found in rural areas, improving rural livelihoods and raising living standards by promoting the key attributes of decent work – most notably opportunities for productive, remunerative employment – would be a major contribution to worldwide efforts to halve poverty by 2015.

Trends in Employment

With a total of over 1 billion people employed in the sector, agriculture is the second greatest source of employment worldwide after services and occupies the greatest portion of the rural workforce. With over 700 million agricultural workers, Asia accounted for more than 70 per cent of the world total, and sub-Saharan Africa, with 192 million workers for almost 20 per cent. With 510 million and 276 million people engaged in agriculture respectively, China and India together represented almost 60 per cent of the world's total agricultural labour force.

Table 1: Total employment in agriculture ('000)

	1991	*2001*	*2007*	
World	1 036 584	1 086 886	1 036 330	
Developed economies&European Union	30 126	24 090	18 468	
Central and South-Eastern Europe&CIS	40 732	36 717	31 787	(3%)
East Asia	387 010	362 734	309 797	(30%)
South-East Asia and the Pacific	118 308	117 769	120 825	(12%)
South Asia	256 371	299 488	286 085	(28%)
Latin America and the Caribbean	45 321	42 734	46 383	(5%)
Middle East	7 697	10 502	11 282	(1%)
Sub-Saharan Africa	136 841	176 837	192 007	(19%)
North Africa	14 178	16 015	19 697	(2%)

Source: ILO: Global Employment Trends

Agriculture is the most important sector for female employment in many countries, and especially in Africa and Asia. It has been estimated that rural women produce more than half of the food grown worldwide. Women are typically more likely than men to work in the agricultural sector. In rural Africa women produce, process and store up to 80 per cent of foodstuffs while in South Asia and South-East Asia they produce and process 60 per cent of food production.

The share of agriculture in total employment is declining. In 1991, 45.2 per cent of total employment was in agriculture. By 2007, this share had fallen to 34.9 per cent, with women making up 41.3 per cent of the total. In all regions, the portion of agriculture in total employment declined during that period, sometimes sharply as in East Asia, South-East Asia and the Pacific and Central and Latin America and the Caribbean. This reflects the shift towards industry and services, growing urbanization and demographic changes in the rural labour force.

Despite agriculture's declining share in employment in all regions, the number of people working in the sector in 2007 was almost the same as in 1991. However, in North Africa, sub-Saharan Africa, the Middle East, Latin America and the Caribbean and South-East Asia and the Pacific the number of people employed in agriculture actually grew. In fact, East Asia was the only developing region which saw a decline in agricultural employment in the same period from 387 to 309 million. Since 2001, South Asia has also witnessed a small decline in total numbers. Two-thirds of the ministries of agriculture that responded to the Office questionnaire – most of which were in developing countries – expected the number of persons engaged in agriculture to remain stable or grow over the next ten years, with a strong majority expecting growth. The forestry and fishing sectors, which in many countries are also under the responsibility of ministries of agriculture, are both expected to require a growing workforce in the coming decade.

Table 2: Share of agricultural employment in total employment and female share of employment in agriculture

	Employment in agriculture (%)			*Female share of employment in agriculture*
	1991	2001	2007	2007
World	45.2	40.3	34.9	41.3
Developed economies and European Union	7.2	5.4	3.9	36.2
Central and South-Eastern Europe (non-EU) and CIS	26.6	24.0	19.5	44.0
East Asia	57.3	47.9	38.4	47.4
South-East Asia&the Pacific	60.2	48.3	43.9	41.4
South Asia	60.5	57.1	48.0	36.6
Latin America & Caribbean	27.5	19.9	19.1	22.7
Middle East	22.5	20.9	17.5	47.7
Sub-Saharan Africa	72.1	70.1	64.7	44.4
North Africa	37.5	32.9	32.8	23.9

The highest rates of employment in agriculture are found in sub-Saharan Africa (64.7 per cent), South Asia (48 per cent) and South-East Asia and the Pacific (43.9 per cent), which together with East Asia, account for some 60 per cent of the world's working-age population. Hence, the preponderance of employment in agriculture in total employment. In contrast, agriculture only accounted for 19.1 per cent of employment in Latin America and the Caribbean, 17.5 per cent in the Middle East and just 3.9 per cent in the developed economies and the European Union. Women's share of total agricultural employment varied from 47.7 per cent in the Middle East to

22.7 per cent in Latin America and the Caribbean. Nowhere did women constitute the majority of those working in the sector.

Historically, agriculture has been the largest employer of youth in sub-Saharan Africa. In 2005, young people accounted for an estimated 65 per cent of agricultural employment. However, low and precarious incomes and the lack of useful work experience are driving many to look for work in cities, despite the great disadvantages they face in urban labour markets. Ministries of labour that responded to the Office questionnaire cited better job opportunities in urban areas as the most frequent reason for rural–urban migration. Nonetheless, the number of unemployed youth in Africa grew by almost 30 per cent between 1995 and 2005, underscoring the need for labour market policies that provide young people with the skills they need to earn a living, whether in rural or urban areas.

The challenge of providing decent employment for young persons is immense. In developing countries as a group, the number of 15–24 year-olds is expected to rise by 10 per cent between now and 2050, but in the LDCs where poverty is most widespread and the vast majority of the population resides in rural areas, the number is expected to double. During the same period, as this age cohort advances through life, the overall working-age population comprised of 15–64 year-olds will rise from approximately 450 million today to 1.1 billion, or 65 per cent of the total population of the LDCs. In 2030, almost 60 per cent of them are expected to be in rural areas. Addressing the challenge of rural youth employment today will set the stage for decent work for generations to come.

Regional averages offer an overview of the general structure of the economy over wide areas, yet they conceal the great diversity in the nations comprised in the grouping. In sub-Saharan Africa, for example, in 2007 employment shares in agriculture ranged from 82 per cent in the United Republic of Tanzania to 10 per cent in Mauritius. In South-East Asia and the Pacific, 72 per cent of employment was in agriculture in Papua New Guinea compared to 0 per cent in Singapore. In Latin America and the Caribbean, Haiti and Puerto Rico represented the two ends of the spectrum with 51 and 2.1 per cent, respectively.

Globally, the male and female shares of employment in agriculture, compared to their employment rates in other sectors, are quite similar, with only a slightly higher portion of females working in agriculture (36.1 per cent) than males (34 per cent). In the Middle East and North Africa, the share of women working in agriculture rose between 1997 and 2007, the only regions showing such a trend. This trend was accompanied by an overall rise in waged employment for women in those two regions along with a drop in female own-account workers and contributing family workers, suggesting that women in those regions are engaging increasingly in paid employment in the sector.

In Latin America and the Caribbean, agricultural employment accounts for only 10.7 per cent of female employment, a far lower portion than the 24.7 per cent of male workers in the sector. In contrast, in the Middle East and South Asia employment in agriculture comprises a much greater portion of female employment than male (31 versus 12.5 per cent and 60.5 versus 42.9 per cent). In both East Asia and sub-Saharan Africa, female employment rates in agriculture are also higher than male although the difference between them is smaller (41 versus 36.3 per cent and 67.9 versus 62.4 per cent). It is noteworthy that the two regions with the highest shares of female employment in agriculture – sub-Saharan Africa and South Asia – are also the regions with the lowest shares of female waged and salaried workers, with 15.5 per cent in each region. Noteworthy too are the consistently higher shares of women workers, compared to men, classified as "contributing family workers". South Asia provides a particularly striking example of this.

Research on the micro level has shown that there is a strong correlation between the status category "unpaid contributing family members" and the share in agricultural employment: the higher the share in agricultural employment, the higher the share of "contributing family workers" in most countries. In other words, unpaid contributing family workers, who are usually women and children, are typically found in the agricultural sector, especially in developing countries.

This is true for both sexes but to a stronger extent for women than for men. Therefore, if a high share of women in a country work in agriculture, the likelihood of their being unpaid contributing family workers – and thereby being in extremely vulnerable employment situations – is very high. In the case of Pakistan (2005–06), for example, agriculture accounts for more than two-thirds of female employment and contributing family workers account for 57 per cent of all female employment. Cross tabulations show that more than 90 per cent of all female contributing family workers (across all sectors) are in agriculture.

Returns to Labour

Agriculture continues to provide the predominant source of employment in many regions, accounting for 63 per cent of rural household income in Africa, 62 per cent in Asia, 50 per cent in Europe and 56 per cent in Latin America. However, non-agricultural activities have come to provide a much larger share than in the past. For example in Kenya, smallholders derive approximately 40 per cent of their income from off-farm activities, of which 7 per cent comes from remittances, 12 per cent from commercial activities, and 21 per cent from salaries or wages. While non-farm income had contributed less than 50 per cent of household income in seven out of eight instances in the 1980s, by 2003–04 the portion of household income derived from non-farm activities surpassed that derived from agriculture in five out of eight instances, often by significant amounts. This was the case in both high potential and in marginal agricultural areas.

Income from farming increased at the very low annual rate of only 0.3 per cent, amounting to less than 4 per cent in total over the 13 years. The rise achieved was due largely to diversification away from rice farming towards the cultivation of other higher value crops, the value of which rose at a rate of 4.3 per cent annually, compensating to some extent for the fall in agricultural wages. In contrast, income from non-farm sources rose by 70 per cent during the period, from US$348 to US$591, an annual increase of 4.3 per cent. The share of non-farm income in the total household income thus increased from under 40 per cent in 1987 to over 51 per cent in 1999–2000. Two main factors account for this: the greater engagement in trade and business activities, which contributed 19.9 per cent of household income, up from 12.6 per cent; and the growth in remittances, which rose from 4.7 to 11.8 per cent of household income. Out-migration and declining birth rates contributed to smaller average household size and thus to the faster rise in per capita, compared to household, income as well.

During the same period in Bangladesh, the portion of households reporting agriculture as their primary occupation fell from just under 70 per cent to just under half. This did not represent the abandonment of agriculture, however, but rather a greater diversification of economic activity among household members. Indeed, the portion of households reporting some income from farming and other agricultural activities both rose to high levels, to 69.9 and 86.2 per cent respectively. Agricultural wage labour declined in importance both as a primary occupation and as a contributing source of household income.

India seems to have followed a similar pattern in the 1990s with increasing agricultural output, relatively little growth in farm jobs, but a much larger rise in earnings from non-farm activities. In the 16-year period from 1983 to 1999–2000, employment increased by 16 per cent in agriculture, but by 57 per cent in rural non-farm activities. Indian agricultural trade unions have reported large declines in opportunities for work, ranging from a 20 to 77 per cent drop in various regions of the country. The Bharatiya Khet Majdoor Union (BKMU) in Haryana stated that harvest work that had offered one month's employment in the mid-1990s had fallen to seven days by 2001 and the Andhra Pradesh Vyavasya Vruthidarula Union (APVVU) in Anantapur, Andhra Pradesh stated that availability of employment had dropped from 180 days per year to fewer than 90. The Working Peasant's Movement (WPM) in Tamil Nadu had seen work opportunities in irrigated areas fall from 240–270 days to 60–70 days per year within a ten-year period. Declining opportunities for waged employment were attributed to mechanization, changes in crop patterns and conversion of land to non-agricultural purposes. Also, small and medium farmers lacked the means to hire labour due to the increased costs they were facing for inputs, such as high yield seed varieties, inorganic fertilizers and pesticides. By 2002, casual workers had come to account for 80 per cent of male employment and 92 per cent of female employment in agriculture.

Declining opportunities for regular waged employment were reported by agricultural trade unions in a number of other countries as well. The majority of those that replied to the Office questionnaire stated that in the companies with whom they had collective bargaining agreements, the number of regularly employed women workers had declined over the past five years and more than 40 per cent said that the number of temporarily employed women workers had grown.

Wage work in agriculture is generally low paid. Most of the ministries of agriculture that responded to the Office questionnaire reported that the average wages in agriculture, fisheries and forestry – the principal occupations of rural people – were lower than the average wages for urban informal workers. Indeed, a number of countries exclude agricultural workers from minimum wage protection and others exclude specific types of workers or occupations frequently found in agriculture or in other rural activities, for example, casual workers, part-time workers, piece workers, seasonal workers, or tenant farmers who give part of their crop as rent to their landlord. Payment systems can exacerbate this situation. Many agricultural workers, particularly casual, temporary or seasonal workers, are paid at least in part on a piecework basis – i.e. per kilo of crop picked, row weeded, or hectare sprayed, rather than by the day, the week or the month. For example, on rubber plantations in India, 65 per cent of workers were paid on a piecework basis; on tea plantations the figure was 90 per cent. Men accounted for 57 per cent of those paid on a piecework basis on rubber plantations, where their earnings averaged 90 rupees per day; women accounted for the same percentage of pieceworkers on tea plantations, but their daily earnings averaged only 63 rupees. Indeed, gender pay gaps are the norm in many countries in agriculture.

Real earnings of waged agricultural workers can also be volatile. For example, a series of six wage surveys undertaken between 1958 and 2004 among Indian tea plantation workers found real earnings falling by as much as 31 per cent or rising by as much as 79 per cent between rounds. The World Bank has reported falling agricultural earnings in a number of Latin American countries, for example in Brazil, where temporary workers saw their income fall by 30 per cent between 1980 and 2004. Daily paid rates for fruit workers in Chile were reported to vary 50–60 per cent between peak and slack seasons.

Research carried out in Ghana found that the typical daily farm wage in 2000 was just US$0.71, and even the maximum daily farm wage of US$1.42 was below the daily earnings of a vegetable grower and less than half what a farmer of food crops would earn. Research in Mexico in 1996–98 showed that the median hourly wage for agricultural workers was US$0.41, slightly higher than artisans, but less than half the median earnings of traders. The average wage in non-agricultural employment was 56 per cent higher than that in agriculture. In Uganda, agriculture and fishery workers had the lowest median wage of all major occupational groups, averaging just 20 per cent of the earnings of a clerk. In India in 1999–2000, wage rates for male rural casual workers in non-farm activities were 50 per cent higher than for those in agriculture.

Trade unions in four Indian states reported wage rates for women of 50–60 per cent of those of male workers. In Andhra Pradesh, male agricultural labourers had largely abandoned agricultural wage work, going in for petty commodity production and non-farm employment instead. In some cases, this involved tied labour arrangements, whereby an indebted male worker withdrew from low-paid agricultural work and delegated debt repayment and household provisioning to women family members.

Agriculture can be an engine of economic growth and social progress, but the right policy mix must be in place for it to play that role. Empirical evidence has demonstrated that employment growth and productivity growth in agriculture can go hand in hand paving the way for a more balanced development process supported by a healthy agricultural sector. The experience of ILO member States in this regard is mixed, with some incurring declines in value added per person employed in agriculture while others have raised that figure over time.

Access to Land

Most people who work the land work on small farms. These are variously referred to as smallholdings, family farms, subsistence farms or resource-poor farms. There is no common definition of what a small farm is. The size of the landholding is often cited, but the scale varies tremendously from one country to another, and in any case, says nothing about the quality of the land, its productive use, or the natural, social, political or commercial environment in which it is found.

The World Bank's Rural Strategy has defined smallholders as those with a low asset base operating less than 2 hectares of cropland. On the basis of that figure, 85 per cent of the world's 525 million farms are smallholdings, and three-quarters of these are made up of less than 1 hectare of land. Asia accounts for 87 per cent of the world's small farms, with China alone accounting for half and India for 23 per cent. Farms of less than two hectares make up 95 per cent or more of all farms in Bangladesh, China and Viet Nam. Some 80 per cent of African farms are small-scale. Farms of less than 2 hectares make up 97 per cent of farms in the Democratic Republic of the Congo, 90 per cent in Egypt and 87 per cent in Ethiopia.

Sharp inequalities in the distribution of land remain a major source of extreme poverty. In Latin America, for example, the average farm size is 67 hectares, yet 58 per cent of Peruvian farms and 49 per cent of Mexican farms are smaller than 2 hectares. In Ecuador, smallholders make up 43 per cent of all farmers yet they cultivate only 2 per cent of the land. In Brazil,

20 per cent of farmers are smallholders, but together their share of cultivated land amounts to 1 per cent.

Land reform is inevitably controversial, as it alters not just the distribution of land, but also of economic and political power. It is therefore unlikely to be successful without the active support of the State in response to the demands of the landless poor. State-led land reform undertaken from 1945 onward – whether through the confiscation of large landholdings, progressive taxation of land or publicly subsidized land transfers – has generally resulted in the redistribution of a larger portion of total agricultural land to a higher percentage of households than the market-led reform programmes undertaken from the mid-1990s onward. The success of reform, however, relies on two key factors: the breadth of political support that reform commands, and substantial state support in the form of public investment, credit and technical assistance to enable the many newly endowed small farmers to use their land productively, access markets and to raise themselves from poverty.

In Africa and Asia, the trend is towards further subdivision and fragmentation of landholdings. In the Democratic Republic of the Congo, for example, average landholdings fell from 1.5 hectares in 1970 to 0.5 hectares in 1990 and almost two-thirds of households operated holdings of less than 0.5 hectares. The number of farms more than doubled during the period. This suggests that small-scale agriculture has come to play the role of safety net, providing a degree of food security, but forming only one part of family livelihood strategies which count increasingly on diversification of income sources to ensure well-being.

Indeed rural households tend to adopt livelihood strategies that respond to the particular blend of human, social, natural, physical and financial capital available to their members. The combination of asset endowments – whether in terms of family members' skills and education, the social networks to which they belong, the quality and quantity of land available to them and their access to other resources, such as water, social services, infrastructure, credit, or cash provided through remittances – and the degree of vulnerability to which households are exposed are key elements in the strategies they adopt. Households require a range of assets to achieve positive livelihood outcomes; no single category of assets on its own is sufficient to yield the many and varied outcomes that people seek. This is particularly true of poor households, whose access to any given category of assets tends to be limited. Cultural factors can strongly influence household livelihood strategies. For example, when rights of ownership, access, use or inheritance of land or other productive resources are defined or delimited on the basis of sex, female-headed households may be unable to convert their assets into positive livelihood outcomes.

Gaps between people's decent work aspirations and their daily reality are particularly pronounced in poor rural communities. Decent work deficits are seen in the fact that incomes are lower and more unevenly distributed than in the rest of the economy. Low-skill, low-pay, low-quality jobs make it hard for the working poor to work themselves out of poverty. High levels of informality, ineffective labour markets and lack of investment in rural enterprise and job creation contribute to widespread underemployment and offer young school leavers too few viable options for their future well-being. Such decent work gaps are interconnected with lack of social protection, lack of rights, and lack of voice.

Social Protection

There is much room for improvement in the labour and social protection currently provided to rural workers, whether in terms of their conditions of work or their vulnerability to livelihood risks. In agriculture, for example, conditions of work can be arduous. Much agricultural work is by its nature physically demanding, involving long periods of standing, stooping, bending, and carrying out repetitive movements in awkward body positions. The risk of accidents is increased by fatigue, poorly designed tools, difficult terrain, exposure to the elements and poor general health. Even when technological change has brought about a reduction in the physical drudgery of agricultural work, it has introduced new risks, notably associated with the use of machinery and the intensive use of chemicals without appropriate safety measures, information and training. Unsurprisingly, the level of accidents and illness is high, accounting for half of the global total. Yet, rural workers are among the least well protected in terms of access to basic health services, workers' compensation, long-term disability insurance and survivors' benefits. Poverty and dependency are the plight of those who grow too old to work, since pension schemes rarely cover the rural population in developing countries. Innovative thinking is required to extend coverage to those at risk of falling into poverty as well as to those prevented by poverty from participating fully in economic and social life.

Rights at Work

Fundamental principles and rights at work apply to all. They ensure freedom of association, the right to collective bargaining, the elimination of child labour, the abolition of forced labour and non-discrimination in the world of work. In the rural world, however, even fundamental rights are often denied. This is seen in the violence perpetrated against those who organize and represent the rural poor, in the high levels of child labour in agriculture, estimated at 70 per cent of the global total, in the perpetuation of bonded labour practices from one generation to the next, and in unequal treatment before the law.

Much rural work is currently ungoverned by national labour law. Absence of an employment contract results in exclusion from the protection of the labour code. Lack of minimum wage rates and competition for paid work under any conditions leave the rural working poor – poor. The multiple aspects of poverty that affect them – the lack of access to safe drinking water, sanitation, health services and basic education – not only raise important human rights issues, but also reduce the capacity of the rural poor to work their way out of poverty.

International labour standards provide policy guidance as to the type of legal framework that supports decent work. While economic forces tend to favour some to the detriment of others, social policy measures derived from international labour standards can help redress the balance by widening opportunities for productive employment, increasing access to public goods and services, providing fairer access to resources and promoting greater participation in decision-making.

Social Dialogue

It is through social dialogue that governments, employers and workers are able to voice their concerns, participate in decision-making and improve governance in the world of work. In rural areas, closing the representational gap is crucial to addressing the inadequate legal and social protection, lack of access to productive assets, and lack of public services from which they suffer. This may require innovative approaches to organization and representation in order to suit rural constituencies. New methods may be needed to increase economic capabilities and strengthen voice, to defend rights and to generate and transfer sufficient resources to provide social protection. Government policies can support or hinder collective representation and social dialogue, but the formation and unimpeded functioning of representative organizations are critical to the success of social dialogue. Workers' and employers' organizations have a role to play in defending the right of all workers and employers to organize and to join organizations of their own choosing so that institutions of social dialogue can address decent work deficits in rural areas.

Towards Decent Work in Rural Areas

In summary, agriculture continues to provide a major source of income for most rural households in developing countries, although in many instances, small-scale farming is only part of a diversified livelihood strategy, which combines on- and off- farm waged work, service activities and remittances. Earnings from agricultural wage labour are low and volatile and opportunities for regular employment appear to be in decline as workers are increasingly engaged on a casual or temporary basis. Decent work deficits in rural employment need to be addressed urgently as the rural population in developing countries will continue to grow, in absolute terms, for another generation.

References

European Commission, (2008).*Report on the EU contribution to the promotion of decent work in the world*, Staff working paper.

ILO, (2009).*Protecting people, promoting jobs: A survey of country employment and social protection policy responses to the global economic crisis*, Report to the G20 Leaders' Summit, Pittsburgh.

OECD DAC, (2009).*The Role of Employment and Social Protection: Making Economic Growth More Pro-Poor*, Policy Statement of High-Level DAC meeting.

Papola, T. S. (2007).*Employment in the development agenda: Economic and social policies,* International Institute for Labour Studies.

Rémi Bazillier, 'Core Labour Standards and Development: Impact on Long-Term Income', *World Development* 36(1), 17-38.

Stuart Bell and Steve Gibbons, (2007).*Decent Work: Implications for DFID and for the Labour Standards and Poverty Reduction Forum.*

3

Employment Generation through Sustainable Rural Growth

Evidence consistently shows that agricultural growth is highly effective in reducing poverty, not least because so many of the world's poor live in rural areas and in low-income countries, where agriculture typically constitutes both a large share of gross domestic product (GDP) and employment. Large numbers of poor people depend either directly or indirectly on agriculture for their livelihoods. Agricultural growth reduces poverty by raising incomes and employment and by reducing food prices. Historically, agricultural growth has been the precursor to industrial growth in Europe and, more recently, in parts of Asia. Agricultural growth runs in parallel with the structural transformation of economies that, somewhat paradoxically, is normally associated with a decline in the share of agriculture in GDP. However, the labour share in agriculture typically declines at a much slower rate than the share of agriculture in national GDP.

Agricultural growth has strong linkages to other economic sectors, most obviously to agro-processing and food marketing and to the demand for intermediate inputs and services. However, agricultural growth also has much broader linkages or multipliers and allows poor countries to diversify their economies to sectors where growth may be faster and where labour productivity and wages are typically higher. Where agricultural productivity has grown slowly, as in many parts of sub-Saharan Africa, non-farm activities have also tended to grow slowly and to offer low wages. Creating jobs and livelihoods outside agriculture is vital to both rural and urban areas and to poverty reduction generally. Thus, generating more and better jobs through growth in rural areas must involve policies targeted at both on-farm and off-farm employment.

There is no one-size-fits-all solution to the design and implementation of policies to promote rural employment, but generating more and better quality jobs in rural areas is predicated on economic growth. Even though the relationships between growth and job creation (employment intensity of growth) and growth and poverty reduction are complex and far from automatic, a high growth rate creates a more favourable environment to achieve employment and poverty reduction objectives, including in rural areas. By providing more resources overall, economic growth widens opportunities for decent work, makes economic choices and adjustment processes less painful and, especially in developing countries, enhances opportunities to facilitate the transition from the informal to the formal economy. However, economic growth is a necessary but not sufficient condition for promoting rural employment and poverty reduction. Although for many of the poorest countries, the fundamental issue is simply to achieve growth, it is important to remember that the pattern and distribution of growth will determine the degree to which it translates into job creation and poverty reduction.

There are many drivers of growth but the principal ones are capital investment, human capital development, expanding markets through trade and economic integration and good governance. An effective growth strategy requires policies in each of these areas. This calls for policy coordination and coherence across a range of institutions and areas. Particular attention needs to be paid to increasing productivity, improving domestic market integration, as well as access to foreign markets and promoting the diversification of income and employment opportunities in rural areas.

Sound and stable macroeconomic policy and good management of the economy is essential. Monetary, fiscal and exchange-rate policies should guarantee stable and predictable economic conditions. Sound economic management should balance the twin objectives of creating more and better jobs with combating inflation and providing for policies and regulations that stimulate long-term productive investment. Attention should also be given to increasing aggregate demand as a source of economic growth, contingent on national conditions.

Growth and poverty reduction are undermined when public expenditure management and taxation are weak and when the fiscal deficit and public debt are not well managed. Good fiscal policy can raise economic growth through well-chosen public investments. Growth itself increases the tax base generating the potential for higher public spending on, for example, rural development and poverty reduction. Poverty reduction in rural areas is predicated on an appropriate fiscal system which enables governments to improve equity, efficiency and social inclusion.

Growth in agriculture and in rural areas more generally depends on investments in essential public goods such as physical infrastructure like roads, ports and telecommunications, in agricultural research and extension and in public health and education. In most developing countries, public (and private) investment in rural areas is very low. In sub-Saharan Africa, for example, levels of agricultural spending are simply insufficient for sustained growth. In many countries – not just in Africa – inefficiency and inequitable subsidies crowd out investments in core public goods and services. Thus, underinvestment in agriculture is often further compounded by misinvestment, including provision of input subsidies and transfers that effectively serve to benefit richer farmers.

There are strong welfare arguments for helping those who stand to lose or are most vulnerable to structural change or shocks to their livelihoods. Public policies and funding may be required to overcome market failures, offset the fixed costs of providing public infrastructure and reduce risks. Thus, a reform agenda is required in many countries to promote more and better quality expenditure and investment in rural areas. This requires "improved budgetary processes aligned to well-articulated agricultural strategies. Greater public disclosure and transparency of budget allocation and impacts are needed to mobilize political support for budgetary reform".

National development strategies, including poverty reduction strategies and national employment frameworks, should embrace agriculture and the rural economy both in terms of developing policies to stimulate growth in rural communities and of assessing the impact of policies on rural areas. The challenge is to determine what policies to put in place to promote pro-poor growth in rural areas: growth that is sustainable, friendly to the environment, that increases living standards for the present and for future generations, and that is inclusive, shared equitably, with more social justice and solidarity. This is the type of growth embedded in the ILO's GEA.

Importance of Off-farm Income and Employment

While agriculture is a source of livelihood for an estimated 86 per cent of rural women and men and provides jobs for 1.3 billion smallholders and landless workers, agriculture alone cannot alleviate rural poverty. Rural off-farm employment is vital. In all rural communities, the promotion of sustainable off-farm enterprises is necessary to generate more and better jobs. There is a substantial body of research and evidence showing the importance of non-farm enterprises as engines of rural development and their role in income growth and poverty reduction. Increases in non-farm employment opportunities imply a potential reduction in the supply of agricultural labourers, thereby increasing wages. So, policy measures that encourage non-farm employment are likely to generate spillover benefits to rural labourers.

Diversifying into non-farm incomes can be an important survival mechanism for rural households, especially landless households that otherwise would have to rely on casual agricultural wage employment. However, the demand for rural wage labourers and wage rates are obviously affected by the seasonality of production, with the demand for labour highest at harvest. Environmental fluctuations also cause uncertainties in agricultural incomes. For example, in India, an analysis of 257 districts from 1956 to 1987 showed that wages are very sensitive to rainfall shocks. This will be compounded by climate change, which has increased the risks of unpredictable weather cycles.

In many developing economies, non-farm activities have traditionally constituted a relatively low-productivity supplementary activity that households undertake to diversify their income sources and insure themselves against shocks to their agricultural income. However, off-farm activities are increasingly important in many rural societies not just to complement or supplement on-farm activities but as sources of strong income and employment growth. This is especially true for rural regions that enjoy high levels of physical infrastructure and human capital. Indeed, rural non-farm enterprises are likely to perform better in more densely populated areas, where demand is higher and where there are economies of agglomeration, while they are likely to be constrained by low market demand in areas with low population densities, dispersed populations and in areas where liquidity is limited by high rates of poverty. Generally, rural non-farm employment is of growing importance to the livelihoods of rural households.

Evidence suggests that the development of rural small and medium enterprises is likely to be pro-poor, as they tend to be labour-intensive in nature, reducing unemployment, helping to smooth income seasonally and bidding up local wages. They tend to generate more employment per unit of capital than big firms and typically produce goods and services that are affordable to the poor, thereby increasing their access to goods and services which otherwise might not be available to them. However, it is retailing rather than manufacturing that typically constitutes by far the largest share of off-farm income-generating activities.

It is important to assess the impact of rural non-farm employment on poverty reduction and gender relations. For example, there is evidence to suggest that rural non- farm activities are more often undertaken by the better-off members of a rural community (studies have shown that wealthier households in rural areas have a higher share of income from non-farm activities). In most countries men appear to dominate non-agricultural employment and in some countries this leads to the "feminization of the agricultural workforce". Systemic competitiveness: The key to generating more and better jobs both on- and off-farm Making rural economies more competitive requires increasing agricultural and off-farm productivity and enhancing access to domestic and international markets. There are many dimensions to improving rural competitiveness including factors largely internal to the enterprise or farm activities and those more external or structural factors such as macroeconomic policies, trade policies and the investment climate. Obviously, the particular factors driving growth or constraining it will be context specific. Smallholders, for example, may lack access to key inputs and services and be constrained by weak human capacity and inappropriate technologies which limit their capacity to diversify production into higher-value products. Larger producers targeting export markets, for example, may find themselves competing in markets which are increasingly demanding in terms of quality and food safety and distorted by developed countries' agricultural subsidies or trade barriers.

In some poor countries there may well be growth potential for small producers in the food staples sector. This will have the effect of raising incomes and reducing food prices. However, even producers of traditional food staples are likely to have to compete against cheap food imports from abroad. In less poor countries, opportunities for growth in food staples are likely to be more limited and growth is more likely to be linked to demand for livestock feed or exports than to domestic consumption of staples. In this case, the emphasis is likely to be on diversifying rural economies to include more off-farm activities and to non-traditional high-value agriculture such as horticulture, which can be labour intensive and generate substantial employment. For example, from a low base, Ethiopia has emerged as a major exporter of cut flowers in recent years and in the process has created about 50,000 new jobs. Other countries, such as Ecuador, Colombia and Costa Rica, have also experienced rapid growth in the cut flowers export market. Growth potential may also exist in niche markets such as organic or ethically sourced products.

However, because of the particular nature and characteristics of rural labour markets, market forces alone are likely to lead to outcomes which are not pro-poor and which, in fact, disproportionately benefit larger and commercially oriented producers and those with good connections to markets and infrastructure. Hence, pro-poor growth in rural areas is likely to warrant active policies to ensure equitable outcomes in terms of decent work opportunities for all, including for disadvantaged or marginalized groups such as women or ethnic minorities. This will entail policies to support smallholders and to strengthen producer organizations so that farmers can achieve economies of scale in production and marketing and upgrade their technical capacities. Where commercial agriculture dominates, fair and efficient labour markets are fundamental to reducing rural poverty.

Improved labour productivity (through improving the skills of workers) and improved land productivity (through better irrigation, soil fertility and improved seed varieties) are key to pro-poor and pro-decent work agricultural growth. The relationship between labour and land productivity is critical and will vary depending on factors such as natural resource endowments, type of farming system, geographical location and levels of economic development. For example, smallholders typically exploit labour using technologies that increase yields and hence also increase land productivity and they may use labour-intensive rather than capital-intensive methods. Thus, in this case, land and capital productivity is likely to be higher but labour productivity lower than in larger production units. In contrast, some types of modern commercial farming place emphasis on capital-intensive production and on labour-saving technologies and thus, productivity improvements may not lead to significant employment growth, although they may lead to increased wages and better living conditions for the workers in such establishments.

Generally, in the early stages of growth, both land and labour productivity must rise in order to reduce poverty but land productivity must rise faster in order to create additional employment on farms that benefits the poor and, in turn, stimulates demand for non-farm goods and services. For innovation to benefit farmers, it must stimulate the demand for their produce by reducing food prices but it must also reduce the costs of production by a greater amount. In later stages of growth, as employment opportunities outside agriculture expand, labour is increasingly drawn away from agriculture and wage rates for agricultural work tend to rise. In order to maintain an affordable supply of food, it becomes more important to raise labour productivity, in the absence of which increasing food prices will jeopardize ongoing economic transformation.

Fostering systemic competitiveness in rural areas calls for public policies to ensure balanced and equitable development. Unless policies and investments are put in place to foster agricultural productivity, there is a danger that the decline of agriculture will be accompanied by increased rural poverty. At the same time, policies and programmes which increase the human capital of the rural poor and allow them to enter potentially more remunerative labour markets are powerful tools to facilitate diversification in rural areas and, where appropriate, to ensure a smooth transition of people out of agriculture without increasing poverty through unemployment or underemployment on the land.

Business Environment and Investment Climate

Good governance is essential to create the conditions for generating more and better jobs through growth in rural areas. Good governance provides the framework for a conducive policy environment. This includes strengthening the capacity of support institutions including ministries of agriculture, producer and worker organizations, enhanced research and extension services. A key vehicle for reforming the business environment and investment climate is through public–private dialogues (PPD) and through social dialogue between government and representative bodies of producers/employers and workers. Dialogue should give voice to groups which are often excluded or marginalized such as smallholders, rural women and agricultural labourers. Freedom of association, the right to collective bargaining, elimination of discrimination at the workplace, the right to information and freedom of the press are all essential preconditions for the effective engagement of all stakeholders.

Rural markets can be made to work better by addressing the external constraints faced by agricultural and rural enterprises, including cooperatives. The investment climate reflects the many location-specific factors that shape the opportunities and incentives for firms to invest productively, create jobs and expand.

A good investment climate is not just about generating profits for enterprises - if that were the goal, the focus could be limited to minimizing costs and risks - it is also about improving outcomes for society as a whole. This includes reducing the potential negative impacts of some types of investment projects, such as in the case of displacement of poor people or investments which entail environmental degradation. This implies that some social and environmental as well as economic costs and risks need to be borne by enterprises. Competition plays a key role in spurring innovation and productivity and ensuring that the benefits of productivity improvements are shared with workers and consumers.

The business environment can be defined as those policies, laws, regulations and organizations that affect the performance of the agricultural and business sector. It includes the administration and enforcement mechanisms established to implement government policy, as well as the organizational arrangements that influence the way key actors operate (i.e., government agencies, regulatory authorities, business membership organizations, civil society organizations, trade unions, etc.). The enabling environment comprises a large array of factors. The relative importance of these factors may vary at different stages of development and in different cultural and socio-economic contexts.

A good business environment will support farmers and businesses of all types to invest and innovate and provides incentives for the creation of more and better jobs by:

- reducing business costs: to increase profits (and thereby investment and real wages) or increasing market share (and thereby output and employment);
- reducing policy risks: to reduce the cost of capital (and thereby increasing the number of attractive investments in the market);

- increasing competitive pressures through new entry: to stimulate the efficiency and innovating incentives of the market; and
- strengthening predictability by securing property rights and the rule of law.

Property rights and, in particular, land rights are an important dimension to the business environment in rural areas. In many countries insecure property rights, poor contract enforcement and other legal impediments limit economic performance and foment economic and social inefficiencies and inequities. Land reform and broader agrarian reform can promote smallholder engagement in markets, reduce inequalities, increase efficiency and enhance rural competitiveness.

New mechanisms to increase the security of property rights and facilitate land re-allocation will help improve rural incomes. Providing landowners or users with security against evictions enhances their competitiveness by encouraging land-related investments. Legally binding land ownership allows rural households to use land as collateral to obtain credit, which can be used to invest in non-farm enterprises: conversely, once a household relies primarily on non-farm activities for income, it can lease its land to others.

Over the last decade a number of African countries adopted new land laws to recognize customary tenure, make alternative (oral) forms of evidence on land rights admissible, strengthen women's land rights, and establish decentralized land institutions.

With greater knowledge of such laws, land-related investments and productivity increased, as evidence from Uganda suggests.

If the environment for doing business is volatile, precarious or constraining, then even with access to extension services and credit, farmers and business people will be discouraged from taking reasonable risks in, for example, hiring labour or investing in training or skills development of workers or in terms of maintaining acceptable standards of safety and health at the workplace. Experience indicates that a good business environment encourages investment and promotes higher levels of growth while inappropriate regulations, excessive red tape and bureaucratic obstacles, lengthy business registration procedures, ineffective safeguards of property rights, corruption and weak commercial justice systems constrain businesses, especially in poorer countries.

Information: A Vital Resource

Information about markets is vital and among the range of policy tools which can be employed to promote rural employment are market information systems, including those on labour markets, which can improve rural labour market outcomes by assisting rural households in finding more and better employment and training opportunities. Market information systems can provide farmers and traders with timely and accurate prices, buyer contracts, buyer and producer profiles and trends, import regulations, standards specifications, and so forth. Market information systems have been facilitated by the advances in communications technology and the liberalization of telecommunications and broadcasting.

A key objective of labour market institutions is to provide regulations for the effective and equitable functioning of labour markets. Within broader labour codes, special provisions or legislation may be required to address the particular circumstances and challenges inherent to rural labour markets, as in the case of the United Kingdom's Gangmasters (Licensing) Act which was set up to avoid the exploitation of (mostly) migrant agricultural workers.

Rural Finance for Income and Employment Growth

Poor people in rural areas typically face a triple burden when it comes to finance. First, an inability, especially for women, to access credit on competitive terms to invest in their agricultural and off-farm income-generating activities means that their incomes and employment opportunities are constrained. A recent multi-country study found that in most countries surveyed, no more than about one in ten agricultural households had access to credit. Secondly, the rural poor are also likely to lack access to appropriate savings instruments, implying that their investments are put into less productive or more risky forms which may further reduce rural liquidity. Thirdly, without adequate access to risk reduction instruments (such as crop insurance) rural households are likely to withhold on innovation, on adopting new activities or expanding existing ones, even if they have adequate liquidity.

A number of factors constrain the development of rural finance markets such as the high transaction costs associated with dispersed populations and the seasonality of household income flows, which typically peak at harvest time but fall away at other times, making credit repayment which is not tied to seasonality factors a challenge for poor households. Another fundamental reason why rural finance and especially credit markets typically do not function well in rural areas is because land institutions and markets often do not work well in the sense that land titles – if they exist at all – are often not easily transferable and so cannot, or not easily, be used as collateral.

The situation regarding rural finance for poor people is a clear example of market failure. The situation is particularly serious in much of rural Africa where a combination of agricultural risk, scarce borrower information, cumbersome legal procedures and high transaction costs means that many financial service providers are reluctant to serve poor farmers and business people, leaving the market open to informal institutions and operators like traders and processors who may well be less scrupulous and supportive in the way they operate. This context provided the rationale for the state subsidized and targeted agricultural finance schemes which flourished in the 1970s and 1980s but which, with a few exceptions, turned out to be rather ineffective and inefficient.

In contrast, in more recent times, microfinance programmes (credit, savings and, to a lesser extent, microinsurance and leasing services) have expanded and proven powerful means for addressing rural poverty and for income generation in rural areas. Given the typical small size of loans and the nature of the activities financed, the employment effect of microfinance is generally seen in terms of self-employment and intra-household employment rather than on non-family waged employment. But microfinance is only one tool. Bringing financial services to rural communities implies the need for reforms that both broaden and deepen rural financial markets and this may justify government subsidy and guarantees (but not interest rate subsidies which should broadly reflect the cost of lending) in order to build the capacity of a range of different rural and agricultural finance providers.

Education, Skills and Training

People in rural areas tend to be more disadvantaged in accessing education and training than people in urban areas. Girls and women are likely to be particularly disadvantaged. With respect to formal education in rural areas of poor countries, it is often a challenge to get skilled and motivated teachers to work in rural areas, especially if they are in remote locations; teaching materials and school infrastructure are often poor; and children themselves may live far from school or, for a variety of reasons, be discouraged from attending school. The result is that enrolment, completion and literacy rates all tend to be lower in rural areas than in urban areas, among rural women. Thus, poor-quality basic education, low levels of educational attainment and low levels of adult literacy hold back the generation of productive employment and poverty reduction in rural areas.

Improving basic education is essential and often a necessary condition for other programmes and policies targeted at improving skills and knowledge in rural areas and for making the most of vocational and technical training opportunities. Education may also be the most important variable for entry into the non-farm economy. Evidence from China and India indicates that better education enables rural workers to find high-paying non-farm employment, whereas a lack of education tends to force them into agricultural employment or low-wage non-farm employment at best. Generally, schooling is positively and significantly associated with participation in rural non-agricultural wage employment, and negatively related to participation in agricultural activities in most countries.

A key factor for accelerating productivity growth is the availability of workers with appropriate skills. Strengthening human capital facilitates the transfer, adaptation, absorption and dissemination of technologies that accompany investment and technological change in rural areas. Of great importance are the quality and accessibility of training and learning opportunities for rural people, as well as the relevance of the training to labour market needs. In addition to improvements in human capital, good working conditions, innovations in work organization, continuous workplace learning, good labour–management relations and respect for workers' rights, are important ways of raising productivity and promoting decent work.

Rural skills development, including extension services and promoting technological change in rural areas, is also vital for enhancing food security and protecting the environment. More and better technical vocational education and training (TVET) oriented to both on-farm and off-farm activities and aligned with market-based outcomes and market demand, is vital to enhance rural productivity and competitiveness. However, many of the obstacles to achieving more and better quality schooling in rural areas (such as dispersed populations, poor infrastructure, perceived or actual returns to schooling and so forth) also inhibit the development of more and better TVET. Also, all too often, TVET policies tend to be gender biased, focusing on men more than women.

Given that changing patterns and organization of work in rural areas and the use of new technology create different demands for skills, there is often a critical need for reform and reorientation of national training policies and systems and for the upgrading of traditional (and typically informal) apprenticeships. Greater involvement of the private sector in skills development is necessary, both in the delivery of training as well as in the delivery of extension services. Increasing the productivity of rural workers may require greater emphasis on linking formal with informal training, recognizing acquired skills, and finding new ways to expand skills and entrepreneurship training for the informal economy.

Successful diversification of rural livelihoods requires investment in human capital. This includes encouraging entrepreneurship, especially among women and young people, and building the capacity of individual enterprises through training programmes such as the Small Enterprise Programme's Start and Improve Your Business (SIYB) range of tools, and the Training for Rural Economic Empowerment Programme (TREE), a community-based training methodology. Such tools require the development of business service providers, the provision and coordination of extension services in rural areas and skills development programmes specifically targeted at rural areas. They also need to be customized to take into account that levels of basic education and literacy are typically lowest in rural areas.

Attracting Public Investment into Rural Areas

Investment in physical infrastructure including, where appropriate, through Public Private Partnerships, is vital for making rural markets work better and for generating employment opportunities in rural areas. It is important to distinguish the employment effects of investment and to plan investment so as to capitalize on the comparative advantages of both rural and urban areas to optimize the spatial and regional dimensions of these employment impacts. This implies the need for systematic employment-impact assessments of public investment programmes. Such employment impact assessments can then be a concrete first step for optimizing and increasing the employment impact of investment decisions.

Infrastructure investment for rural employment should strengthen rural–urban linkages by helping rural producers (especially of agricultural or perishable goods) to get their products to market in a timely fashion. Difficult market access restricts opportunities for income generation. Remoteness increases uncertainty, reduces choice and results in restricted marketing opportunities, reduced farm gate prices and increased input costs. It also exacerbates the problem of post-harvest losses. Good transportation infrastructure also helps to get rural goods and services into potentially lucrative global markets.

A wide variety of infrastructure can directly support agricultural productivity and lend itself to implementation using labour-based methods. Such infrastructure includes feeder roads, irrigation, land reclamation, erosion control, small water-retaining earth dams and reforestation, among others. These categories of infrastructure are also likely to be environmentally friendly but they require strong collaboration between the public and private sectors. Investment-driven rural employment strategies should identify the respective roles of the public and private sectors: they should not be inflationary; they should not interfere with the micro-decisions of individual firms; they should not rely on the "fine-tuning" of the aggregate demand approach; they should be consistent with the premise that, to the extent possible, socially productive work is preferable to income maintenance; and they should not replace existing jobs.

The ILO has a wide range of experience in supporting integrated rural development programmes, through its Special Public Works Programme in the 1970s and 1980s, and its Integrated Rural Community Access projects, which supported government strategies to address disequilibrium between rural and urban labour productivities. Such programmes can have a multiplier effect by injecting wages and sources of new demand into rural areas. As well as being labour-intensive and local-resource based, they also improve the productivity of agricultural workers.

One avenue for employment creation which is gaining renewed interest, especially for rural areas is that of government-sponsored employment guarantee schemes, in which the Government acts as employer of last resort. While the public sector takes responsibility for funding and oversight, such programmes can provide new opportunities for private-sector involvement in direct job creation and can put in place much needed economic and social infrastructure, and therefore help support a sound investment climate and decrease the cost of doing business. Recent research indicates that an employment guarantee or employer of last resort programme can be put in place for between 1 and 2 per cent of GDP. One of the most well-known programmes of this type is the one established by the Indian National Rural Employment Guarantee Act through which, as a legal right to work, every rural citizen able to meet means-testing requirements has the right to 100 days of remunerated, productive and socially or economically useful employment per annum. Such programmes can be seen as a concrete measure which governments can take, in close consultation with social partners, to implement a policy of full, productive and freely chosen employment, as called for in the Employment Policy Convention, 1964 (No. 122).

Agriculture, Trade and Sustainable Economic Integration

Given that two-thirds of the world's agricultural value added is created in developing countries, relatively significant gains in income, employment and poverty reduction can be made from trade reform. But agriculture is at the heart of many of the most complex and difficult trade reform negotiations. The liberalization of trade requires the removal of trade-distorting policies. These include export subsidies and limiting market access through import tariffs, quotas and non-tariff barriers that protect local producers from competing imports. The World Development Report 2008 warns that: "The economic and social costs of today's trade, price and subsidy policies in world agriculture are large. They depress international commodity prices by about 5 per cent on average (much more for some commodities) and suppress agricultural output growth in developing countries. They consume a large share of the government budget and distract from growth-enhancing investments." Agricultural tariffs and subsidies in developed countries alone cost developing countries the equivalent of about five times the current level of overseas development assistance to agriculture.

Agricultural subsidies and tariffs on rice and sugar, aggregated across all countries, are estimated to account for 20 per cent and 18 per cent, respectively, of the global costs of all agricultural trade policies – the highest of all commodities. Although the equivalent global cost of cotton subsidies and tariffs is much smaller, the absolute cost to developing countries is large, an estimated US$283 million a year. However, there have been some recent changes to rice, sugar and cotton policies in Japan, the EU and the United States respectively, all at an early stage of implementation. There have also been initiatives taken to facilitate market access for goods imported from some developing countries. In addition to the troubled Doha Development Round of trade negotiations – where discussions concerning agricultural trade have proved particularly contentious – other examples include the Africa Growth and Opportunity Act (AGOA) of the United States and the European Union "Everything but Arms" agreement which allows for duty-free and quota-free access to its markets for UN Least Developed Countries – although it excludes services and has delayed the opening of sensitive markets for bananas, rice and sugar.

The liberalization of agricultural trade has the potential to improve the livelihoods of rural households. According to a 2006 World Bank study, full trade liberalization is estimated to increase international commodity prices on average by 5.5 per cent for primary agricultural products and 1.3 per cent for processed foods. Developing countries are estimated to gain 9 percentage points in their share of global agricultural exports. But these aggregate results hide big differences across commodities, according to types of production system and between countries. The largest estimated price increases are for cotton and oilseeds, with significant estimated trade share gains to countries exporting these products.

The removal of trade-distorting agricultural policies in developed countries has mixed terms-of-trade effects on developing countries. Terms of trade improve for developing countries exporting commodities currently protected in developed countries, but worsen for net importers of these commodities, i.e. trade liberalization that raises the price of food will hurt net buyers (such as Bolivia and Bangladesh) while benefiting net sellers (such as Cambodia and Viet Nam). Similarly, the poverty effect of price changes from agricultural trade reforms will depend on where the poor are, what they do for a living and what they consume.

Developing countries have seen their absolute share in world agricultural exports decline from 40 per cent in 1960 to 30 per cent in 2005. Many traditional agricultural commodities, including coffee, cocoa and tea, sugar and textile fibres, have experienced significant declines: between 1982 and 2001 the price index of traditional commodities declined by 47 per cent and real prices for tea, coffee, cocoa, sugar and bananas are expected to remain stagnant at least until 2010. These price declines are linked to problems of oversupply, low-demand elasticities and, in the case of a protected product like sugar, to expanded production in industrial countries.

However, there has recently been a rise in food prices for certain commodities.

Many farmers in developing countries are faced with adverse conditions and an uneven playing field stemming from differences in conditions such as the quality and quantity of land and other agro-ecological resources and access to technology, inputs and equipment, finance, and other ancillary services. Globalization has accentuated the challenge of global competition whereby farmers from many different parts of the world, facing very different production conditions, become, willingly or not, part of the same market, with their products open to the same world price discipline. Such competitive pressures tend to hit mostly farmers from developing countries with low labour productivity. This is a competitiveness issue separate from, but amplified by, the inequity that these farmers may face from the farm protection systems of OECD countries (and is further exacerbated by the erosion of trade preferences and the phasing out of commodity agreements). Policies that seek to improve the "initial conditions" of poorly endowed farmers and help them make as much as possible of these conditions would have a favourable effect on their competitive position.

To address this challenge, consumption patterns will need to change and food production will need to rise, especially in poorer countries such as those in sub-Saharan Africa. However, if the policy of providing heavy subsidies to farmers in some rich countries for fuel production from maize and soybeans is not revised and more serious efforts are not made to develop long-term environmentally sound technologies to substitute for scarce oil and gas and for fuels produced from farmland then the world's poor will be hardest hit by the combination of rising world food prices and long-term climate change.

Although enhanced access to international markets is necessary to generate employment and reduce poverty in rural areas in the developing world, "the varying development levels of countries must be taken into account in lifting barriers to domestic and foreign markets ... trade integration can also lead to job dislocation, increased informality and growing income inequality .... (Thus)... measures must be taken by governments, in consultation with the social partners, to better assess and address the employment and decent work impact of trade policies. Actions are also needed at regional and multilateral levels to remove trade distortions and to assist developing countries in building their capacity to export value added products, manage change and develop a competitive industrial base".

Expanding Employment through Agricultural Value Chains

A value chain is a set of businesses and their interactions that bring a product (or service) from raw material to final consumer. Vibrant value-chain systems grow and continuously incorporate new businesses, generating ever-increasing jobs, income and assets. In this manner, value-chain systems have significant potential to integrate farmers and rural enterprises into national and global production systems (in some countries there is considerable potential for growing urban food demand to drive increased agricultural production). Value chain development forms a core part of a range of private sector development strategies, from export promotion to local economic development and clustering strategies. At the heart of value-chain development is the effort to strengthen mutually beneficial linkages among enterprises so that they work together to take advantage of market opportunities.

Most value-chain initiatives work with a range of business types to strengthen both vertical linkages – among enterprises that buy from and sell to one another – and horizontal linkages – among enterprises that serve the same functions in the value chain. Positive outcomes occur when there is a strong market drive for linkages, strong investment from many enterprises in the chain and a market system in place to replicate improved models and practices. Clearly, a chain cannot be moved by pushing it; in order to move a chain, it has to be pulled. In this sense, a value-chain system will only develop if linked to strong consumer demand. Furthermore, value chains typically thrive when businesses in the chain come together to market themselves using a common competitive strategy.

Although global value chains do have the potential to generate quality employment, they can also be vehicles for passing on the costs and risks to the weakest links in the chain. Sometimes, under pressure from investors, among others, governments in poorer countries have allowed labour standards to be defined by the demands of supply chain flexibility, including easier hiring and firing, more short-term contracts, fewer benefits and longer periods of overtime which may bring short-term advantage for trade but at the risk of a long-term cost to society. Also, women agricultural workers can be affected differently by the organization of production due to their limited ability to take advantage of existing opportunities or due to their disadvantages in terms of skills and access to knowledge among other factors. Thus, distinguishing the costs and benefits of value chains, and identifying how best to promote value chains which have the potential to nurture rural employment for all and reduce poverty levels requires careful analysis and a conducive policy framework.

Agricultural value chains can play a key role in generating employment and reducing poverty in rural areas. Fresh fruit and vegetables make up 17 per cent of world agricultural exports, and are among the largest and fastest growing of all traded agricultural products. Compared to other agricultural sectors, trade protection for fruit and vegetables is much lower. The creation of the North American Free Trade Agreement (NAFTA), for example, stimulated massive growth in US imports of fresh fruit and vegetables from Mexico and Canada during the 1990s; Mexican growers' shipments of winter tomatoes grew from 28 per cent of the US market in 1991 to 42 per cent in 1997. Horticulture is also more labour intensive than other food sectors, with many crops being hand-picked and processed. Consequently, many US and European traders have increased their sourcing and investment in production and processing activities in developing countries, where labour costs are lower.

Trade in fresh fruit and vegetables has seen important success. For example, Kenya currently supplies 25 per cent of the world's green peas and together with Guatemala is the world leader in this market. However, exports are heavily concentrated amongst a handful of middle-income players in Latin America (Argentina, Chile and Mexico) and, increasingly, China. Chile, Costa Rica, Ecuador and Mexico account for 43 per cent of developing country exports of fresh fruit, while for fresh vegetables, 67 per cent of developing country exports come from just four suppliers: Argentina, China, Mexico and the Syrian Arab Republic.

Involvement in global value chains and the expansion of export trade has generally had a beneficial impact on employment in agriculture and off-farm work. Even if small farmers do not participate directly, they can benefit from increased farm employment opportunities. The proportion and rate of increase of waged workers in the agricultural labour force are highest in regions enjoying export-oriented horticultural booms. For example, in Chile the percentage of waged workers in such areas has risen steadily since 1990, in contrast to areas with greater emphasis on traditional activities (wheat, dairy and beef) which have experienced a decline in the number of waged workers over the same period.

In Senegal, despite tight export standards that led to a shift from smallholder contract farming to large-scale integrated estate production, the higher horticulture exports increased incomes and reduced regional poverty by about 12 percentage points and extreme poverty by half. Poor households benefited more through labour markets than through product markets, as employment in estate farms increased from 10 per cent of households to 35 per cent. In Guatemala, studies found that lettuce farmers participating in modern supply chains hire 2.5 times more labour than those who do not and this labour is typically sourced from local asset-poor households. Studies of tomato growers in Indonesia and kale growers in Kenya found similar results.

Broadly, there are four key functional activities involved in fruit and vegetable value chains: growing, processing, distributing and selling. Stage one is crop production and harvesting. Producers range from small family farms to medium- and large-sized commercial farms. While some operate independently, others may be contracted to large farms and exporters, or owned by a vertically integrated exporter. Stage two involves processing and packaging the produce, before storing and transporting it to the importing country. Stage three entails distribution (import and export) and further processing and stage four involves the final retail sale to the consumers.

The same study found that global agri-food systems are characterized by four key trends:

- Growing vertical integration means that the industry is dominated by a handful of large firms. Rise of powerful global buyers, which can dictate terms to their suppliers. Increased concentration at multiple stages of the value chain, from input supply to retailing. This increases the pressures in production segments of the chain, which are generally more fragmented and drives consolidation there.
- Growth in private and public standards, which set increasingly stringent production and management processes for farmers and exporters to follow.

The study described fresh fruit and vegetable chains as "increasingly short, integrated and buyer-driven". The strong governance by large retailers has led to growing concentration at all stages and the imposition of tough quality-

and food-production standards, all of which raise entry barriers, exposing producers to high costs and risks while squeezing incomes. As a result, it is increasingly the large and better resourced farms and exporters which are able to access global buyers, leading to the marginalization and exclusion of many medium-sized and smaller producers.

Farm incomes are also threatened by global over-supply in some products, like bananas and apples, which is driving down prices and sometimes having an adverse effect on the terms and conditions experienced by workers at the base of the supply chain. This is linked to a complex mesh of factors, including trade liberalization, deregulation of domestic markets, the end of producer-led commodity agreements, ongoing producer subsidies in rich countries, trade rules restricting market access (e.g. tariffs on processed products from developing to industrial countries) and technological change and falling transport costs, which facilitate global sourcing and increased competition.

Buyer demands in terms of product quality, just-in-time supply and environmental standards can incur significant costs which are prohibitive to many smaller firms and farms. For example, buyer demand for product freshness will require investment in field-level cooling facilities. Research on African horticulture points out that the capital and land needed to make such purchases viable are prohibitive to many small-scale growers. Smallholders seeking to source global supply chains are also faced with the need to comply with strict standards. For importers, private standards serve two main functions. They help coordinate supply chains by standardizing product requirements for suppliers over many regions or countries, enhancing efficiency and lowering transaction costs; and they help ensure that public food-safety standards are met in all markets served by the retail chain.

The internationalization of food safety and quality standards is taking place not only through the increase in the world trade of foods but also through the internationalization of food retailing systems, mostly by supermarkets. Supermarket chains are now the dominant food retailers in the urban areas of many developing countries. These chains, many of them global, tend to impose more or less uniform quality and safety standards throughout the countries where they operate. A favourable consequence has been the improvement of these standards to the benefit of consumers. The issue is that most farmers in developing countries, particularly small ones, find it difficult to satisfy the standards nowadays required to participate in international trade or to sell to supermarkets in their own countries. Their capacity to compete is thus diminished.

However, while there is concern that sanitary and phytosanitary standards result in compliance costs that will disadvantage developing countries, recent studies find that compliance costs tend to be small relative to the scale of most export industries. Fixed, non-recurrent costs are generally 0.5 per cent to 5 per cent of three-to-five year exports, while recurrent costs tend to be 1 per cent to 3 per cent of annual exports. There are also the benefits that exporters gain from compliance with standards, including environmental benefits and workers' safety, as well as the value of continuing market access.

An important avenue for smallholders to gain access to value chains is through their involvement in producer organizations. These are membership-based organizations or federations of organizations with elected leaders accountable to their constituents. They take on various legal forms such as cooperatives, associations and societies. Often they are commodity-specific organizations. These can also provide technical assistance to ensure quality, delivery and compliance with standards. Smallholders may also get better access to global value and on better terms through participation in fair or ethical trade systems.

Employment Generation Strategies in Developing Countries

While many formal studies have been prepared to assess the growth and employment potential in developing world's private sector, less attention has been given to the conditions and strategies to promote rapid expansion and job creation in the rural and informal sectors. This section focuses on strategies to increase employment opportunities in developing world's informal sector, with special emphasis on Indian agriculture, agro-industry, rural services and related vocations.

Although accurate measures of employment and unemployment are difficult in India's largely informal economy, the current labour force consists of approximately 400 million men and women. It is estimated that the work force is currently growing by 7 million persons per year. Of these, about 56% are engaged in agriculture as their primary occupation which is down from 65% in the early 1990s. Another 13% are engaged in manufacturing and the balance are employed in the service sector, which has grown from 25% to 32% of total employment over the past two decades.

The organized sector provides less than 8% of the total jobs, about 3% in private firms and 5% in the public sector. The informal/unorganized sector is provides the other 92%. Only 6-8% of India's workforce has received formal training in vocational skills, compared with 60% or more in developed and most rapidly developing countries.

Depending on the survey measure applied, unemployment is estimated to range between 25 and 35 million. Youth unemployment is 13%, but reaches a high of 35% in Kerala. Unemployment as a percentage of the workforce fell in the 1980s and rose slightly in the 1990s. Authoritative published data was not available to indicate trends after 2001-2.

According to sample survey estimates, approximately 27% of India's population are migrants, including those who move from one rural or urban area to another or between rural and urban areas. Approximately 57% of urban male migration is for seeking better employment opportunities. The net migration from rural to urban areas is approximately 2 million per annum, of which about 1 million may be job seekers.

In spite of a large influx of youth into the workforce, unemployment is not rising dramatically. This indicates that the Indian economy is generating a very large number of additional employment opportunities by natural processes that are not well documented or understood. An understanding of these processes is will assist the formulation of effective strategies to accelerate employment generation and eliminate the remainder of unemployment and underemployment in the economy. If the unconscious process of employment generation can achieve this much, surely a conscious understanding and application can accomplish far higher rates of job growth.

Since high rates of urban unemployment would almost invariably lead to rising discontent and violence, the relative stability of India's urban environment suggests that the urban economy is generating sufficient employment opportunities to absorb most new entrants and migrants from rural areas.

While the number of employment opportunities is rising more or less as required to keep pace with the growth of the workforce, the type and quality of these opportunities does not match the expectations of many educated job seekers, which reflects inadequacies both in the type of employment generated and type of education being imparted to youth. Ironically, despite the surging number of graduates, many firms report difficulty in recruiting educated persons with the required work capabilities to meet the growth in demand for business process outsourcing, automotive component production and many other fields.

At the other end of the labour spectrum, it is increasingly difficult to obtain workers with basic skills in carpentry, masonry, electricals, mechanics, and many other trades. Although India operates a large vocational training system, it provides training to less than 2 million persons annually, which is grossly insufficient to impart skills to the 7 million new job entrants as well as the huge number of current unskilled workers. Absence of reliable information on the actual growth in employment by specific occupational categories makes it difficult to determine either the number of jobs being created in each field or the unsatisfied demand for various types of skills.

Evidence of an increase in casual and migratory employment reflects a deterioration in the quality of jobs in rural areas as well as rising expectations of the workforce that impels increasing numbers to abandon traditional occupations in search of better employment opportunities.

While the percentage of the workforce employed in agriculture is declining, total employment in this sector continues to rise, though at significantly slower rates than in the past. A reduction in the proportion of the population employed in the primary sector is a natural and inevitable trend that is spurred by rising expectations and changing attitudes as much as by rising levels of farm productivity and mechanization. However, this does not mean that the potential for employment in this sector is being fully exploited.

The traditional path of economic development was a progression from agriculture to manufacturing to services. India's recent success in IT and IT-enabled services is only one indication that this formula need not necessarily apply in the context of today's global economy where the demand for services internationally can rapidly expand employment opportunities domestically. In addition, changing social expectations within the country are stimulating rapid growth in demand for services that become prevalent in advanced industrial countries at a much later stage in their development, as indicated by the proliferation of courier companies, Xerox shops, Internet cafes, fast food restaurants and retail boutiques. The rampant clamour for education at all levels, surging demand for health care services, telecommunications, media, entertainment, and financial services are other expressions of this phenomenon. The publication of six English dailies and six Kannada dailies in the city of Bangalore is only one reflection of this wider trend. Research is required to more carefully document growth of the service sector, particularly its informal portion, to assess the potential demand and most effective strategies for accelerating growth of employment. *These trends suggest that rural India has the opportunity to leapfrog over the traditional path to development, moving directly from agriculture into services.*

Theoretical Basis for Full Employment

The International Commission on Peace and Food, in its report entitled *Uncommon Opportunities: Agenda for Peace & Equitable Development,* examined the process of employment generation in society and concluded that full employment was a realistic and achievable goal for all countries in the foreseeable future. It observed that efforts to achieve full employment are constrained by a vague sense of helplessness or inevitability based on the erroneous perception that the number of employment opportunities generated in society is determined by forces that are either beyond the control of government and public initiative or too complex, costly and difficult to manage without severe adverse affects on the economy. Therefore, it may be useful to examine some of the major factors that presently limit the creation of new employment opportunities and the practical scope for action at these specific points.

Economically, employment generation is determined by how fully and productively society utilizes the material, technological, organizational and human resources at its disposal. The more productive the society is, the greater the quality and efficiency with which it produces goods and services, the greater the demand for those goods and services in the marketplace, the more employment opportunities and purchasing power created. This increased purchasing power then acts as an additional stimulus to the creation of new demand and employment opportunities.

Although early economists perceived that resources were limited, we now know that the potential for enhancing the productivity of resources is not. The Commission's report points out that the productivity of resources is the result of human resourcefulness. Since no society can or does fully exhaust its potentials for enhancing social productivity, the potential for employment generation is unlimited. Land, water and minerals may be limited, but the scope for increasing their productivity is not. Land is limited in India, but the scope for raising farm yields is not.

If this is the case for purely material resources, how much more true is it of technology, organization, knowledge, skill and other less tangible society resources? The enhancement in computer performance over the past 35 years according to Moore's Law is only one dramatic instance of a general truth about technological productivity in all fields. While the power of computers keeps increasing, the cost of producing them keeps falling because of technological developments that reduce their size, material consumption and labour inputs.

Technology alone does not result in human development. The application of technology through innovative social organizations has been the chief cause for the phenomenal gains of the past century. It was not the invention of the automobile but rather the innovation of a new organization of mass production by assembly line that enabled Henry Ford to transform the car from a luxury of the idle rich into a necessity for middle and working class families. It was not the invention of the computer, but the innovation of a new organization for electronic exchange of information in a standardized format that converted the Internet from the medium of academics and military planners into the most powerful communication tool in history and led to the emergence of the World Wide Web as a global library and global marketplace. India's dairy cooperatives, micro-finance self-help groups, STD booths, export processing zones, technology parks, and private computer training centres are all examples of organizational innovations that have stimulate development and create jobs.

What is true of technological and organizational resources is even more true for other social and human resources. Information is a resource that improves the quality of decision-making and makes possible the tapping of new opportunities. The quantity, quality and speed of all types of information exchange is multiplying exponentially. Through the enhancement of skills, knowledge and attitudes, the productivity of the human resource is growing by leaps and bounds. The USA, which awarded only a single PhD in 1880, now awards for than 35,000 annually. India produces more software engineers than the USA. Tamil Nadu, which had less than a dozen engineering colleges in 1980, has more than 200 today. Five lakh Indians are taking software training courses every year. Tens of thousands of four and five year old Indian children are surfing the internet or playing chess like future grandmasters. At the same time 45 per cent of the Indian population is still illitreate, only 60 per cent of 11-14 year olds are enrolled in school, two-thirds of children drop out before completing 10th Standard, and only five per cent of the workforce in the 20-24 age category have undergone formal vocational training, compared to 28 per cent in Mexico and 96 per cent in Korea. There is enormous scope for enhancing the knowledge and skills of India's workforce.

If the technological, organization and human potentials are unlimited, what is it that determines the actual extent to which a society develops these potentials? It is the awakening of the society. Socially, employment generation is determined by the aspirations of people, by rising expectations, by the urge to achieve and enjoy more. The higher the aspirations of society that actively yearn for fulfilment, the greater the energy and activity of the society and the greater the potential for employment generation. Government does not create jobs. No government can create and sustain full employment primarily by means of programmes. What government can and should do is to help awaken the people to the opportunities for higher accomplishment and to formulate policies and programmes that will help to release the initiative and support the efforts of the population for its own upliftment.

Social Factors Responsible for Employment Generation

Society progresses by the development of new activities and their gradual integration with all other existing strands of the social fabric. Therefore, employment generation is not so much a question of finding out where to engage people in work, as it is how to stimulate the natural growth of the factors that result in job creation. These factors are innumerable and their interactions are very complex. They include, for example,

- *New products* - motor vehicles, cell phones, cut flowers, designer clothes
- *New services* - Xerox, courier, yellow pages, Internet cafes, credit cards, neighborhood newspapers, various insurance products
- *Growth in domestic demand* - energy, motorcycles, cars, tourism, pharma, health care, insurance, financial services
- *Growth in export demand* - textiles, software, automotive components, mangoes, grapes, fish
- *Technological innovation* - Internet, mobile phones
- *Higher quality &/or productivity* - automotive and farm exports

- *Organizational innovation* - STD booths, World Wide Web, Internet cafe
- *Higher skills* - software, BPO, journalism, sales & marketing
- *Better access to information* - Internet job sites, E-choupals
- *Increased speed* - money flows, transport, communication, decision-making
- *Legislation & law enforcement* - e.g. safety and environmental regulations
- *Administrative responsiveness* - speed, transparency, less red-tape
- *Environment/health consciousness* - bottled water, recycling, organic foods
- *Change of attitudes* - regarding consumption, investment, entrepreneurship

Approaches to Accelerate Employment Generation

There are three broad approaches can be adopted to stimulate greater employment generation:

Expand existing activities

Introduce measures to stimulate more rapid proliferation of existing activities that are already growing rapidly, such as nursery schools, tutorial institutes, English language teaching, etc.

Adopt activities prevalent in other countries which have not yet come to India

Examples of new activities that have recently been adopted by India include credit rating agencies for businesses and individuals, collection agencies, trade shows, network marketing, health clinics, etc.

Promote culturally compatible activities based on Indian environment

Examples include mini-power plants, rural information centres, contract farming agencies, STD booths, chit funds, marriage halls, etc.

Several different modes of action can be adopted to stimulate these activities:

- Increase access to credit
- Provide incentives for new initiatives
- Strengthen or enforce legislation

- Impart training
- Use insurance as a stimulus
- Publicize opportunities in the media

Development of agriculture is critically important for ensuring food and nutritional security for the hundreds of millions of people that still live below the poverty line, for raising rural incomes and generating employment opportunities, and for stimulating industrialization and overall economic development of the country. Raising the productivity of irrigated and rain-fed agriculture, combined with rainwater harvesting and water conservation techniques and assured access to remunerative markets for agricultural produce through linkages with agro-industries can dramatically raise rural incomes, generate millions of on-farm and non-farm employment opportunities, eradicate poverty and usher in a prosperity movement throughout rural India.

In 1991 the International Commission on Peace & Food (ICPF) conducted a country study of employment potentials in India and drew up a strategy entitled *Prosperity 2000* to generate 100 million additional employment opportunities within 10 years. The strategy was adopted by the then Government of India and the *Small Farmers' Agri-Business Consortium* was established by the Government for implementation. Two subsequent studies were conducted that confirmed the feasibility of this strategy at the local level: a study of Pune District by the Agricultural Finance Corporation for the Government of Maharasthra and a study of Pondicherry by the Mother's Service Society. Although Rs 100 crores were allocated in the 1992 Union Budget by the then Finance Minister, Dr. Manmohan Singh, for a variety of reasons the Prosperity 2000 strategy was never implemented.

The thrust of the *Prosperity 2000* strategy was to directly utilize agriculture as an engine to raise on-farm incomes and purchasing power, generate additional on-farm employment opportunities, and stimulate rural industrialization and services. These would in turn increase demand for agricultural products, manufactured goods and services throughout the economy, creating a multiplier effect that generates jobs in other sectors. The specific focus on the strategy was on raising on-farm productivity and fostering closer linkages with industry and markets through innovative approaches to the organization of the rural economy.

In reviewing ICPF's strategy 13 years later, we find that some of the potentials it identified have been partially exploited, such as the dramatic increase in production of fruits and vegetables, export of grapes and mangoes from Maharashtra to Western Europe, the rise in production and per capita consumption of sugar, and grow of inland aquaculture. The report examined the current levels of food consumption and dietary nutrition among the Indian population-at-large and projected growth in demand that would result from the gradual rise in living standards for fruits, vegetables, sugar and dairy products. The actually rise in demand for fruits and vegetables has nearly matched ICPF's projection.

In retrospect, we find that the technological and market potentials identified in the original study remain valid today. The scope for improving farm productivity, the potential for improving linkages with processing industries, and the scope for dietary enhancement is as great as before. However, the organizational mechanisms required to fully tap these potentials need to be re-examined in the light of the current role of government and private agencies in the development process. In addition, we need to take into account changing external conditions that open up new opportunities and present new challenges, especially the rise in international energy prices and the increasing opportunities for textile exports after the removal of quotas in January 2005.

Vocational Training

The speed of a nation's development is directly related to the quantity and quality of vocational skills possessed by its workforce. The wider the range and higher the quality of vocational skills, the faster the growth and more prosperous the society.

In the coming decade, an additional eight million young people will enter India's labour force every year in search of employment. Currently only 5% of the country's labour force in the 20-24 age category have formal vocational training, compared with 28% in Mexico, 60 to 80% in most industrialized nations, and as much as 96% in Korea.

The availability of employable skills is one of the major determinants of how readily new job seekers find employment. The very low level of employable skills makes the search for work much more difficult. It reduces the market value of the job seeker and adds to the costs of employers that must train new recruits from scratch.

India has over 4200 industrial training institutes imparting education and training 43 engineering and 24 non-engineering trades. Of these, 1654 are government run ITIs (State governments) while 2620 are private. The total seating capacity in these ITIs is 6.28 lakh. Most of this training is conducted in classroom style in the form of 1 to 2 year diploma courses.

In addition, about 1.65 lakh persons undergo apprenticeship vocational training every year in state-run enterprises. If a wider definition of applied courses is taken that includes agricultural, engineering and other professional subjects, the total number receiving job related training is about 17 lakh per annum, which still represents only 14% of new entrants to the workforce.

The limitations in the existing approach to vocational training have been highlighted in the Planning Commission Report of the Task Force on Employment Opportunities (2001). They include outdated courses for which there is little demand, shortage of suitably trained faculty, inadequate infrastructure, and unreliable testing.

There is a great unmet need for shorter vocational training programmes that job seekers can take on their own time and at their own pace and at relatively low cost. In addition there is also need for a wide range of vocational courses for those who are already employed but seek to broaden or upgrade their skills to keep pace with changing needs and to further their career opportunities.

The ITI's offer training on a very narrow range of skills, primarily those required by manufacturing industries. These include 43 engineering related skills and 24 non-engineering trades. But the range of skills required by the country for its development includes literally hundreds for which no formal training is presently offered.

The lack of vocational training applies at all levels, from basic mechanical skills needed for operating and repairing equipment to jobs in sales, administration and management, including specialized occupations such as bookkeepers, insurance agents, pharmaceutical marketing, travel agents, food service managers, journalism, etc. It applies also to a wide range of value-added skills for enhancing the performance of workers in different occupations, such as safe driving, industrial safety, quality control, pollution control, water conservation, rainwater harvesting, energy conservation, customer service, etc.

Guaranteed Employment

The generation of employment opportunities is as natural for a society as the spontaneous growth of plants on fertile soil. Every person born brings with him an assortment of material and other needs that natural create employment opportunities for himself and others to meet. The problem of shortage arises only when the structure of society prevents the spontaneous growth of employment opportunities. Employment is a problem of reconciling the potential with the actual. Like the shortage of water for agriculture in India, it is not a genuine question of economic scarcity but rather a problem of management.

Information about the actual process of employment generation in India is severely limited. We know that some seven to eight million persons are entering the labour force every year. We know that the rate of unemployment is relatively stable over time. Therefore, we must conclude that the society is spontaneously creating approximately seven million jobs a year, of which only a few percent are in the private organized sector. This fact shows that the Indian economy is vibrant and fully capable of creating the additional employment opportunities necessary to absorb the unemployed and underemployed. Minor adjustments in the structure of laws, policies and institutions can accomplish it.

It was with this understanding that the International Commission on Peace & Food first proposed to the United Nations in 1994 that employment be considered a basic human right to be constitutionally guaranteed. At the time, the proposal appeared visionary and unlikely to be given serious consideration. Now, a brief decade later, the proposal has been endorsed by the Government of India and is in the process of being converted into law. Naturally, it is neither possible nor desirable that Government tries to directly create all the necessary jobs. What it can do is to make the necessary adjustments in laws, policies and institutions and supplement them with some selected programme initiatives that will accelerate the creation of new employment opportunities by the society.

The growth of any sector of the economy depends on the growth of and support it receives from other sectors and the extent of integration between activities in different sectors. Until now the growth of Indian agriculture has been severely constrained by the weakness of its linkages with other key sectors, including industry, agricultural education, banking, insurance, marketing and infrastructure. A conscious effort to strengthen these linkages can stimulate rapid growth in this sector resulting in rapid growth in employment opportunities.

REFERENCES

Foster A.D and Rosenzweig M.R. (2004). "Agricultural productivity growth, rural economic diversity and, economic reforms: India 1970–2000", in *Economic Development and Cultural Change*, Vol. 52, No. 3.

Hurst P. et al. (2005). *Agricultural workers and their contribution to sustainable agriculture and rural development* (FAO–ILO–IUF).

ILO: (2005). "Why agriculture still matters" in *World Employment Report 2004–05*, Ch. 3. Geneva.

Lanjouw J. and Lanjouw P. (2001). "The rural non-farm sector: Issues and evidence from developing countries", in *Agricultural Economics*, Vol. 26, No. 1.

Mellor J.W. and Lele U. (1973). "Growth linkages of the new food grain technologies", in *Indian Journal of Agricultural Economics*, Vol. 28, No. 1, pp. 35–55.

Panda B. et al.(2007). *Some issues in rural labor markets,* Rome, FAO, mimeo.

World Bank, (2007). *More and better investment in agriculture, World Development Report 2008 Policy Brief,* Washington, DC.

4

Rural Development and Agriculture

It is not an exaggeration to say that the battle to achieve the global society's stated objectives on hunger and poverty reduction will be won or lost in the rural areas of the developing countries. Globally, extreme poverty continues to be a rural phenomenon despite increasing urbanization. Of the world's 1.2 billion extremely poor people, 75 percent live in rural areas and for the most part they depend on agriculture, forestry, fisheries and related activities for survival. The promotion of the rural economy in a sustainable way has the potential of increasing employment opportunities in rural areas, reducing regional income disparities, stemming pre-mature rural-urban migration, and ultimately reducing poverty at its very source. In addition, development of rural areas may contribute to the preservation of the rural landscape, the protection of indigenous cultures and traditions while rural societies could serve as a social buffer for the urban poor in periods of economic crisis or social urban unrest.

However, public policies at national level and resource mobilization at both national and international levels have not always recognized the multiple potential of the rural economy. Public policies and investments in developing countries have historically favored industrial, urban and service sectors at the expense of agricultural and other rural sector development. In many cases, a coherent rural development policy (by its very nature cross-cutting) has fallen victim of the lack of a cross-sectoral institutional framework.

The past 20 years have witnessed a steep decline in the availability of public resources for agriculture and rural development. Between 1983-1987 and 1998-2000, the annual average allocations of Official Development Assistance (ODA) for agriculture in the least-developed and other low-income countries fell by 57 percent from USD 5.14 billion (2002 prices) to USD 2.22 billion. Lending from international financial institutions followed a similar pattern while domestic public spending has remained stagnant at best. The result has been reduced incentives for rural investment. Serious questions have also been raised as to the efficiency and effectiveness of public resource mobilization for agriculture and the rural space. For example, López and Galinato show a consistent bias in rural spending in Latin America in favor of subsidies and against investment in public goods which has translated into lower agricultural growth in the region.

An important question in the development debate regarding rural development has been the relationship between agriculture and the rural economy. In certain respects, past policy perceptions and practice have often equated rural development with agriculture, and rural development policies have been subsumed under an agricultural policy package. The issue of how and under what conditions agriculture is a driving force of rural growth has received scant attention or has given mixed messages including in the position of major multilateral financing institutions.

Recently however, the emergence of national and international commitments on poverty and related targets (as for instance in the Millennium Development Goals and the Poverty Reduction Strategies at country level) coupled with the failure of past paradigms to make mass reductions in rural poverty, have given a new impetus to the role of agriculture in development and poverty reduction. While at the same time, new rural development models have emerged (especially in the context of Latin America) emphasizing a more broad approach in which rural and urban space are viewed as a continuum and their interactions are emphasized (de Janvry and Sadoulet.

The principal objective is to present in a concise way, some of the conceptual issues regarding the role of agriculture in both rural and overall development, emphasizing its role in poverty reduction; and to explore if agricultural development can be an engine of growth and poverty reduction in developing countries, and under what conditions.

Agricultural and Rural Development

The definition of rural development has evolved through time as a result of changes in the perceived mechanisms and / or goals of development. A reasonable definition of rural development would be: development that benefits rural populations; where development is understood as the *sustained* improvement of the population's standards of living or welfare. This definition of rural development, however, has to be further qualified.

In the 1960's and early 1970's the consensus was that intense industrialization was the main characteristic of the perceived development path. In this context it seemed natural to define rural development as precisely leading into that path: "Rural development is essentially a part of structural transformation characterized by diversification of the economy away from agriculture. This process is facilitated by rapid agricultural growth, at least initially, but leads ultimately to a significant decline in the share of agriculture to total employment and output and in the proportion of rural population to total population.

Later during the 70's, mostly based on equity considerations, the focus and definition of rural development turned to the provision of social services to the rural poor. This shift was partially founded on the recognition that even under rapid growth of income in rural areas, the availability or equitable access to social services and amenities was not guaranteed. Lacroix exemplifies this line of thought when he explains the difference between agricultural and rural development: "Agricultural Development generally tries to raise agricultural production and productivity and is of a technical nature. It is similar to other efforts to develop physical capital as a means for economic growth... Rural Development, though, by definition is oriented more toward benefiting primarily the poor... Thus, the fundamental distinction between pure agricultural and rural development is the emphasis on capital development for the former, and human capital development for the latter."

Since the 1970's rural development as a concept has been highly associated with the promotion of standards of living and as a precondition for reducing rural poverty. This pro-poor bias was born from the understanding that, particularly in societies where wealth is extremely concentrated, mean incomes could grow without improving the well being of the most dispossessed. Thus, if the general definition of rural development is accepted, i.e. the improvement of the welfare of *all* members of the rural populations, then this pro-poor bias is justified.

On the other hand, the focus on human capital formation, through the provision of social services in rural areas has been constantly stressed since the 1970's. Originally, this focus stemmed from social equity considerations: it is fair that all of society's members have access to services like education and health. However, the development of endogenous growth theory in the late 1980's provided macro-foundations for this priority, as this theory proved how permanent growth / development is possible (even in the presence of constant returns to scale) when there is balanced investment in both human and physical capital at the same time.

Having defined rural development it is essential to define what is rural. Unfortunately there does not exist a single methodology, much less a single definition of what constitutes rural. The problem is that patterns of spatial occupation are, *inter alia*, culturally and historically determined and vary among regions of the world. A natural definition of rurality is to define it by exclusion, as that which is not urban, where urban is defined on the basis of population agglomerations.

In practice there are two main methodologies to define rural. The first methodology is to use a geopolitical definition. First, urban is defined by law as all of the state, region, and district capitals (centers), and by exclusion all the rest is defined as rural. Countries like Colombia, El Salvador, Dominican Republic, and Paraguay follow this methodology. In all of these countries urban population is defined as that living within the "*cabecera municipal*" the municipality's head or center. The drawbacks of this methodology are obvious: populations that live outside the geopolitical limit of a city (specially in a growing city) are miscounted as rural; while population living in tiny municipalities in sparsely populated regions is miscounted as urban.

The other popular methodology is to use observed population agglomeration to define urban. In this case populations that live within an area where contiguous households form populations larger than, say 2,000 inhabitants are considered urban, while by exclusion the rest is defined as rural. This methodology seems more attractive because it establishes a clear threshold; unfortunately this threshold varies widely around the world. In countries like Uganda, an agglomeration of only 100 inhabitants constitutes an urban settlement, while in countries like Nigeria and Mauritius the minimum agglomeration for urban areas is 20,000, and even 30,000 in Japan. In spite of these large variations certain thresholds are popular, like 2,000 in Chile, Argentina, Bolivia, Israel, and France; 2,500 Mexico and USA; and 5,000 in Belgium and Switzerland.

Other less popular methodologies consist of counting agglomerations of homes; for example, 100 contiguous dwellings constitutes an urban area in Peru. Other countries consider the availability of services as defining urban. For example in Honduras, an area is urban if, in addition to having a population of 2,000 inhabitants, it possesses services of water, electricity, education and health infrastructure. This definition is relevant from a poverty analysis standpoint because the absence of these services is usually associated with poverty; thus, this particular definition of rurality provides elements for characterizing poverty. In comparison, rural areas in developed nations have availability of all of the above mentioned services, spatially more scattered, but still available.

The limitations in comparability imposed by the differing definitions of rurality have spurred efforts to create internationally comparable measures of rurality. These projects merge satellite imagery, which shows population agglomerations, together with census data to spatially distribute populations. The GRUMP project (Global Rural Urban Mapping Project) is one major effort of the type, identifying cities with night-light satellite imagery and using census data to distribute population inside and outside those cities. Although the effort is important, it is still not an ideal measure because it depends on the reliability of the original census (and its degree of sub-administrative unit detail), and because it uses official (and therefore different) rurality figures in the model used to assign rural and urban populations. For Latin America, Chomnitz et al. created a rurality indicator based on population densities and distance to a major city. The cutoff point to define rurality is areas with populations living in densities below 150 inhabitants per squared kilometer *and* living more than 1 hour of travel away from a major city.

Although it seems easy to think of what is urban and rural, the multiplicity of definitions shows that it is not as easy to define. Furthermore, the fact that the definitions vary so greatly, creates a problem for making meaningful comparisons, when "rural" refers to a variety of different contexts. Finally, the beneficiaries of a successful rural development strategy, the rural populations could be larger than what official figures indicate.

Most of the world's poor live in rural areas. IFAD estimated in 2001 that among the poorest 1.2 billion people in the world, surviving with less than a dollar per day, three out of four lived in rural areas. They constitute the poorest fifth of world population and do not earn enough to cover their food needs. In a recent World Bank study, Ravallion et al. estimate that in 2002, 75% of the developing world poor still live in rural areas. As one of the most accepted characteristics of development is a secular decline in the share of agriculture, countries with larger rural populations shares are expected to be poorer since the main activity in the rural economies is likely to be agriculture.

Importance of Agriculture in Development

Economist as early as the beginning of the 20th century observed that wealthier countries were characterized by a smaller portion of their output coming from agriculture and relatively less labor resources tied to the same sector. They also noted that the process of development itself was characterized by a monotonic decline in the relative importance of agriculture and the primary sector in the economy, both in terms of GDP and employment.

Therefore, if the process of development is characterized by a shrinking agricultural sector, should the development "recipe" then suggest policies that are biased against agriculture (in favor of other sectors of the economy) to accelerate development? Or should agricultural growth be promoted to facilitate this structural transformation? If one looks at history, and recounts the policies that developing countries implemented from the late 1950s until the 1980s (particularly in Africa and Latin America), it would seem that they followed the first strategy.

Some economists argued that agriculture plays an important role in development. One of the first arguments in favor of the role of agriculture in development was placed by Lewis who suggested that "there are large sectors of the economy where the marginal productivity of labor is negligible, zero, or even negative." Of course these labor resources are tied to the primary sector, and are a key ingredient for industrial growth, which will occur thanks to a growing labor force coming from the primary sector. Hence, the primary sector plays, although passive, an important role in development. Later, Johnston and Mellor, identified some active roles that the agricultural sector performs throughout the development path: *i*) agriculture provides food necessary for a growing economy, as food demand, although at a decreasing rate, grows with income (Engel's Law); *ii*) agricultural exports generate the foreign exchange necessary to import capital goods; *iii*) agriculture, as the larger sector in less developed countries, is the only sector capable of generating the savings mass that the non-agricultural sector needs for capital accumulation; and *iv*) a growing agricultural sector creates a larger local market for the non-agricultural sector. These Johnston-Mellor linkages still remain relevant for developing economies with a large primary sector.

Johnston and Mellor were perhaps also the first to note that successful industrialization experiences are usually preceded by periods of dynamic agricultural growth. Although this does not amount to a causality link, the authors observed that countries that embark in a successful industrialization path, first experience fast agricultural expansion, fueled not by absorbing resources from the rest of the economy, but by rapid increases in productivity. The authors tell the story of Japan in the early 20th century.

However this was not a widely accepted message. During the second half of the 20th century there was no widely shared optimism concerning the role of agriculture in development. Agriculture was in practice condemned mainly by two separate schools of thought. The *structuralist* school (particularly strong in Latin America) provided arguments against agriculture. What eventually became to be known as the Prebisch-Singer hypothesis, states that the commodities that developing countries (the periphery) produce and export (i.e. primary commodities) have an income elasticity of demand less than one; as opposed to the demand elasticity of the industrial goods produced by the developed countries (the center) that have income demand elasticity that is not less than unity. Therefore in the long run the price of the primary commodities exported by developing countries relative to the price of the industrial goods imported by these same countries (i.e. the barter terms of trade) is doomed to fall. Thus, specializing and exporting these primary commodities is a losing development proposition.

This hypothesis was disseminated before reliable price time series were available. Today with good statistics it is a contentious debate if this hypothesis holds or not; principally because it depends on the primary commodity and the industrial/manufactures price index used as deflator. Also, should one account for changes in quality? Recent long-term analysis

(Ocampo and Parra) suggest that for most commodities the hypothesis does not hold. In the short-run most commodity prices are pro-cyclical. In the long-run some commodity real prices are non-stationary and thus move around a stable mean, while other commodities show one time falls in early 1920s and 1980s, and some other commodities show an upward trend like the relative price of meat. Therefore, the Prebisch-Singer hypothesis may apply to explain the failed development experience of any one particular country, dependent on a particular commodity, but it can not be generalized to all developing countries and to all commodities.

The second main hypothesis that condemned agriculture is related to the belief that agriculture has low potential for growth and its multiplier effect, its ability to "pull" the rest of the economy, is very low. The first part of this hypothesis can be traced back to Rosenstein-Rodan. He proposed that industrialization can be achieved by investing in several different industries separately, even if none of them *alone* generates enough rents to break even. This is possible because there exist economies external to the industry (i.e. increasing returns to scale) that spill-over to the rest of the economy. If there are enough industries generating this type of positive externalities, the "big push" into industrialization can be generated. Agriculture here lies in its absence, it is a sector that does not generate these economies external to the industry.

Also part of this agro-pessimism, and perhaps more influential in condemning the sector is Hirschman's work *The Strategy of Economic Development*. Hirschman opposed what he called a "balanced growth" strategy, of all sectors growing at the same rate, i.e. Rosenstein-Rodan "big-push" argument. Hirschman advised promoting the growth of the sector with the greater ability to pull the rest of the economy. He focused on the production backward linkages, that is the links in production that one sector has with the rest of the economy as a purchaser of inputs. If a sector A with high backward linkages expands, the rest of the economy will consequently experience a larger expansion, as it sells the inputs that sector A needs to grow. To uncover the backward linkages, Hirschman analyzed the input-output matrices of countries with available data: Italy, United States and Japan, and discovered that agriculture has high forward linkages, but among the lowest backward linkages of any other sector. "Agriculture – argues Hirschman – certainly stands convicted on the count of its lack of direct stimulus to the setting up of new activities through linkage effects: the superiority of manufacturing in this respect is crushing".

Below, evidence is presented to show that neither of these two propositions is really corroborated by the data. If (other) industries are inherently superior to agriculture, they would manifest a long-term productivity growth rate higher than agriculture. This appears not to be the case. Faruqui et al., for example, estimate the annual labor productivity growth of the primary industries in the USA at 3.1% while that of the manufacturing sector at 3.3% per year. A simple observation of the development process, in which labor employed in the agricultural sector falls, while output still grows, shows how there is a considerable increase in labor productivity in the primary sector during development. This simple observation is corroborated in studies like Parry that show high labor productivity growth in resource industries. Of course, one can find examples of the contrary, low or even negative productivity growth in primary industries, but this is by no means an inherent characteristic of the sector.

Agriculture's Production Linkages and Development

Linkages in the agricultural sector are easy to identify: forward linkages are mainly in the agricultural and food processing industries, in the service industry with the restaurant and hotel industries and, sometimes, public schooling. Similarly the main backward linkages are with the agricultural industries that produce animal feed, with the chemical and mineral industry for purchased fertilizers, and, depending on the degree of sophistication of the agricultural sector with the financial and business services sector and the industry of machinery manufacture. In many developing countries, backward industries consist of a large number of small firms (fertilizer mixing, small scale transport, agricultural implement repair, commerce, etc.) largely labor intensive and vital for the rural economy.

Common wisdom, as reflected in Hirschman's indictment of agriculture, suggests that as the agricultural sector becomes more developed, its backward linkages increase, by requiring more financial services, machinery and other purchased inputs. Also, the forward linkages are more important in a developed economy, where there is an existing and more developed food industry, and equivalently a hotel and restaurant industry. Therefore, common wisdom suggests that in terms of linkages, agriculture would not be a good sector to promote in early stages of development, because its linkages (and thus its multiplying effect) is low. These are important questions of rural and overall development that have rarely been studied systematically. *Testing the "linkages" hypothesis*

The place where the linkages between sectors are recorded in an economy is the input-output (I-O) matrix, which shows how the total output of each sector is distributed between final consumption, from households and the government, and intermediate inputs sales; describing how each sector sells inputs to all the other sectors of the economy. In the 1950's, when there was more faith in planning, these I-O matrices where used to discover the sector with the higher backward linkages, that is the sector that could have a greater effect in "pulling" the rest of the economy. The method applied was to calculate and find the higher Leontief multiplier. When a sector expands it demands inputs from other sectors to grow; in turn, these other sectors to supply these inputs need to expand and demand more inputs from yet some other sectors. This process continues infinitely, but in each round the size of the expansion is smaller. The limit of this process of expansions generated by the growth in one sector is given by inverting a transformation of the I-O matrix, which solves for the Leontief multipliers. This method has been usually criticized because as inputs are calculated in values, and not in units, any I-O analysis assumes fixed relative prices, an unrealistic assumption when the relative size of sectors change significantly. This criticism is valid, but the I-O analysis still provides relationships that are valid at the margin.

In spite of the mathematical beauty of the inverted Leontief multiplier matrix, the problem with the multiplier analysis is that the second, third and *nth* round of backward linkage caused expansions, although progressively smaller, may not realize; either because of frictions in the economy, or because these rounds take time to complete, and by the time they do, the economy may have changed. Furthermore, this multiplier analysis does not take into account the relative importance of sectors in the economy. For example, the sectors "multiplied" by another sector may be relatively insignificant for the economy in terms of income generated.

The fact that the value of linkages drops at higher levels of income makes sense, because the share of agriculture in total income is falling, and so does the value of the connections with the rest of the economy. Simple regression analysis, demonstrate that this correlation is statistically significant. That is, both forward and backward linkages are higher for countries at earlier stages of development (note that no causality is implied). Thus as countries are in their earlier stages of development, agriculture has a higher effect in national non-agricultural income. These results seem to contradict the intuition that as agriculture modernizes, forwards linkages should become more important, as countries develop an industrial food processing sector. This intuition, though, can be supported by looking at the relative size of the backward with respect to the size of agriculture. These latter results altogether convey that although linkages fall with development, the size of these linkages fall less than the decline in the relative size of agriculture.

These results are rather surprising, and deserve a closer inspection. The backward linkages, the focus of early development economists, not only are higher at earlier stages of development, but these linkages are among the highest of any sector at earlier stages of development. In the case of Bangladesh actually the highest, since Rice Milling is totally linked to agriculture, and agriculture itself is second in the ranking. Furthermore, even in middle-income countries, agriculture still has high backward linkages, as in the case of Chile, where the sector represents 4% of national GDP, but ranks 10th out of 71 sectors in importance of its backward linkages.

Understanding Structural Transformation as a General Equilibrium Process to agriculture as a key sector to promote development as its backward linkages are highest at earlier stages of development. Therefore, a development strategy that promotes agriculture will indirectly "pull" the rest of the economy towards development. However, looking at output linkages may not be the key for the design of long-term development policies. As Timmer states, part of the controversy of the role of agriculture in development stems from the fact that structural transformation is a general equilibrium process that can not be explained by looking at agriculture alone.

López et al., explain the process of reduction of the relative size of agriculture, i.e. structural change within the context of a two sector endogenous growth model. The authors show that even when labor productivity grows at the same rate in agriculture as in the industrial sector, and even if there is no declining income demand elasticity for the agricultural good, agriculture will relatively contract because one of its production assets can not be indefinitely accumulated. This asset is of course a renewable resource, which can be understood as water, land, soil quality, etc., which is limited in its supply by nature. The income maximizing path is achieved by equating the returns to assets. The relative contraction of agriculture, and the migration of assets from agriculture into the industrial sector is a result of this equating of marginal returns to assets that can be employed in agriculture or industry, like labor.

The equation of marginal returns to assets, that at the aggregate level are always decreasing can be considered as the *golden rule of development*, not the promotion of the sector with high multiplier effect. While this has rather obvious policy implications and one that most economists would recommend intuitively, unfortunately if one looks at the "import substitution" era one finds the most egregious anti-agricultural bias and incredible disparities of returns to assets within the rural and urban world. For example, in China and India, the pursued industrialization policies implied a strong pro-urban bias leaving the returns to investment in the rural areas with much higher rates of return. In a very influential work, that is partially responsible for turning the anti-agricultural tide Krueger et al. (with main results summarized in Krueger et al.) show that on average (over 16 developing countries for the period 1975-1984) the exchange rate overvaluation and import tariffs on industrial goods were the equivalent to at least an 11% export tax on each country's agricultural export.

Another important lesson that can be obtained from a general equilibrium development analysis, is an interpretation of poverty traps, i.e. those countries that are unable generate enough savings to lead them into the development path. These countries are characterized by overstretching their natural resources, a manifestation of this overstretching being an excess of labor resources employed in resource using sectors. The general equilibrium view suggests two ways to exit a poverty trap: On one hand, there is implicitly low productivity in the industrial sector, and investing in non-agricultural productivity can help increase the demand for labor in the industrial sector and reduce the pressure on the resource. However, another possibility is to increase agricultural productivity to make the operation sustainable. Today most of the rural poor live in fragile tropical ecosystems, and where labor is not a major economic constraint. Most of the human and financial resources, public and private, that are devoted to agricultural R&D, are employed in research that is relevant for capital intensive and temperate climate agriculture; i.e. which are the needs of developed countries' agriculture.

Agriculture's Pro-Poor Role

Not all growth experiences are equal. There is a growing focus on the importance of a "pro-poor growth" defined as growth (an increase in average income / purchasing power) that is also accompanied by an improvement in the distribution of income. To help in the understanding of a formal definition of the concept, let imagine a rural world with only 100 inhabitants. One person owns the only farm, and earns 101 monetary units, while the rest are 99 laborers that earn 1 currency unit each. If the poverty line is 2, then the headcount poverty rate in this rural economy is 99%. Let consider 2 growth possibilities: (*i*) the owner earns 151.5 and the workers earn 1.5 each; and (*ii*) the owner earns 201 while the laborers still earn 1 each. Initially, the average income is 2, so on average nobody is poor. In both growth possibilities, income grows exactly by an striking 50%, however in both cases poverty remains at 99%. In the first case, all incomes grow exactly by 50%, so there is no change in the distribution of income, and all inequality measures commonly used (which are sensitive to the distribution and not to the level of income) remain constant. On the second case, while growth is the same, the distribution of wealth deteriorates, and income inequality measures rise.

The above example serves to highlight some important facts about growth. First, when the initial distribution is extremely unequal, growth is not enough to reduce poverty, even if there is "trickle down" of the benefits of growth, as in case (*i*). Given that many examples of growth that resemble cases (*i*) and (*ii*) have been documented, with limited or no reduction of poverty, is that researchers have turned their attention to "pro-poor growth". In example assume case (*iii*) all incomes grow by 1. In case (*iii*), growth is also exactly 50%, but the distribution of income has improved, and more importantly poverty has been reduced to 0%. Case (*iii*) is an example of pro-poor growth.

Different formulas have been proposed to formally define pro-poor growth. Both Ravallion and Chen and Kakwani et al. propose formulas to measure "pro-poor growth" that involve scaling up or down the observed growth rate by a factor that is greater (less) than one if inequality has been reduced (increased).

There is ample theoretical support and empirical evidence that suggests that agriculture is pro-poor, and that growth based on the expansion of the sector is pro-poor growth. Four main channels by which agricultural growth helps poverty alleviation:

- *Directly increasing the income/own consumption of small farmers*: Small holders are usually not only inadequately endowed with land, but usually also lack other assets, like physical and human capital, and thus are usually poor. Expansion of the agricultural sector may benefit also the small-holder sector and pull some of them out of poverty. Small farms are, with respect to capital and land utilization, labor intensive (own family labor), and therefore are likely to benefit from technological progress that is labor intensive. When land distribution is equitable, it will be the case that expansion of agriculture will benefit the small-holder sector; when the land distribution is inequitable there could be agricultural growth fully based on large farm output expansion, in which case the small holder sector would not necessarily benefit.

- *Indirectly by reducing food prices*: Most measures of poverty are based, directly or indirectly in the cost of access to food. When the price of food is reduced, there is a two-way accounting improvement in the welfare of the poor. In the first place their real income increases, and more so than the wealthier, because food is the main component of their consumption basket. At the same time, the poverty line which is usually used to measure poverty is decreased, which acts to alleviate poverty. In a completely open economy without any additional transaction costs, the price of food should not be affected by agricultural growth in the same country. However, not all food is tradable, many perishable vegetables are for all purposes non-tradables. In addition, the bulk of cereal staple foods produced and consumed by the poor in rural areas are traded in local markets which, due to high transactions costs are disconnected from larger (including international) markets.
- *Indirectly by increasing the income generated by the non-farm rural economy*: The rural non-farm economy in most regions is either: mostly composed of goods and services that directly serve agriculture, or indirectly depend of the demand of those tied to agriculture. The more disconnected the rural economy is from urban markets, the more dependent is the rural non-farm sector on the income generated by what is usually the main engine of the rural economy: agriculture. Hence, agricultural growth can increase the demand for the goods and service of the rural non-farm sector and help pull out of poverty households tied to this sector.
- *Indirectly by raising employment and wages of the unskilled*: Agriculture is usually intensive in unskilled labor. Thus, agricultural growth through an increase in unskilled labor demand will increase

unskilled employment and/or the wages of the unskilled, most of which are poor. There is here a general equilibrium effect, because raising the unskilled wages in agriculture pushes upward the unskilled wages in urban areas also. This latter general equilibrium effect will be higher the more integrated rural and urban labor markets are.

Given these channels through which agriculture reduces poverty, it should come as no surprise that the overwhelming empirical evidence shows that agricultural growth is not only pro-poor, but more pro-poor than other sectors of the economy. The key in this fundamental result lies in that all four channels described benefit the poorest households of the economy more than the rest. In a seminal study Ravallion and Datt used a long time series data from India, to explain poverty with output from the different sectors of the economy. They found a large elasticity of poverty with respect to primary output (-1.2), with the sector being more effective at poverty alleviation than industry. Kakwani used the additive property of the most popular poverty indicators, the FGT (Foster, Greer, Thorbecke) class, and decomposed the effect of sectoral growth in poverty. Using the information of a 1985 Côte d'Ivoire household survey she shows that the elasticity of poverty with respect to agricultural output is much larger (-1.8) than other sectors such as services (-0.1) and industry (-0.1). Thorbecke and Jung used the additive property of the FGT poverty measures and a Social Accounting Matrix (SAM) to decompose the contribution of each sector to poverty alleviation. The authors apply this methodology to Indonesia, and find that the primary sector has a larger contribution to poverty alleviation than the industrial sector, and slightly larger than the services sector.

The fact that agriculture is more pro-poor than other sectors seems to be substantiated in poor countries like India and Côte d'Ivoire; as well as in middle income countries like South Africa. It is reasonable to expect that at different stages of development different channels dominate the pro-poor role of agriculture. The four channels described above are ordered in their likely importance from earlier stages of development, a ranking that can be corroborated by the scattered evidence. In very poor countries, most agricultural output comes from small holders, and therefore, this is likely the most important pro-poor channel of agriculture, for example, for poor Sub-Saharan nations. This intuition is consistent with the results of de Janvry and Sadoulet, who show that following a (simulated) technological improvement, the direct effect of technical progress on poor farmers is the main poverty reducing factor in Sub Saharan Africa, larger than price and employment effects. In Asia employment effects dominate, while in Latin America indirect effects on the rest of the economy are more important in the poverty reducing effect of agricultural technological progress. The food price effect is also likely to be more important in poorer regions, because they are likely to have a food basket highly dominated by 1 staple crop, like in some poor Asian nations. Timmer shows that in the case of Indonesia 80% of the variability of the poverty to growth elasticity can be explained just by changes in the real price of rice. Note that when the price of rice falls, it adversely affects poverty by reducing income of poor farmers; however, when the price fall is caused by gains in productivity this is not necessarily the case.

As rural economies develop, the non farm economy becomes more sophisticated and diversified, and as show below more important within the rural economy. Therefore, this indirect effect becomes more important. On the other hand, with development, the rural non farm economy becomes more tied to the rest of the economy, diminishing this indirect effect. This is consistent with the very high demand multiplier from agriculture found by Haggblade et al. in poor Sub-Saharan rural economies; but also consistent with the high indirect poverty elasticity of agriculture found by de Janvry and Sadoulet for Latin America in general.

Finally, as agriculture makes its transformation into commercial farming, the direct effect of the sector on small and poor farmers becomes much smaller, but commercial farmers are employers of unskilled labor; and concomitantly with the commercial farm transformation and their interaction with world markets, generally rural economies become interlinked with the rest of the economy, in particular with urban markets. These are the preconditions for agriculture to have an important effect on the employment and wages of unskilled workers. Anríquez and López show that in Chile, where the lion share of agricultural output comes from medium and large commercial farms, agriculture is still more pro-poor than other sectors of the economy, and that this poverty to agricultural growth elasticity is mostly explained (90%) by the effect of agriculture on unskilled labor markets.

Agriculture vs. Rural Development

To what extent is rural development the same as agricultural development? In other words, in which case does a sectoral (agricultural) driver to rural growth is indispensable? To answer this question need to have an idea of the importance of agriculture within the rural world. There is no direct measurement to uncover the importance of agriculture within the rural economy, but will show alternative roads which indirectly point to that measure.

Agriculture, is an important component of most rural economies especially in the developing countries. It was shown above that the size of agriculture within the local economy is sometimes used to define rurality. Therefore, any successful rural development strategy will contain an agricultural development component; but they are not the same thing. While agricultural development aims at improving the welfare of populations through sustained improvements in the productivity of the agricultural sector, rural development aims at the improvement of welfare of rural populations through the sustained growth of the rural economy, which includes agriculture, but may not be its only component and not necessarily the most dynamic.

Ideally, if wanted to know the importance of agriculture within a rural area, would look at the GDP or output figure for that region, and measure the share of agricultural output within the total value added of the region. Unfortunately only few countries have aggregate output figures available by region (state or province), and even at this regional level, output is aggregated for both rural and urban areas.

We show above that the importance of agriculture within the national economy falls with development, but this does not necessarily mean that the relative importance of agriculture in the rural economy also falls with development (given that rurality also falls with development). Poorer countries, with lower per capita income, and with higher incidence of poverty, not only are more rural, but in their economies agriculture has a higher relative weight. Thus, the poorer the economy, the more important agriculture is for its rural and overall development.

Another road to measure the value of agriculture in the rural economy is to examine the share of income from agriculture to total rural income. This can be done, thanks to household surveys that measure income, most of them implemented in developing countries since the 1950's to understand poverty. Unfortunately, the way researchers have measured rural agricultural income *vis-à-vis* non-agricultural income (also known as rural non-farm income) has varied too much. Examples of these conceptual inconsistencies are: to add remittances (which in countries like Pakistan and in Central America can amount to more than 5% and even 10% of household incomes) to rural non-farm income, when remittances are not *rural* (sometimes not even national) income. Other inconsistencies arise with income from wages of agricultural labor. Some authors add wages accrued in farms outside their own to non-farm income, when it is clear that this is agricultural income. Further problems arise when wage income due to the absence of information can not be assigned to any particular sector, in these cases all of wage income can be added to either the farm or non-farm sector. Some authors even add food sales to non farm income. Then there are gray areas, like the way in which to value own agricultural consumption; or income from fishing and forestry that could be added to either farm or non-farm income. These conceptual differences and inconsistencies highlight the need for comparable measures of agricultural and non-agricultural rural income to make further meaningful cross-country comparisons and studies.

However, for purpose of uncovering any links between rural agricultural income and development, these measures, alas inconsistent, will be helpful. For this study have collected share of rural agricultural income for 120 country-year combinations. Three country-year combinations are repeated with different figures, and keep all the information as are in no condition to discriminate the inaccurate information. The main sources are, FAO, and Lanjouw and Feder, that made comparable recollections of rural non-farm income shares, and own collection from more than 30 monographs, mostly from rural household survey studies. This database contains information from four continents and it spans the period 1950 to 2002.

As per capita GDP increases, the share of agricultural income in total rural income tends to fall, although at middle income level (medium for the sample) the share seems to lie relatively stable. Per capita GDP may be a good indicator of overall development for a country, but not necessarily an equally good indicator of rural development. When the share of agricultural income in total rural income is ordered by agricultural GDP per rural inhabitant categories, there is clearly a diminishing trend for the share as income increases.

The results confirm that more developed rural economies have a lower share of agricultural income in total rural income. This relationship is statistically significant, and the estimated elasticity indicates that a 1%

growth in rural per capita agricultural income reduces the share of agriculture in total rural income by about 0.12%. Also, the differences in income (development stage) explain one fifth of the variability of the share of agricultural income in total rural income, which is a good fit considering the possible inconsistencies in the measurement of agricultural income; and that geographic, agroecological and climatological differences probably explain a lot of the observed variability.

The negative relationship between rural development and the share of agricultural income can also be confirmed by examining time series data for particular countries. In Japan for example the share of agricultural income in rural income dropped from 82% in 1950 to 30% in 1980; similar drop can be observed in India, 92% to 62% in the period 1958-1994; and in China from 90% to 67% in the period 1980-1997. In Bangladesh the share of agricultural income in rural income actually went up in the period 1963-1982 from 82% to 92%, but real income also dropped in this Asian country during this same period.

Spatial Constraints to the Promotion of the Non-Farm Economy

In general, in the rural space find activities that require proximity to the point of extraction or production: primary activities like agriculture, fishing, forestry and mining; industry that may benefit from proximity to the sources of raw material like food and other processing ; and services that need proximity to the resource like eco and agro tourism. In less developed countries scant evidence indicates that most non-farm activities are closely linked to agriculture and cluster regionally in small and medium-sized towns, Haggblade et. al.

The realization that non-farm activities enjoy economies of agglomeration and tends to cluster throughout the rural space has motivated the promotion of rural development strategies that promote the non-farm sector but with regional focuses. One early such strategy was the clusters promotion, which focused on the development of regions specialized in one industry or non-farm sector (i.e. wine industry or steel industry cluster). More recently, the territorial approach to rural development has proposed a more integral approach by seeking the promotion of both agricultural and non-agricultural activities jointly at a regional level, de Janvry and Sadoulet. Both strategies presume the existence of rural-scale agglomerations that make viable the promotion of a particular non-farm sector. A successful territorial approach strategy requires the existence of the agglomerations and/or infrastructure which will facilitate the reaping of benefits from economies of agglomerations and scale.

In this latter spatial context it is hard to argue in favor of a territorial strategy. Not only are densities very low, but they are *de facto* compounded by a very poor standing communications infrastructure. In these contexts a sectoral, agricultural based rural development strategy is still the necessary first step.

Some Policy Implications

The last few years have seen an increased attention of the international development community on agriculture and rural development. If the data for the last 3 years constitute a real trend then are witnessing a real increase in official development assistance to agriculture and rural development. The emergence of private donors and foundations (such as the Gates foundation) with keen interest in transferring resources to agriculture is a welcome development. Major multilateral donors (such as the World Bank) are looking at agriculture as an engine for poverty reduction for most developing countries and regions and a fundamental component of a growth and poverty reduction strategy for the poorest, agriculture based economies. There seems to be increased interest by domestic and foreign private capital (including multinational agro-industrial firms) for investments in sectors up and downstream of production agriculture. The potential of agriculture as a source of bio-energy promises to attract further attention to the potential of the sector to produce and address global food and energy needs.

It provides analytical evidence and arguments in support of the proposition that agriculture and the rural economy are fundamental for obtaining substantive and sustainable gains in the fight against poverty. Even using the existing, highly imperfect measures of "rurality" (which very likely underestimate the economic importance and dimensions of the rural space and the extent of rural poverty) poverty is intrinsically linked to rurality. What the evidence shows is that even when population movements and demographics reduce the share of the rural in total developing country population, poverty will still be a predominantly rural phenomenon. The experience of Latin America (the most urbanized of the developing regions) is instructive in this regard: even in countries where the number of rural poor are less than the number of urban poor, the poverty rate is nevertheless higher in the rural areas.

It also shows that the analytical underpinnings of a development strategy with a strong anti-agricultural bias do not hold in light of new data and evidence. Agriculture has strong links with other sectors in many countries and, a productivity-induced agricultural expansion can "pull" other sectors with it, increase economic activity and employment opportunities in the rural areas. It also shows that, while a regional or spatial approach to the development of the rural economy is a reasonable proposition for countries with good infrastructure, functioning labor and other markets, there is substantial scope for a sectoral (agricultural) entry point for rural and possibly overall development and poverty reduction. This proposition is further corroborated by the results of Davis et al., who show that despite income diversification by rural households; households in the lowest expenditure categories have a larger share of agricultural in their total income than households in higher income groups.

The balance of entry points for rural development and poverty reduction is bound to change, as food systems change both globally and, especially in developing countries. However, such a change hides both opportunities and threats. First, the role of agriculture in the structure of the economy will decline in the process of development. However, the data on the agricultural transformation shows that the labor share of agriculture declines much slower than the share of agriculture in national GDP. Unless policies and investments are put in place to foster agricultural productivity, there is a danger that the decline of agriculture will be accompanied by increased rural poverty some of which will find its way into the urban areas. At the same time, policies and programs which increase the human capital of the rural poor and allow them to enter a more remunerative labor markets are powerful tools to ensure a smooth transition of people out of agriculture without increasing poverty.

At the same time a transformation of the agricultural sector itself is underway. Growing per capita incomes have increased and will increase further the demand for high value food products and for the quality and safety characteristics of foods. Such shifts in demand are reflected in the structure of the food systems even in some of the poorest developing countries towards the spread of the modern food chains and consolidation of the production, distribution and retail segments of food markets. The role of the more traditional "chain" will shrink overtime. Therefore, while increasing productivity for food staples oriented agriculture will still be an important anti-poverty entry point for many poor areas in the world, the high requirements in terms of skills and capital by the "new agriculture" point to the need for increased access to modern technologies (research and extension systems) which promote the higher quality and safety standards demanded by consumers.

Will trends towards (domestic) market integration, and globalization affect the strength of the links between primary agriculture and up-stream and down-stream sectors? On one hand, market integration will sever the links between agriculture and the local economy, but will open new links to larger markets (regional, national or even global). Opening the agricultural sector to foreign but also domestic competition will challenge the position of smallholders in national markets. The non-farm rural economy will also be subjected to competition pressures from cheaper consumer goods distributed by supermarkets and similar retail outlets as they expand to the rural areas of developing countries. Small scale and artisanal food processing may give way to more organized, capital intensive processing plants and a similar scenario may be thought for other activities up or down-stream primary agriculture (such as transport or input processing, etc.). The speed and extent to which these changes will occur will vary by context as will vary the net effects on employment etc.

In such cases, even if the "inverse" relationship between size and productivity were to hold in primary production (commodity production) especially of staples, larger farmers will more than likely have an advantage in producing what will be increasingly demanded: high value products requiring capital intensive technologies and human and managerial capital.

However, the future of smallholders and rural livelihoods is not without opportunities: access to larger markets and higher value alternatives will also be available for those who innovate and are able to take up opportunities presented by the changing system. Public policy will have a significant role to play in this context. In addition to providing the "traditional" public goods it also needs to provide assistance to farmers in dealing with new product requirements, and creating the proper institutional and regulatory framework to enable smallholders to organize so as to exploit available economies of scale and promote competition.

References

Edward J Blakely & Ted K Bradshaw, (2003). *Planning Local Economic Development: Theory and Practice,* Vistaar Publications, New Delhi.

Katar Singh, (2009). *Rural Development: Principles, Policies and Management,* (3rd Edition) Sage Publications, New Delhi.

Meenakshisundaram S S, (1994). *Decentralization in Developing Countries,* Concept Publishing Company, New Delhi

Stan Burkey, (1993). People First: *A Guide to Self-reliant, Participatory Rural Developmen*t, ZED Books, London & New York.

5

Rural Non-Farm Employment

With the process of development, the share of non-farm income and employment in the total income and employment of the rural households increases in the developing countries. A combination of farm and non-farm income at the household level provides resilience against adverse situations in either of the sectors, though agriculture is known for more frequent adversity. There are also evidences to show that productivity and profitability in the non-farm sector is generally higher than in the farm sector; as are the average wages and working conditions that obtain in the non-farm sector. A greater reliance on the non-farm sector would therefore provide a demand-pull to rural economy and also ensure welfare for rural workers.

A comparative account of the non-farm sector in the rural *vis-à-vis* the urban sector however, shows significant disparity in terms of its size and growth. The lopsided nature of growth of the non-farm sector is causing a problem of rural - urban migration. The small base of the rural non-farm sector located within a large rural population is in fact indicative of the employment potential in the rural non-farm sector (RNFS). Achievement of employment growth as per its potential may require a more favourable policy environment; and the present study attempts to search for these policy options.

The rural non-farm sector (RNFS) encompasses all non-agricultural activities: mining and quarrying, household and non-household manufacturing, processing, repair, construction, trade and commerce, transport and other services in villages and rural towns undertaken by enterprises varying in size from household own-account enterprises to factories. The RNFS thus comprises diverse activities while sustained growth in the RNFS depends on a varied set of factors, depending on the kind of impetus, positive or negative, that these factors provides to the rural economy RNFS will experience development- and distress- related rural diversification. For a better understanding of rural diversification it is necessary to study the participation of rural households in particular non-farm activities; the motivation behind the decisions as well as the ability of the households to participate in these.

The state plays an important role in encouraging positive rural diversification. The rural economy includes several heterogeneous rural activities having different demand and supply conditions in their input and output markets. Government policies therefore, in most of the cases are industry specific. In a labour surplus country like India, the government also has a role to play in regulating and mediating in the rural labour market.

Macro Trends in Rural Employment

In this section, an effort has been made to understand the pattern of rural non-farm employment at aggregate and disaggregate levels using the National Sample Survey (NSS) quinquennial data on employment. The study also utilizes Economic Census data from the Central Statistical Organization (CSO). Previous studies related to the rural non-farm employment suggest that construction, trade, and transport have emerged as the engine of rural employment growth; these industries together account for only 11 per cent of the rural workforce. Can these industries with such a small base sustain the growth of the rural non-farm employment in a country such as India? How have women benefited in terms of employment growth in the rural non-farm sector is another question that this section attempts to answer.

Though the share of agriculture in the economy has declined during the planned development of the country, it still assumes a pivotal role in the rural economy since three-fourths of the rural work force is dependent on it. The bulk of employment in agriculture is rural-based (97 per cent) and it is astonishing that rural employment growth in agriculture is abysmally low (0.06 per cent) and insignificant during the 90s. The corresponding growth was moderate and significant (1.1 per cent) during the 80s. It is however interesting that the growth of agricultural income during the 90s is higher (0.02 per cent) than in the 80s. These trends suggest job-less growth in agriculture during the 90s. An enquiry into the pattern of growth in agricultural income suggests that growth in agricultural income during the 90s is largely because of value addition in agriculture. Whereas, intensity of employment in agriculture depends more on cropped area and crop area indices have decreased during the 90s. Further, livestock which has emerged as an important source of rural employment during the 80s has undergone structural changes, as the livestock population in fact declined. The recent livestock census shows that population of cattle and goat has declined after the mid-90s. As a matter of fact, rearing of cattle and goat is highly labour intensive; a decline in absolute number of population suggests decline of employment in the livestock sector.

The annual compound growth rate (ACGR) of employment in the non-agricultural sector, unlike for agriculture, has been positive and significant during the 90s; this has held true for both rural and urban sectors. The ACGR of employment in the non-agriculture sector during 1994-2000 has been less than in the previous reference period, 1983-1994. The non-agriculture industrial categories where employment growth during the 90s was positive and also higher than in the previous reference period were manufacturing, construction, trade, transport, and business services. This trend in employment growth was slightly different at the level of the rural and urban sectors. In the urban sector, manufacturing, trade, transport and business services were the industries where employment growth during 90s was higher than in the previous reference period; while in the rural sector, construction, transport and business services, recorded a higher growth during the 90s as compared to the previous decade. It must be noted that the base of these industrial categories in the rural sector was very low.

In manufacturing, employment growth during the 80s was similar in both the rural and urban sectors; disparity in the rate of growth between these sectors has surfaced in the 90s. The possible reasons for disparity in the rural and urban rate of growth of employment in manufacturing during the 90s are as follow: (a) burgeoning gap in rural and urban infrastructure facilities with regard to assured power and telecommunications; (b) increasing focus on cost-competitiveness with trade liberalization which discourages rural manufacturing that is generally small scale in either the organized or unorganized categories; (c) uncertain policy environment for small-scale industry has also discouraged some village resource-based manufacturing activities in the rural sector; and (d) with trade liberalization and growing consumerism the relative importance of goods produced in the urban sector has increased even for the rural masses.

A detailed study by Uma Rani *et al.* lists reasons for particular trend of employment and income in the manufacturing sector. The study found that in manufacturing activities undertaken in the organized and unorganized sectors during the years 1984-1999 the growth of employment, value-addition and capital in the organized manufacturing sector has grown during 1984-95 and declined subsequently. The unorganized sector presents a different trend. Growth in this sector has peaked up during the 1984-90, flattened during the 1989-95 and surged ahead in subsequent years (1995-00) following the adoption of promotional policies towards unorganized segments of small-scale industries. This growth has been particularly high for the organic as compared to the inorganic manufacturing units. It is significant that organic manufacturing is mostly village resource-based and with favourable infrastructures for manufacturing in the rural sector, organic manufacturing industries can be attracted.

Employment growth in construction peaked during the 90s, though it was fairly high (1.75%) even in the 80s. In the urban sector, construction activity has peaked early (in the 80s) while in rural India a high growth was experienced during the 90s. The extension of basic infrastructure like roads in rural India might have encouraged employment growth in rural construction during the 90s. A state-wise analysis of data would throw light on the possible factors favouring the robust growth in construction activity. Certain economic policies might also have encouraged construction activities in the 90s.

Transport-storage-communication (TSC) and finance-insurance-real-estate-business (FIREB) services are the industrial categories where employment increased in both the rural and urban sectors. Employment in TSC appears to be more influenced by increased investment in infrastructure such as roads which are being prioritized in recent years. Increased investment in infrastructure increases the quality of real estate and consequently, the income and employment in real estate. This in turn has spread effects on the growth of business services. Trade, hotels and restaurants (THR) are the other industrial categories where employment growth was positive and significant in both the sectors, though the rate of growth was higher in the urban sector.

In the 90s, employment growth was negative in mining and quarrying, utilities and community services. These industries largely fall within the domain of the public sector. Since there is already an effort to downsize the role of the public sector, a decline of employment in these industrial categories is obvious. Incomes in these sectors are in fact salaries and with an implementation of the Fifth Pay Commission recommendations during the late 90s, salary in this industrial category has increased. In mining, the decline in employment could also have been accentuated because of the strict environmental regulations and an increased focus on clean technologies. Strict environmental regulations have in fact, caused the closure of many mining units. Again the focus on cleaner technology, which essentially means a greater use of gas and oil-based technology rather than coal, has discouraged the production of coal. As a matter of fact, coal is labour-intensive while gas and oil is capital-intensive; so this substitution could also have caused a decline of employment despite increase of income in mining.

Growth of employment in agriculture plateaued, though agricultural income has grown during the period. Job-less growth in agriculture is on account of value-added growth in this sector. A continuous process of transformation from subsistence to a commercial mode of production in agriculture and livestock has also contributed to this trend. Manufacturing, which is another source of employment growth, was also insignificant in the rural sector in the 90s. Employment growth in the rural sector was propelled by construction, trade, transport and business services. It is interesting to note that employment intensity in these industrial categories also increased during the 90s. These industrial categories however, account for only 11 per cent of rural employment; therefore employment intensity in the non-agriculture sector could not increase during the 90s.

Rural Employment Trends in States

The above discussion gives a comparative account of employment for major industries at the aggregate level. Certain trends, which were evident at the aggregate level, may emerge robust with the help of state-level information. Over a span of 17 years, the share of agriculture in rural employment has declined by only 2 per cent at the aggregate level. There are mixed trends from the states; the percent share of agriculture has not declined in the states of Andhra Pradesh, Bihar, Karnataka, Madhya Pradesh, Maharashtra and

Orissa. The reasons for non-decline of rural employment in agriculture could be different for these states. In certain states like Bihar and Orissa, a dearth of opportunity in the non-agricultural sector could have pushed rural workers towards agriculture whereas in states like Maharashtra the pull factor could have attracted the rural workforce in agriculture. These issues need further probing.

In the non-agriculture employment categories, manufacturing is the most important, accounting for more than 7 per cent of rural employment in the country. With economic development, one would expect manufacturing to become more important in the rural sector; however there is only a marginal increase in its share during the reference period. The share of manufacturing in rural employment has in fact declined in some states like Andhra Pradesh, Bihar, Goa, Karnataka, Kerala, Madhya Pradesh, Maharashtra, Orissa and Punjab; whereas, in Assam, Delhi, Gujarat, Haryana, Tamilnadu and West Bengal, the share of manufacturing has increased during the reference period.

Though the reasons responsible for these trends may be different for different states; changes in infrastructures to a large extent explain these trends. In the latter group of states, rural infrastructure has increased significantly during the reference period. This does not necessarily mean that the rural infrastructure in the earlier group of states is poor. A significant increase of rural infrastructure in these states might not have taken place during the reference period. There is evidence at least from Punjab to suggest that even with relatively better rural infrastructure, manufacturing activities have shifted away from the rural sector. It may be noted that the rural sector here is defined on the basis of census classification rather than the revenue records. Urbanization and better infrastructure facilities like assured power could also have lead to this situation.

The state of Delhi presents a different pattern of growth in which rural manufacturing has increased significantly. The developed world arguments to justify manufacturing in the rural sector as for example, low cost of living, etc, in the rural sector probably hold good for Delhi. While the difference in rural and urban infrastructure from the view-point of manufacturing is not there in Delhi; nevertheless, manufacturing activities in the rural sector of Delhi has certain advantages; these units escape some regulations imposed by municipal corporations.

The utilities (consisting of electricity, water), mining and quarrying are the employment categories not very important from the rural employment perspective. Both these categories registered negative growth during 90s at the aggregate level. The share of mining in rural employment has however increased at the aggregate level, whereas the share of utilities in rural employment like its share at the aggregate level has declined.

Construction has provided an important impetus for the growth of rural employment; its share in most of the states barring Karnataka, Madhya Pradesh and Maharashtra has increased. The states of Bihar and Orissa, which have not performed well otherwise have done well in construction. It appears that population pressure in these states accompanied by a favourable policy environment for building construction material during the reference period has encouraged construction activity. There can be other reasons such as increase in per capita income for improved construction activity in the country.

Trade is another industry group, in which evidence of rural employment increase is apparent for most of the states. The states of Andhra Pradesh, Orissa and Tamil Nadu were exceptions. The share of transport in rural employment has increased for all the reference states. The creation of basic infrastructure like roads is obviously increasing in recent years in the rural sector; subsequently rural employment in transport has also increased.

Services in rural employment are grouped into two categories namely; community social and personal (CSP) services, which largely fall under the domain of the public sector; while finance insurance real estate and business (FIREB) services are subsumed under the private sector. The share of CSP services in rural employment has also declined in the country, though Assam was an exception. It may be noted that in the recent decade there has been a greater focus on the North-Eastern states including Assam, which may have led to an increase in the share of CSP services. The share of CSP services in rural employment also might have declined on account of a rural-urban classification in the census as well. There is a possibility that with an increase of rural employment in the community social and personal services of a place, the population around that place increases and with an increase of population beyond 5000, the village (rural) gets reclassified as town (urban) sector.

The share of FIREB services in rural employment has increased marginally at the aggregate level; though this has emerged as important for some states such as Andhra Pradesh, Bihar, Gujarat, Haryana, Kerala, Maharashtra, Rajasthan. The share of FIREB services has also declined in many states like Delhi, Goa, Karnataka, Orissa and West Bengal. There could be a variety of reasons that vary across states for this decline in the share of FIREB services. Increase of employment in FIREB services requires slightly different kinds of skill and infrastructure, for example, better literacy, more communication-related infrastructures. Basic infrastructure like roads is almost a precondition for the growth trajectory of the non-agriculture sector to take-off.

The nature and pattern of rural employment across states, shows that various independent factors influence employment in the non-agricultural sectors. Demography or population pressure for instance, influences construction activity, while rural literacy in general promotes FIREB services.

The study found that employment in trade and transport is highly correlated and is more influenced by basic infrastructure such as roads. The expansion of rural roads appears to both increase rural employment in trade and transport, while there is also evidence that availability of roads encourages employment of skilled rural work-force in urban centers in selected industries like manufacturing and business services. Infrastructure as such is important for employment in most of the industrial categories. The kind of infrastructure however, varies across industries; for instance, employment in manufacturing requires more of assured power /electricity; while employment in transport and trade requires basic infrastructure like roads; employment in finance-insurance-real estate-business services require more of communication- related infrastructures.

Gender Aspects of Rural Employment

The gender dimension in rural employment has become important in recent decades following growing concerns about the deteriorating status of females in a society. In all major industrial categories, males dominate by accounting for around 70 per cent of rural employment. The bulk of female workers are concentrated in agriculture, manufacturing and community services. Approximately 30 per cent of the rural work force is female at all industry levels. The corresponding share has increased marginally (0.5 per cent) at the aggregate level during the reference period. Industrial category-wise gender proportions indicate that females are concentrated more in agriculture followed by manufacturing and community services. The proportion of females in these industrial categories has increased significantly; by more than 2 per cent in agriculture and community services while less than 2 per cent for manufacturing at the all India level.

The trend in gender-wise employment in many states is different from that of the country. In agriculture for instance, the proportion of females has declined in Bihar, Madhya Pradesh and West Bengal. Amongst these in Bihar and Madhya Pradesh the share of agriculture in rural employment did not decrease during the reference period; this suggests that pressure on agriculture for rural employment is quite high and in this kind of situation males are generally preferred over females for employment. This reason does not hold good for West Bengal as this has experienced a spurt in agricultural growth during the 80s, though this growth tapered off in subsequent years. Since participation of females is often specific to particular agricultural operations any significant change in the structure of agriculture and allied activity can also change woman's share in agriculture.

In community social and public services, though the share of females in rural employment has increased at the aggregate level, the corresponding share has not increased in the states of Assam, Haryana, Orissa and Rajasthan. These states barring Assam and Rajasthan have registered a sharp decline in the share of CSP services in rural employment. Since the bulk of employment in CSP services is under the organized sector, this is considered better than many other employment categories for workers of similar qualification. In this situation, competition for getting employed in this category increases and probably males dominate in this competition since the difference between genders in human development related statistics like literacy is sharper in these states.

In manufacturing, an increase in the share of females at the all-India level was observed, the corresponding share declined in the states of Delhi, Goa, Haryana, Punjab, Gujarat, Maharashtra, Karnataka and Himachal Pradesh. As many of these states have a good road infrastructure, there is a possibility that urban manufacturing units are doing well with the provision of cheap labour from the rural sector to these manufacturing units; while males have it appears, some distinct advantages over females in commuting from rural to urban places.

The share of females in the total rural employment has increased marginally during the reference period. Many states in fact report a decline in the share of females in the total rural employment; some of these states are Bihar, Madhya Pradesh, Rajasthan, Delhi, Goa, Haryana and Kerala. These states present different reasons for a decline in the share of female employment. The first group of states suggests push factors as possible reasons for a decline in the employment share of females whereas the latter group of states suggests urbanization and a high mobility of the work force as possible reasons for a decreasing share of females in rural employment. The share of females in rural employment has increased in relatively well-off states.

It must be noted that the proportion of females in the total rural employment has increased (0.52%) marginally; though the corresponding share has increased significantly in agriculture, manufacturing and community services. This difference in the temporal share of females in rural *vis-à-vis* gender-wise important industrial categories like agriculture, manufacturing and community services suggests that in rural India the share of females in industries other than the above has declined. In this regard too, varying trends from different states are present.

Quality of Rural Employment

The quality of employment is as important as the quantity and in the rural sector disguised unemployment is probably the most important issue while discussing the quality of rural employment. The NSS data presents a comparative account of usually employed persons and persons employed on the basis of current daily status (CDS) during a year; the difference in the level of employment reveals disguised unemployment in the rural sector.

Disguised unemployment here means that persons employed on the basis of their usual status are not getting employment for a sufficient number of man days to be termed as employed on the basis of current daily status (CDS). Out of one hundred usually employed rural males more than 10 per cent of rural males were either unemployed on the basis of CDS or are not in the labour force during the year 1999-2000.

The relative proportion of different categories of workers, self-employed, regular and casual also explains the quality of employment. The present study assumes that with an increase in the proportion of casual workers in the total work force, the quality of employment decreases since social security measures for casual workers are less effective in the country. In 1999-2000, in the rural sector, a large proportion of the male (54.4%)

workforce is self-employed, the group of casual workers is a distant second while regular employed workers account for only a small proportion (9%) of the total workers and occupies the last place. The urban sector presents a different picture, the regular employed is the most dominant class of worker closely followed by the self-employed workers; casual workers are the least important in terms of their proportions. Across gender, the problem of casualization is more acute for females, especially, the rural female. A temporal comparison of employment categories suggests that casualization, that is, the per cent of casual to regular employed workers, is on the rise.

The quality of employment is often influenced by enterprise type, for instance, an enterprise employing more than 20 workers is covered under the Factories Act, 1948 and this Act to some extent protects employee's interests. It may be noted that the quality of employment is better for salaried workers, and the proportion of salaried workers increases with the size of enterprises. Enterprise trends would generate more evidence about the pattern of rural employment in the country.

There can be different ways of classifying enterprises. On account of social security provisions for its workers, enterprises are of two types; one, organized sector enterprises which include factories that have better social security provisions; while the unorganized sector consists of smaller enterprise that are devoid of satisfactory social security provisions. Enterprises classified on the basis of the number of persons hired are own account enterprises (OAEs) and establishments. Again establishments identified on the basis of number of people hired are Directory and Non-directory enterprises; these enterprises vary on the basis of type of regulations. Enterprises can be further classified on the basis of location namely; rural and urban; and type of activities being performed namely; agricultural and non-agricultural enterprises. The present study discusses the trend in enterprises on the basis of the above criteria. Enterprise-level information is obtained from the Economic Census, and is available for the years 1980, 1990, and 1998. The Economic Census does not include enterprises engaged in crop production and plantations.

In the urban sector the difference between agriculture and non-agricultural enterprises is even higher. As far as distribution of enterprises according to the size-class of employment is concerned, agriculture and non-agriculture enterprises are similar in both the sectors, rural and urban. The difference between these enterprises becomes significant when the distribution of employment in various size classes of enterprises is taken into account. In non-agricultural enterprises, the concentration of employment is higher (33.6%) towards larger establishments; this trend is more pronounced in the case of the urban sector. This particular trend explains the presence of high regular / salaried workers in the urban sector.

The per cent share of non-agricultural enterprises and its trend during the last three economic surveys 1980, 1990, and 1998 suggests a trend almost similar to that of the NSSO quinquennial survey on employment. In rural enterprises, the per cent share of construction, trade, transport and business services has increased, while the share of manufacturing enterprises has declined in both the sectors. Even though the number of enterprises is on the rise, for the sake of quality of employment one would expect that the average size of enterprises should grow.

Pattern of Wages and Salaries

The wages and salaries to some extent explain the productivity of labour in different sectors and in the economy. The trend in labour productivity across industries and over the years can be studied by comparing real wages in these sectors during different years.

The average wage for a male worker is significantly higher than that of the female worker for most of the industrial categories; this difference in wages is at a maximum in the manufacturing sector. The wage difference appears to be related to the differences in the productivity of male and female labour in these industrial categories. A higher wage for female workers in certain employment categories as that of transport and storage, agriculture in the urban sector may be ignored on account of the small sample size for these specific categories of workers.

In rural India, the growth of real wages across industries suggests different trends. This growth in real wages is based on three points of time, namely, 1987, 1993, and 1999. Agricultural wages have grown at a faster rate as compared to the non-agriculture wages during the first period (1987-93), whereas growth in non-agriculture wages has been higher than agricultural wages during the later period (1993-99). This trend has probably a lot to do with the real performance of the respective sectors during the reference periods. Several indices related to agriculture suggest that performance of agriculture was better during the earlier period. A comparison of real wages during the entire period (1987-99) suggests that rural wages in agriculture, construction and trade doubled during the reference period. Certain studies also report an abrupt increase in agricultural wages during the late 80s. A relatively higher increase in real wages for these industrial categories might also have been because of an abnormal base year (1987-88).

A comparison of male wages between rural and urban sectors shows higher urban wages for most of the industries. The real wage in the urban sector was significantly higher than for the rural sector during the year 1993-94. This difference in wages was only marginal for most of the industries during the year 1999-00. Given the general belief that wages in the rural sector are low as compared to the urban sector, this trend is alarming. The real wage for agriculture in the urban sector and that of non-organic manufacturing in the rural sector is significantly higher than its counterpart during the year 1999-00. These extreme cases may be ignored since the sizes of samples in these instances are too low.

Analysis of wages and salaries suggests that real wages have increased uniformly in all the employment categories during the reference period (1987-1999). In most of the employment categories, the real wage in the rural sector was significantly lower than for the urban sector in the early 90s; the difference in wages between the rural and the urban sectors has however tapered-off in non-agriculture employment categories during the year 1999-00, negating the general belief that rural wages are significantly lower than the urban wages.

In sum, the employment situation in the rural non-farm sector has deteriorated in the 90s. Manufacturing, the most important non-farm sector is marked by a decelerating rate of growth of employment during the 90s. Though mining, utilities, and community services account for only a small proportion of rural employment; employment growth in these sectors was negative. Construction, trade, transport, and business services emerged as the most important sources of rural employment growth in the 90s. These industries have however, a small base, which accounts for around 11 per cent of rural employment in the country. Nevertheless, employment figures in these activities have been associated with various development-related indicators; these are not autonomous. The NSS survey of enterprises presents a trend similar to the NSS quinquennial survey on employment. The situation on the quality aspect of rural employment is also not encouraging; there is persistently high underemployment, casualization has risen manifold. In spite of all these discouraging trends, the real wages of rural workers have increased while the gap between rural and urban wages in non-farm activities has decreased during the 90s.

Rural Diversification

Rural diversification may be defined as the economic development of non-agricultural activities. At the micro-level this refers to a livelihood which has multiple, part-time components. In the previous section, the nature and pattern of rural employment across states shows that rural diversification may be associated with a booming or recession economy or with accumulating or immiserating livelihood strategies. These trends, with typologies and implications for rural welfare would be clear from an analysis of disaggregate level data.

The available studies explain positive or negative outcomes of rural diversification with pull and push factors. In the pull or development-led proposition for rural diversification there are again different strands of arguments. Mellor for instance, argues that technology-led growth in agriculture gives rise to several linkages, which lead to an expansion of employment in the non-agriculture sector. Visaria *et al.* argue that development of urban centres give impetus to non-farm employment in the adjoining rural areas because of low factor (land, labour) prices in the rural areas. These areas however, need to be integrated with the nearest rural town. In the development-led proposition for rural diversification, some researchers argue that infrastructure facilities and supportive institutions encourage rural non-farm employment. In general, the urbanization and extension of infrastructure facilities in a region are highly correlated. Several human resources related parameters like education and skill development of rural workers, credit availability for non-farm activities have also encouraged the process of rural diversification.

The second set of arguments explains the phenomenon of employment diversification in rural India with distress-related indictors. Vaidyanathan found a positive association between the unemployment rate and the incidence level of rural non-agricultural employment in states. He argues that in a situation where the labour absorptive capacity of agriculture becomes limited and the urban industrial sector is not able to accommodate the ever-growing labour force, the RNFS tend to act as a 'sponge' for the surplus labour. The RNFS thus acts like a residual sector in which rural workers concentrate on account of their distress conditions. This is popularly known as the push phenomenon or distress hypothesis which was subsequently, supported by several scholars.

The above discussion suggests that pull as well as push-related factors promote rural non-farm employment (RNFE) growth. However, the pattern of RNFE growth in either of the situations would be different. The present study argues that the non-farm sector consists of several heterogeneous industries, and is influenced by a host of separate factors often independent of other industrial categories. The state-wise employment trends in non-agriculture industrial categories and several related indicators at the level of state also support this premise. Demographic pressure accompanied by increase in per capita income, for instance, influences construction activities; whereas, rural literacy and infrastructure facilities by and large promote finance-insurance-real estate and business services (FIREB). Employment in trade and transport is highly correlated and is most affected by basic infrastructure facilities like roads. From certain states there are also evidences of road facilities encouraging employment of the rural work force in urban industries like manufacturing, business services. Infrastructure other than roads is also important for employment growth in other non-farm sectors. Manufacturing for example, requires assured power, business services require more reliable communication facilities, etc.

The above findings are obtained from state-level figures. The state-level data, especially for the bigger states, are too aggregate; in many states small poorer regions coexist with the prosperous region. Considering the kind of disparity present within a state, the process of RNFE has been studied with a mixture of state and district-level information. In each state, two districts representing low and high concentrations of RNFE have been chosen.

A perusal of these districts and of the socio-economic parameters associated with these districts shows that districts with a very high concentration of non-farm employment are good in at least one of the income-generating industries like agriculture as in Ludhiana or urbanization-led manufacturing activities as in Gurgaon, Baroda or tourism-related activities as in Kanniyakumari. These trends suggest that income-infusing sectors like agriculture, manufacturing, tourism, etc. provide income in the hands of rural workers / persons, and promote the growth of non-farm activities like construction, trade and services. These non-farm activities are income-absorbing in nature.

In order to investigate the possible determinants of rural non-farm employment (RNFE); the RNFE per cent in selected states and districts are plotted separately with agriculture income per hectare (PHAI), agricultural output per capita (PCAO), infrastructure indices (INFI) in per cent and population density (PDS) per sq. km. In the above instances, the observations, which depict RNFE as more than 40 per cent appear to be outliers for the above sets of relationships. Even if we ignore these observations, a distinct relationship between agricultural development and RNFE is not observed. This is so with both the variants of agricultural development, per capita agricultural production and per hectare agricultural income. This trend is not in accordance with the theory of agriculture-led rural non-farm growth.

The pictorial presentation shows the relationship between RNFE and one of its determinants at a point in time; the dynamics of rural diversification in actual practice is different since these variables often interact amongst themselves and the collective influence on RNFE growth may be different. The above variables are therefore regressed on RNFE per cent with linear and log-linear specifications. It may be pointed that the regression is accomplished in 10 states with information from 20 districts. In order to get unbiased OLS estimates, information for states is obtained after excluding information for selected districts of the state.

Rural Non-Farm Employment and Poverty

In India, the land-man ratio is decreasing, employment elasticity in agriculture has not only declined but has reached almost zero. In this situation, the rural non-farm sector is generally perceived as the answer for tackling the twin problems of employment and poverty in rural India. From this perspective, the determinant of employment in the rural non-farm sector has been assessed. Rural diversification in India is the outcome of technology-induced growth in the agricultural sector.

Mellor illustrates the presence of production and consumption linkages of agriculture with the non-farm sector. On the production side, a growing agriculture requires inputs of fertilizer, seeds, herbicides, pumps, sprayers, equipment and repair services either produced or distributed by non-farm enterprises. Increased agricultural output in a forward direction also stimulates milling and processing activities. The consumption linkage in agriculture arises when growing farm income boosts demand for basic consumer goods. This linkage increases over time as rising per capita income (PCI) induces diversification of consumption spending into non-foods. Much of the overall increase in demand for inputs, services, distribution and many basic consumer goods can be serviced by firms in the rural areas and towns, though heavy production inputs and consumer durables are more likely to be produced in bigger manufacturing units in large cities. Researchers have also found a third important link between agriculture and the rural non-farm sector, Hossain termed it as the labour market interaction effect. Hossain argues that rising agricultural wages in rural areas in particular raises the opportunity cost of labour in non-farm activities. This induces a shift in the composition of non-farm activity from labour-intensive, low-return activities to more skilled high investment - high return activities. The rising agricultural productivity is thus instrumental in inducing a structural transformation of the rural non-farm economy.

This process of growth in the rural non-farm sector is evident from the state of Punjab where the dependence of labour on agriculture decreased substantially following technology-led growth in agriculture. Transformation of the non-farm sector in Punjab presents a similar example. Increased demand for agriculture labour has resulted in higher farm wages, which led to a decline in low return household manufacturing and a parallel rise in high return modern small factories and service industries (NHHI). As this generally happened in towns with a rural vicinity, it resulted in the urbanization and growth of the non-farm sector.

The above phenomenon prevalent in Punjab is not evident in many other parts of the country due to reasons that are wide and varied. As a matter of fact technology-led growth in agriculture was witnessed across a restricted part of the country only in the decade of 80s. This growth in agriculture, unlike that in the Punjab, does not appear to have given enough impetus to rural manufacturing activities in other states. To find the reasons for this setback it is necessary to discuss the assumptions in the Mellor hypothesis. Agriculture-led growth as propounded by Mellor and a few others presumes at least two necessary conditions; first, close linkage between the agriculture and the non-agriculture sector as it holds in the relatively closer village economy; second, impending conditions for the non-farm sector to take-off.

The closeness of the village economy is viewed as the flow of agriculture income in terms of rural *vis-a-vis* urban sector produced items. It assumes that the expenditure of a large part of the agricultural income on items manufactured in the rural sector would promote non-farm activities in the rural sector. It appears that with the opening up of the economy, leakages in the rural economy, which were significantly high even in the mid-80s, have increased further. Some of the possible reasons for the same may be; first, with trade liberalization the importance of imported products increased in the rural consumption basket, which discouraged domestic and village-based products; second, with the media spread impact of advertisements, rural consumption of these goods increased. Small and scattered rural manufacturing units cannot afford to spend a significant amount in advertisements and are again losers. Third, an uncertain policy environment for small-scale industries discouraged its growth; a significant proportion of such industry is located in the rural sector, so that rural manufacturing is thus discouraged.

Agriculture-led growth of the non-farm sector also presumes 'impending conditions' for growth of sectors other than agriculture. Impending conditions are nothing but the public-good or over-head capital or infrastructure required for promotion of rural manufacturing and similar other non-farm activities. In the 90s, rural infrastructure already in a dilapidated condition has experienced a further disadvantage in that assured power and telecommunication is missing. Nevertheless, Vyas *et al,* argue that skewed income gains in agriculture limited consumption linkages while inadequate rural infrastructure limited the ability of rural firms to supply the modest increase in input and consumer demands.

The relationship between agriculture (AGRI) and rural non-farm employment (RNFE) is formalized by regressing agricultural performance as measured by agriculture income (Rs. per hectare of cultivable land) on rural non-farm employment (per cent of RNFE in total employment) in states for reference years, namely, 1983, 1993-94, 1999-00. The R-square values and elasticity coefficients suggest that the relationship between agriculture and rural non-farm employment is quite strong; though the strength of this relationship reduced over the years. The decreasing role of agriculture on rural diversification is in accordance with the overall trend in studies related to determinants of rural non-farm sector growth.

The above discussions suggest an alternate pattern of growth in rural employment. Such an alternate growth pattern has different implications for a region and also for the welfare of the workers in the region. Though welfare is too subjective a term, poverty as measured by persons below the poverty line is considered as an indicator of welfare for the present discussion. An attempt has been made herewith to understand the welfare implications of employment growth in the rural sector. Some of the important determinants of the quantity and quality of rural employment in states are observed for association with the incidence of poverty in the rural sector. The important determinants for rural employment considered for the present comparison are agriculture performance as measured by the per hectare agricultural income, labour productivity as measured by the per worker agricultural income, real wages in agriculture, and pressure on land. Employment in the rural non-farm sector is also important from the perspective of quantity and quality of rural employment in the country.

Though the effect of agriculture performances on rural employment has decreased over the years, it remains an important determinant of rural poverty following Ahluwalia. The productivity of labour is undoubtedly an important indicator of rural welfare since Lewis and others view that the tenet of rural development rests on surplus in agriculture. Surpluses and labour productivity in agriculture are concepts with similar connotations. The association between labour productivity in agriculture and the incidence of rural poverty is significant at five per cent only. The negative sign suggests that states with higher labour productivity in agriculture have a lower incidence of rural poverty. This is quite plausible. Another similar indicator of the quality of rural employment, that is, real wages in agriculture also has similar results. It is however, interesting to note that the association between real wages in agriculture and rural poverty in states has weakened during the 90s. The correlation coefficient significant at 1 per cent in the year 1983 remained significant at 10 per cent only during the 90s. It may be noted that the growth of real wages in agriculture towards the end of the 90s was not duly supported by the real factors in agriculture. The labour-land ratio, which reflects a distress-like situation in agriculture and the rural sector, has not affected rural poverty significantly, though the positive sign of the coefficient is on expected lines. The association between non-farm employment and rural poverty was not significant in the early 80s; this coefficient however emerged significant (at 10 per cent) in the 90s.

A comparison of changes in the above indicators (agriculture performance, labour productivity, real wage, non-farm employment) with the incidence of rural poverty is needed in an assessment of the welfare implications of growth in rural employment. The larger the decline in negative values the better is the rural poverty situation in the state during the reference period. Poverty at the aggregate level or at the level of the specific sector has declined for all the states during both the decades (1980s and 1990s). Though poverty estimates of 55th round is not strictly comparable with the poverty estimates of 50th round and 55th round; some of the states that show a relatively larger decline in rural poverty during 1990s are Himachal Pradesh (HP), Haryana, Karnataka, Kerala, Maharashtra; whereas, states showing a lower decline in rural poverty are Orissa, Madhya Pradesh, Andhra Pradesh and Assam.

The association of rural poverty with wage and labour productivity in agriculture is significant in alternate decades, the 80s and 90s, respectively. It is interesting to note that whenever the coefficients are significant, the sign (negative) is also on expected lines. Growth of real wages and labour productivity in agriculture had a positive influence on decline in rural poverty. Most astonishingly, the growth of non-farm employment and decline in rural poverty was not associated; though a weak relationship is evident during the 80s. It is difficult to accept that growth of non-farm employment is not associated with a decline of rural poverty during the 90s. It may be that 'growth' and 'decline' in respective parameters and poverty levels are not associated, though non-farm employment and rural poverty is. Nevertheless, a decline of rural poverty during the 90s has in fact initiated a whole range of issues in the debate on rural poverty estimates.

In a nutshell, the regression analysis to find the determinants of rural non-farm employment show that the infrastructure index is the most important determinant followed by population density; both of these variables are significant at the 1 per cent. It is however, difficult to accept that agriculture plays a lesser role as compared to the above parameters of rural diversification. The issues of agriculture and rural non-farm employment growth when discussed separately during the reference years show a decreasing role of agriculture in rural non-farm employment growth. The changing role of these determinants on rural diversification has different implications for rural welfare. The present study considers the incidence of rural poverty as an estimate for the level of rural welfare in the states. The welfare implications of the nature of growth of rural employment has been assessed by computing the correlation coefficient between the incidence of rural poverty and some indicators of the quality and quantity of rural employment in the country. Association between the indicators (agriculture performance, labour productivity, real wage, non-farm employment) of rural employment and the incidence of rural poverty during the reference years is along expected lines; though association between changes in these variables during the reference periods is not very consistent and the same may be ignored. Labour productivity and wages in agriculture have a significant impact on rural poverty emphasizing the importance of agriculture-induced rural diversification in declining the rural poverty of the country.

Imapcts of Rural Diversification

The previous section shows that infrastructure and population density are the most important determinants of rural diversification. The kind of impetus these factors provide to rural diversification is not alike. The consequent impact of development- or distress- related rural diversification on the welfare of workers would also be different. These processes of rural diversification in the rural sector have been studied by means of household-level information as collected by researchers in the Agro-economic Research Centres (AERC) and coordinated by the present investigator. Selection of households involves multi-stage stratified random sampling. In the states, districts with either high and low concentrations of rural non-farm employment are selected since the kind of rural diversification is supposed to be different in the extreme districts of a state. As urbanization encourages non-farm employment growth in the surrounding rural areas, in each district two village clusters based on proximity to a rural town, are selected. In other words, the present study expects different kinds of rural diversification in villages near and away from a town. Finally, in a state there are four village clusters in two districts; and from each cluster 30 households are selected to study the process of rural diversification.

The level of wages / salaries for rural non-farm activities in different village clusters may suggest development or distress-led phenomenon in rural diversification. Other possible indicators for this purpose may include the average number of economic activities for a worker. The available literature suggests that with an increase of penuries the number of activities undertaken by an average worker increases. The presumption is that only after performing many less remunerative casual jobs, does the family income of wage-earners become sufficient to meet the household expenses.

The NSS data suggest that a significant proportion of rural workers are willing to undertake more than one activity and one of the most important reasons for the same as per the survey is to supplement their existing levels of income. The number of economic activities recorded for an average worker suggests the influence of distress - related factors. A relatively higher number of economic activities in low-RNFE concentrated districts by and large support the above hypothesis. In some of the progressive states like Gujarat and Maharashtra also, the average number of economic activities is high in village clusters that are near as well as away from the rural town. In the above example, the large numbers of economic activities are associated with the economic prosperity of the region. The average counts of economic activity thus reflect opportunities as well, though this is widely perceived to represent distress-related situations. In the extreme situation, there are also instances of village clusters too poor to provide any profitable employment opportunity for rural workers.

The average counts of economic activity by itself does not explain distress- related phenomenon, since in an extremely poor region sufficient remunerative economic opportunities may not present themselves for workers to supplement their income with. In this context, the average wage / salary for workers and the average employment of casual workers in man-days can be some possible indicators that reflect the process of rural diversification.

Salary is generally low for a worker in agriculture and its allied activity. In this context the evidence from Maharashtra and Tamilnadu is different. In Maharashtra, the performance of horticulture-based crops has been good in the 90s as value additions for these crops in the recent decade have been quite high and so also is the marginal productivity of labour and the salary of the agriculture worker in this state. A higher wage for agriculture workers in Tamilnadu during the early years of this decade (2002-03) is largely because of the scarcity of agriculture workers in the rural settings. The salary in certain employment categories is abnormally high in some states / districts / villages. These abnormal figures may be ignored or interpreted with caution, as the small size of the sample may be the reason responsible for this.

A comparison of salary across the non-agriculture industrial groups suggests that the salary is high for workers in manufacturing as compared to the services sector (transport, storage and communications). Salary is even lower for the construction workers. Salaried workers in construction are generally less-skilled labour, who help the skilled mason; whereas, the mason is generally self-employed in his own establishment. In non-agriculture industrial categories, salaries are particularly high in Haryana and Punjab. In manufacturing, a certain trend in salary for workers in villages near and away from the town is evident. The salary is generally high for workers near the town as compared to the workers away from the town. This is in accordance with the previous finding that as one moves away from rural town, the distress-related process of rural diversification increases in many regions of the country.

Unlike salary, wages for the casual worker in agriculture is as high as in any industrial category. The spatial trend in wages for casual workers in non-agriculture industrial category by and large support the regional trend in salaries. The average wage in the state of Haryana is higher than for many other states. There are reasons for higher wages in this state. In manufacturing, the wages for workers vary across the states; some of the disparity in wages is also on account of the wide and varied nature of manufacturing activities (processing, services, repair, etc.,) and also the possibility of their differential proportion in the AERC samples of different states. In retail trade and services also, wages vary widely across states. Construction is the one employment category where the average wage is high in all the states. It may be noted that construction, unlike many industrial categories, is demand driven and the higher wages in this category are expected.

Even in a single state, the wage rate varies across selected districts and village clusters. By and large, wages in village clusters away from a rural town are lower than in the village clusters that are near towns. A marginal difference in wages between these villages may be attributed to differences in the cost of living; yet, a relatively higher difference in wages between these villages is perplexing. This disparity in wage suggests distress-led rural diversification in villages away from rural towns. It is interesting to note that in agriculturally prosperous districts like Mehsana, East Godavari, the disparity in wages across village clusters is minimal. The trend from the above districts suggests that agriculture-induced development of a region has better spatial spread across the region. This at least is apparent from the wages of the agriculture workers.

An average employment of more than 60 per cent days in a year is observed in Tamil Nadu, West Bengal, Himachal Pradesh. The average employment for casual workers is particularly low in Gujarat and Madhya Pradesh. This indicates distress-related employment diversification in the rural sector of the latter group of states. In this context, the average employment in certain states like Bihar, which is showing symptoms of distress-related phenomenon, is not very low; there is a possibility of workers involved in some less remunerative work in this state.

Across industrial categories, the average employment is low for activities other than construction work. The average employment in the manufacturing sector was interestingly low, though manufacturing is generally perceived as a skill-intensive activity and the worker / entrepreneur are supposed to be engrossed with their enterprises, which are generally own account enterprises. The average employment trend in these industries suggests that disguised unemployment is not evident in the case of agriculture alone but that this is now spreading to other non-agriculture industries as well.

The employment status of workers, that is, employee employed as self-employed / salaried / casual worker, in an enterprise is one of the most important determinants of employment quality, since this determines the social security provisions of the workers. It may be noted that the NSS employment data at the aggregate level does not reflect the industry-wise employment status of workers. In this context the AERC information is important as this presents the employment status of workers in different industries in a sample village.

The employment status of workers may also be influenced by development- or distress-related phenomenon. Development-induced rural diversification is supposed to encourage bigger enterprises and the proportion of salary workers should be higher in this situation; whereas, in distress-led employment diversification the concentration of self-employed and casual workers would be higher. The employment status of workers across industries in selected states of the country based on the AERC sample-design suggests that agriculture and construction are dominated by self-employed and casual workers, whereas, in trade and hotels the proportion of self-employed and salaried workers is high. In transport, storage and communication, the proportion of salary earners is high.

Employment status in manufacturing displays a definite trend across states. In states where the status of manufacturing or non-household industry (NHHI) is good as in Maharashtra, the proportion of salaried workers is high, while in states with a not-so-good state of manufacturing or NHHI as in Bihar, the per cent of self-employed worker is high. This evidence accords with our hypothesis that development-induced rural diversification leads to bigger enterprises and higher proportions of salaried workers. It may be noted that salaried workers have better social security measures. The results from AERC survey unfortunately do not show any pattern to suggest the effect of village locations on the status of employment.

In brief, the above discussions show that employment diversification in the rural sector even though slow is the result of diverse factors, grouped together as pull- and -push related factors; these result in development or distress induced diversification. The development- or distress- related rural diversification is location specific. Though there can be various reasons for this process, the study shows that demographic pressure with limited resources generates a push force, whereas a high infrastructure base creates pull forces for employment diversification. The alternate situation can be distinguished however on the basis of average wage / salary to workers, average days of employment in a year, number of economic activities undertaken by an average worker. The average wage and salary directly reflects the economic condition of the worker and is the most comprehensive indicator of development- and distress- related diversification in the rural sector.

The other two indicators considered in the present study, namely, the average number of days employed and number of economic activities undertaken, may be inferred cautiously. The number of economic activities a worker has undertaken is said to indicate a distress- related situation in rural diversification; at times this also reflects opportunity for workers in a region. The AERC survey in combination with the NSS secondary information breaks the general perception that agriculture is the only residual sector. Now there are evidences of trade especially, retail trade and services emerging as a residual sector in certain parts of the country. Increased fragmentation of land has made agriculture less viable, whereas, increase in rural literacy encourages people to undertake trade and service activities even though it is not a very profitable proposition.

Policy Options

Rural non-farm employment includes several heterogeneous non-farm activities that have different demand and supply conditions in their input and output markets; the policies therefore have to be industry- (within the broad RNFS) specific. In the present discussion, government policies related to rural employment are essentially industrial policies with a significant bearing on the intensity and productivity of labour in the rural sector. Since employment and output in an industry are highly correlated, it is difficult to separate industrial development policies from those policies that are targeted towards employment generation in an industry. This separation has become even more difficult with the increased importance of cost efficiency in a liberalizing world. The findings of the present study suggest that growth in either agriculture or the manufacturing sector is important for the robust growth of employment in the rural sector; though the debate on the sectoral precedence of agriculture *vis-à-vis* manufacturing in the short run goes on.

Growth in industry is often not sufficient for employment growth especially in terms of quality of employment. Industry often encompasses enterprises of different sizes having different levels of profitability and working conditions for workers / labour. Government therefore mediates in the rural labour market. Inspite of the creation of such infrastructure and environment a significant proportion of the population is left out of the developmental process. As a result, direct employment-generation programmes (EGP) have become part of our development planning since the last few decades. The importance of such programmes has further increased with the high incidence of unemployment.

Sectoral Growth

Though as per CSO classification there are nine industries and the growth in all these industries are important. The present investigator believes that growth in agriculture and manufacturing is important for a remunerative, broad-based growth of employment in the rural sector. Growth in these industries would trigger employment growth in other industries.

Agriculture

Government policies related to agriculture during the planned development of the country have passed through at least three distinct phases. The first shift in policy was evident in the mid-60s with the increased importance given to self-sufficiency; the second line of demarcation marked the opening up of trade in the early 90s. It is really difficult to separate out employment-related policy in agriculture from the sectoral policy. Any government policy, which increases cropped area and crop productivity would increase employment and wages, respectively in agriculture. Some suggestions for increasing cropped area and productivity in agriculture involve technological innovations, infrastructure development, rationalization of farm input prices, besides other issues. There is also scope for increasing vertical integration of farm-firm. The less-exploited options in the form of apiculture, sericulture, rearing of birds and small ruminants need to be encouraged especially on small farms. This will increase the utilization of family labour especially that of women and can make the small farm more viable.

Rural Manufacturing

The rural sector has a definite advantage over its urban counterpart in manufacturing certain groups of commodities. The first set of products, those which utilize local resources and are semi-processed. These are not very scale intensive, while examples in this category include honey and organic foods. The second set of products also based on local resources, is highly processed, and are not scale neutral. In this category, technologies that are capital intensive in nature often play a significant role. Agro-processing and ancillary units near urban centres are examples in this category. The third set of products consists of unmanufactured or semimanufactured items. These are also labour-intensive and examples in this category are traditional crafts by rural artisans. The Government of India has created specific institutions for the promotion of these industries, among which specific mention may be made of the Khadi and Village Industries Commission (KVIC). Certain government schemes specifically targeted towards encouraging rural manufacturing include the reservation for small-scale industry (SSI) and cluster programme.

The KVIC at the national level, Khadi and Handloom Boards at the state level and innumerable institutions and cooperative societies at the disaggregate level were created for the development of khadi and village industries. The khadi and village industries are launched to promote local-resource based products and traditional crafts in the rural areas. Apart from promoting rural entrepreneurship, KVI products which attract fiscal concessions are often not cost-efficient for which the reasons generally cited are inefficiencies of the KVI-system. There have been significant efforts in the recent years to reduce inefficiencies in the KVIC. For instance, a market -development assistance scheme against the prevailing rebate schemes for the KVI products was launched. The KVIC has also introduced a franchise scheme for its products. For KVI products, quality has been a problem. To improve the quality of KVI products, the KVIC in recent years has launched some brands such as 'Sarvodaya' for fast moving capital goods like toilet soaps, pickles, honey; 'Khadi' for the upmarket and essential products such as essential oils and herbal products; and 'Desi Aahar' for organic foods, cereals, and spices. The KVIC in order to promote marketing has further united various product-based producers in a marketing federation (Confederation for promotion of khadi and village industries, CPKVI) to take up the branding and marketing of KVI products.

Government carved out the SSI in its industrial policy resolution which also creates several institutions to promote the small-scale sector (Jha 2005a). A significant proportion of small industries are in the rural sector therefore, robust growth in the SSIs is important for growth of rural manufacturing. Government has taken certain steps in the recent years to promote growth in these industries. Thus, investment ceilings for the small-scale industries have been hiked to Rs. 10 million, for selected items this hike has been to the extent of Rs 50 million. Government has also attempted to revive the sector by infusing credit through SSI specialized bank branches, a small and medium enterprise fund under SIDBI, *laghu udyami* credit card scheme, etc. Certain problems specific to the SSIs however remain. In an open economy, the very concept of reserving industries is not tenable; therefore, the uncertainty associated with the reservation of SSIs must end with some categorical stand regarding this. The performance of small and tiny industries also depends on the economic performance of some public sector monopolies that provide basic goods and services. Many of these units have unfortunately less regard for cost efficiency, while the unit cost of production is becoming important in an open economy.

In a globalizing world when technology, cost and quality have become important, rural industrialization cannot rest solely with the KVI, SSIs. Increased private participation is desired to achieve a robust growth in rural manufacturing. Favorable infrastructures, largely under the public domain are also required. International experiences suggest the creation of industry clusters in the rural vicinity as an effective process of rural industrialization. The union government has identified 60 industry clusters in July 2003 for focused development by including their credit requirements in the state credit plan. More recently, the KVIC with the help of SIDBI and NABARD and support of the Ministry of Agriculture and Rural Industries is trying to implement the National Policy for Agriculture and Rural Industries (NPRI). This consists essentially of technological advancement and skill upgradation for effective development of industrial clusters at the district level. This scheme will promote the participation of private entrepreneurs and NGOs. The Ministry of Food Processing Industry has also set up food parks in different parts of the country. This is to provide capital-intensive common facilities such as cold storage, warehouses, quality control laboratories, effluent treatment plants, etc. to the adjoining processing units. The public sector units or corporate or even cooperatives are eligible for grants up to Rs. 4 crore for the creation of such facilities. So far, 20 food parks have already been sanctioned; implementation in actual fact is however, not known.

In spite of these efforts, the performance of rural manufacturing in the 90s has not been satisfactory. The reasons can be numerous for example; The example policy impediments for specific rural industry, the burgeoning gap between rural and urban infrastructure, or decline in demand for products manufactured in the rural sector. With the opening of the economy and the increasing role of advertisement in the marketing of consumer goods, it is easy to influence the rural expenditure pattern for urban manufactured items. There is always the possibility of creating suitable conditions and institutions for rural manufacture.

The KVIC as discussed earlier plays an important role in the production and marketing of unmanufactured or semi-manufactured products. The performance of the KVIC has however been far-from satisfactory. There are suggestions to convert it into a promotional and development agency rather than a financial agency. The KVIC should provide technical support to the KVI units; this includes product process research and market strategies for the KVI-products. Since the village resource-based products have a niche in the international market, the KVIs need to do some aggressive marketing. There is sufficient scope for also reducing corruption in the KVI-system. Regular vigilance for example, may check malpractices in the khadi rebate disbursal. While adequate checks are needed for irregular release of export incentives, ad-hocism in the provisioning of rebate to the khadi sector may be abolished and a medium-term strategy on rebate must be chalked out so that production and planning are not disjointed.

Since the KVIC has failed miserably in performing its duties there is need to involve the private sector and NGOs in the development of khadi and village industries for an optimal utilization of resources and reap the promise of opportunities in a liberalizing world. In order to increase the cost competitiveness of KVI and similar products often, there are demands for exempting these products from the value-added-tax (VAT). The Department of Agriculture and Rural Industry may pursue this suggestion with the state government; it may be noted that all state governments are to adopt the VAT system.

Though the rural sector has distinct advantages in agro-processing, many large-scale processing units have not emerged in the rural region in many parts of the country. The organized growth of the processing industry also requires an emphasis on post- harvest infrastructures. There is scope for increasing private participation in the development of post-harvest infrastructures such as silos and warehouses, cold storage facilities and air-conditioned transport. In order to remove some of the bottlenecks, contract farming is being practiced in different parts of the country; a wider success of contract farming among other things also requires the promotion of formal relations between growers and industry. In the rural sector there is need for the establishment of small-scale processing units involving the latest technology. Unfortunately efficient technology for small scale processing has not received due attention.

International experiences suggest the formation of industry cluster as a possible way of rural industrialization. In the recent decades, several ministries and departments have also initiated efforts towards the creation of industry clusters. These efforts need to be coordinated as adequate synergy between these schemes may leave sufficient funds to promote many industrial clusters in a large part of the country. Government may also devise ways to encourage private participation in creating some of the common facilities in industrial clusters.

The rural sector in India has a large number of artisans. In this changing world, the demand for some products of the artisans' work has declined, while that of some other skill-intensive, artisan-like work has increased; such shifts in demands need to be assessed. In a liberalizing world, when distance is shrinking there may be a latent demand for an artisan's work in a distant market, the tapping of which requires the help of market professionals. In the context of emerging opportunities rural artisans abilities may be increased on a selective basis; while care is taken to ensure that this training is integrated with the production and marketing of such products. Though some public institutions such as the KVIC have been mandated for similar purposes, they have failed miserably in performing their role. There is a need for alternate institutions and producers' associations to undertake the job of training, producing and marketing the rural artisan's products. NGOs may encourage the formation of producers' SHGs to share the benefits of lucrative prices in distant markets; a good example of which is presented by *lijjat papad.* The formation of clusters would also help artisans' in removing many of their size and scale-specific bottlenecks.

The subject of rural industrialization is related to many government departments/ ministries; for instance, the Ministry of Industries, Department of Agriculture and Rural Industries, Ministry of Rural Development, Department of Food Processing Industries. Similarly, public institutions created for rural industrialization or entrusted with the job of rural industrialization are also numerous. The lack of proper coordination among these institutions also leads to the tardy progress of rural industrialization in the country.

The above discussion shows that the rural sector has an advantage in certain kinds of manufacturing activities. These manufacturing activities depending on the typology require different kinds of institutional support. In labour-intensive, capital-light, local resource-based manufacturing activities, there is sufficient scope of improvement in the functioning of KVIC, there is also need for encouraging producer-based small SHGs. For capital-intensive rural manufacturing activities common-facility centres, and a facility for industry-agglomeration is required. As, rural manufacturing is central concern of many government department plans, poor coordination between these departments often results in duplication of some programmes while tardy progress occurs in other programmes related to manufacturing activities.

Other Sectors

Though agriculture and rural manufacturing bear the onus of employment growth in the rural sector, several other industries like construction, trade, transport and business services have emerged as important in recent years. Employment growth in these industries depends on factors, such as infrastructure, per capita income, population density. Again a host of government policies influence these factors.

Employment declined in utilities and community services; these industries fall largely under the public domain and since government is reducing its staff strength, employment under these categories has also declined. Demand for these services has however not declined, and has in fact increased with the pressure of population and shrinkage of common resources. There is enormous potential for private participation in the delivery of utilities and community services and thereby increasing rural employment in the country.

Infrastructure and Environment for Employment

Certain government policies, though basic for the growth of industry, are not industry-specific, these transgress across industries / sectors. Examples under this category include credit and infrastructure-related policies. Traditionally, the state is perceived as the provider of infrastructure and public institutions as the creator of rural technology. This perception is however changing with the emergence of new institutional alternatives. The sustenance of such institutions also requires government support, which may be in the form of suitable legislative environment. Another set of government policies increases the capabilities of workers by providing better education and health facilities. Still another set of government policies for the social security of the workers attempt to protect vulnerable workers from contingencies such as, illness, accident, untimely death of bread-winner, old age and unemployment. Some of the above issues are illustrated below.

Technology and Skill Formation

Technology generation and dissemination, which is of special of interest to the rural sector is largely confined to the public domain. There is a general feeling that our public-funded research and extension system is less responsive to the needs of the people. The response of the farmer or target groups may be assessed through their willingness-to-pay for the research and extension services. With the user's payment principle, the research and extension system may emerge as more accountable and self-sustaining in the long run. In this regard, the government has made some progress with the agri-clinics; and there are also suggestions for village knowledge centres.

The present investigator believes that information technology (IT) - enabled knowledge dissemination centres can potentially provide a viable solution to individual's problems at a distant isolated place.

The existing training infrastructure that has some relevance for the rural sector, such as the District Industry Centre (DIC), Industrial Training Institutes (ITIs), rural poly-techniques is in a bad shape. These institutions must be revitalized and made relevant to local needs. These rural institutes should also identify newer trades for training taking note of the resource endowment of the region and also the emerging opportunities in a liberalized / globalized context. Such trainings should be coordinated by local institutions, such as, the DIC, District Rural Development Agency (DRDA).

Finance and Infrastructure

In spite of the heavy emphasis on institutional credit for farm and non-farm sector, these remain capital-starved. Financial institutions on the other hand often miss their target for priority sector lending. The supply-demand mis-match in rural credit is often on account of lack of sufficient collateral. The concept of community collateral has emerged as important in recent years. The self-help-groups (SHGs) present a viable mode of arranging community collaterals. The SHGs in addition to serving the needs of individual small-scale finances also resolve some specific problems associated with small-scale production of the non-farm sector. The performance of SHGs due to various reasons has however not been uniform across the country. The skewed distribution of non-banking finance institutions (NBFI), which is instrumental in the disbursement of credit to SHGs in the states, is the most important among these. In order to encourage the activity and distribution of NBFI across the country, the credit limits of the NBFI may be reduced.

There are suggestions to involve the regional rural banks (RRBs) in disbursing credit through SHGs, since the RRBs are relatively better distributed in the country. As there are already discussions about the ways to increase the viability of RRBs, this additional work will spread their portfolios and may help in making these units more viable. A uniform spread of SHGs in addition to other actors also requires many credible NGOs in a large part of the country.

A part of the need for credit will be solved if the community collateral and borrowing for viable industry- / product-specific infrastructure project is allowed on an extended scale. In order to overcome some other problems related to collateral, industry associations and cluster-level units, may also be encouraged to form a mutual credit guarantee fund. Service sector units such as trading houses / agencies which assist in marketing or brand building of rural products may be given due priority by the banks and financial institutions.

The kind of infrastructure required for a specific industry or a product-group varies. Some industry-specific infrastructure like, cool van, quality-control laboratories for agro-processing, etc., may be initiated by private parties or producers' and traders' associations and such initiatives definitely require a favourable incentive structure. Government may focus on basic infrastructure like road, power and communications, since in the rural areas such basic infrastructure would largely remain in the public domain. In this context, there are suggestions that the Rural Infrastructure Development Fund (RIDF) may be used more liberally in making investments in projects other than irrigation as well. The existing RIDF disbursements across states are highly skewed so that for generally prosperous states the share in total disbursement is higher. A better regional distribution requires relatively easy conditions for disbursement of rural credit under RIDF. More recently, government has launched the Bharat Nirman programme precisely to strengthen the rural infrastructure of the country.

Social Security and Labour Welfare

Most of the social security and labour welfare policies in India cater to the organized sector, whereas, it is the unorganized sector which provides the bulk of employment to rural people. There is a general feeling that workers in the organized sector are over-protected, while their counterparts in the unorganized sector lack minimum social security provisions. The nature of rural employment is often cited as a possible reason for such apathy. Employment in the non-farm sector is often seasonal, earnings are also irregular and low, while in many cases, the employer-employee relationship also does not exist. Though the employer-employee relationship exists in establishments, these are often not registered with the state governments.

Minimum wage is an important instrument for the provisioning of labour welfare, though instances of violations of minimum wages are numerous. The legal limitations, definitional constraints and over-burdened courts are often cited as reasons for the violation of minimum wages. In the unorganized sector where workers are regular and an employee-employer relationship exists, the provisions of minimum wages and social security to workers only requires that it may be made obligatory on the employer. This of course requires identification of such establishments; the second National Commission on Labour (NCL) suggests enactment of the Small Entrepreneurs (Employment Relations) Bill to cover all establishments employing up to 19 workers and protection to all aspects of workers including wages, social security, safety and health. The NCL also proposes an umbrella legislation to ensure minimum wages to workers in the unorganized sector. For this purpose a worker is defined as one who is registered with a government agency and would permit the administrative body to decide the matter in case of dispute.

Absence of the employer- employee relationship in certain rural enterprises, requires some innovative schemes suitable for particular micro-settings. Some state government has attempted to create a welfare fund for target groups of producers like, *bidi* workers, by collecting 'cess' from consumers of the finished products. Certain state governments in association with Non-Government-Organizations (NGOs) have introduced social security schemes for specific target groups of workers; some of the successful schemes out of these experimentations need to be replicated throughout the country.

Government has recently introduced the Social Security Group Insurance Scheme for the unorganized workers with the help of the Life Insurance Corporation of India. Often, the reach of government social security schemes is limited because of poor literacy, unawareness of rural workers, they are also less organized. Some of the anomalies specific to rural workers can be reduced by the formation of Self-help-Groups (SHGs) of workers employed in similar activities. The SHGs so formed can participate in certain welfare schemes of the government. The SHGs with the help of NGOs can interface with the government agency in a better way.

In India, the expenditure on social security is also low (less than 2 per cent) as compared to many similar countries like Sri Lanka (4.7 per cent) and China (3.6). Nevertheless, a large part of this expenditure is being incurred for the organized sector. More recently, the National Committee for Enterprises in the Unorganized Sector under the chairmanship of Prof. Arjun Sengupta has drafted a scheme to provide benefits of health insurance, life insurance and old age security to the entire unorganized workforce of the country. An alarming situation on account of social security for unorganized workers suggests that the committee report may be adopted.

Employment Generation Programmes

There has been a general feeling that the benefits of the growth process did not trickle down to certain disadvantaged sections of the society. Lipton illustrated some socio-economic attributes about the disadvantaged section, which restricts them from joining the trickle-down queues. This section of the society requires programmes especially targeted towards them and now for a considerable period of time various income and employmentgenerating programmes are in existence in India. The employment generating programmes largely fall under two broad categories; self-employment generating and wage based employment generating programme. The first set of employment generation programme (EGP) attempt to remove chronic unemployment by providing economic assets to the beneficiary while the second group of programmes provides supplementary employment to stave-off seasonal unemployment.

The self-employment generating programmes have been modified frequently; Swarnajayanti Gram Swarozgar Yojana (SGSY) for instance, was launched in April 1999 after review and restructuring of the erstwhile IRDP and allied schemes. The broad objective and instruments of the programme remain the same as that of the IRDP. A high non-willful default rate of the SGSY beneficiaries in fact, suggests that the assets provided to them in the self-employment generating programme do not remain viable in the long run. In the SGSY, selection of projects for beneficiaries should be such as to consistently increase the productive capacity of individuals in the long run. Assessing the suitability of economic activities / enterprises for individuals in particular micro-settings may require the help of professionals. Financial institutions like the National Bank for Agriculture and Rural Development (NABARD) provides such services at a relatively aggregate level; but their reach in terms of provisioning of consultancy services for the selection of individual projects is limited. In this regard it may be noted that nationalized banks were appointing agriculture specialists for a similar purpose; the practice of appointing an agriculture specialist has unfortunately been discontinued in the recent decades.

The projects related to allied activities are important considering the kind of pressure on the land. It is generally felt that the project fund being released in the SGSY or similar rural development programmes are inadequate for the programme beneficiaries to start their operations on a large scale. Many of the disadvantages of these beneficiaries are in fact associated with the lower-scale of production; this can be improved by creating producers' groups as in the SHGs. Certain innovative arrangements as that of contract farming can also improve the viability of small and scattered production units. The long- run viability of the self-employment generating programme therefore depends on the scale of finance, the kind of projects selected and also the institutional arrangements of the production units.

The wage-based employment generating programmes were also modified frequently, for example, in September 2001, all wage-based employment generating programmes were merged into the Sampoorna Grammen Rozgar Yojana (SGRY). Unlike many other programmes of the present day, the SGRY is implemented through the Panchayati Raj Institutions (PRI). In February 2001, the food-for-work programme was also launched in some backward regions of the country. In SGRY or similar wage-based employment generating programmes (EGP), the rural asset is an important component. These programmes may be recast in a way that the programme apart from providing short-term employment also helps in building the productive capacity of the region. In rural assets, the programme should prioritize community assets whose benefits can be shared by a large number of people. The present investigator believes that the wages in the EGP must not be higher than the minimum wage prevailing in that region; the lower wage may be used as an instrument of self-exclusion for the rural work programme (RWP). Studies suggest that income as a criterion for selection of beneficiary has resulted in various pilferages in the programme.

In spite of the large emphasis on different wage-based employment generating programmes, the scale of employment provided by these programmes has been inadequate. Considering the grim unemployment scenario in rural areas, the United Progressive Alliance (UPA) Government enforced the Rural Employment Guarantee Act that would legally guarantee employment to one person in every poor household for a minimum of 100 days on asset-creating public works. Programmes of such large magnitude have other implications as well, it is generally felt that increase of expenditure in such programmes is often associated with a decrease of public expenditures in the social sectors. Investment in the social sector is however, important for a long-term growth of the rural sector.

Though there have been efforts in recent years to unify many of the wage-based EGP, the present study finds that the possibility of further consolidating employment generation and developmental programmes exists. Examples of some labour intensive rural works programmes undertaken by different government departments are soil conservation, watershed development, construction of schools and *pucca* roads. There is a feeling that if works under these departments are pooled and coordinated at the district level, it would leave sufficient funds for broadening the wage-based employment programmes and for simultaneously creating durable community assets in the rural sector. With decentralization under PRI, the unification of various labour intensive rural works programme (RWP) may not remain a far-fetched idea. This probably requires the formulation of district level plans and proper coordination between elected body, bureaucracy, and professionals like subject matter specialists at the district level. The district-level plan may take some more time to realize. For the time being, a clearing house at the district level may be setup for sharing of information by various agencies administering the employment generation programme so as to avoid duplication of beneficiaries and the creation of durable assets in the programme.

References

Ahluwalia, M. S.. "Rural Poverty and Agricultural Performances in India" *Journal of Development Studies,* Vol. 14, No. 3, April.

Basant, R., B. L. Kumar and R. Parthasarathy. (edited). *Non-Agricultural Employment in Rural India: The Case of Gujarat,* Rawat Publications, Jaipur, India.

Jha, B.. Rural Non-farm Employment in India, A coordinated and consolidated unpublished report, submitted to Ministry of Agriculture, GOI, New Delhi.

Mellor, John W. *The New Economics of Growth – A Strategy for India and the Developing World,* A Twentieth Century Fund Study, Ithaca : Cornell University Press.

Vyas, V. S. and G. Mathai "Farm and Non-Farm Employment in Rural Areas: A Perspective for Planning" *Economic and Political Weekly*, Vol.13, No. 6 and 7, (February annual number): 333-347.

6

Migration and Rural Employment

In developing countries, agriculture provides the basis for a major share of employment and constitutes the main source of livelihood for a large portion of the population. By the late 1990s, on average, more than 75 per cent of the labour force in the least developed and other low-income countries was engaged in the agricultural sector. The importance of agriculture also has implications for other sectors of the economy.

However, in most developing countries, employment in the agricultural sector is decreasing. Many rural areas are undergoing a process of "de-agrarianization", with younger workers seeking to move out of agriculture because of lack of jobs, low incomes and agro-climatic constraints. Increasing numbers of rural people are working in non-agricultural activities in or outside their place of origin in order to diversify their income and reduce risk. In the late 1990s, rural non-farm activities accounted for 42 per cent of rural households' income in Africa, 40 per cent in Latin America and 32 per cent in Asia. One important reason for this is population growth and increased pressure on natural resources, exacerbated by economic reform and trade liberalization that has made it impossible to maintain employment in activities that cannot withstand competition. In areas of intensive farming, increased mechanization of agriculture has also led to a fall in farm employment.

Occupational diversification in rural areas is often linked to migration, whether temporary or long term. Evidence suggests that remittances – the money that migrants earn in urban areas and abroad and send back to their places of origin – are gaining in importance and have in some locations overtaken agriculture as the main source of income for rural households.

There is no consensus on the effects of migration on rural employment and development. Generally speaking, it may be stated that there are two opposing views. The first one considers that the overall impact of rural out-migration on both departure and destination areas is negative. Supporters of this view cite a number of negative impacts in urban areas: the rising levels of urban unemployment; the expansion of the informal sector; and increasing persistent poverty. In rural areas, the negative impact is labour loss and its disruptive effect on the local economy. They recommend designing policies to promote rural employment and development in order to limit population movements from rural areas.

A second view considers that migration can have a positive impact on development at national, regional and local levels. Supporters of this view are opposed to policies aimed at restricting migration, arguing that in the past such policies usually achieved the opposite. They consider migration to be a household strategy involving the maintenance of economic and social links between the migrant and his/her household. This view emphasizes the benefits arising from the transfer of resources to rural areas, such as financial or in-kind remittances, skills and innovative ideas. Individual and collective remittances contribute to the subsistence and well being of rural families and, in some cases, to social and infrastructure improvements. Investment of migrants' income in farm and non-farm activities may also create employment opportunities. Supporters of this view recommend designing policies that increase social, economic and financial links between migrants and sending areas.

However, the reality is more complex. A wide range of variables – such as the local context, the type and extent of migration, the size of remittances –interact with and influence the effect of workforce loss in rural areas and the impact of financial transfers from migrants to their families and community of origin.

Trends in Rural Out-migration and Remittances

The past 50 years have seen a significant increase in rural out-migration. According to the Role of Agriculture Report, during this period, some 800 million people have moved from the countryside to the cities. Large numbers have also migrated across borders in the last decades. In 1965, there were

75 million migrants in the world, a figure that increased to about 192 million in 2005, meaning that in today's world one in 35 people is an international migrant. However, the number of rural-urban and international migrants is many times higher than these numbers might suggest as a significant number of people migrate on a temporary basis or, in the case of international migration, illegally. There are also significant flows within both the rural and the urban sectors. A high rate of rural out-migration is expected over the next 50 years, and many countries will continue witnessing an exodus of the youngest and most productive segment of the rural labour force.

There is also some evidence that an increasing number of women migrate, not only as a result of family reunification but in search of remunerable work. A greater demand for female labour in certain services (for example, domestic work/healthcare) and industries, as well as a growing social acceptance of women's economic independence and mobility, are the main factors behind this increase. Today nearly half of the international migration flow is composed of women. The impact of migration on the status of women depends on the socio-economic, cultural and family contexts in which the migration takes place. But in general, many women enhance their status and position within their family and community as they gain access to employment and income.

The gender and the age of those who move and those who stay can have a significant impact on sending areas in terms of remittances. Migrant women tend to send higher remittances to source areas. However, since in many rural communities women lack access to assets, they have limited control over how remittances are used. This was noted in several studies in Sub-Saharan Africa and in Asia.

Rural out-migration is influenced by a combination of economic, political and socio-cultural factors. However, many researchers agree that economic considerations prevail, among them wide disparities in job and income opportunities and in access to superior services, such as health and education. The expanding urban informal sector represents a significant pull factor for rural people who have a very low asset-base and skills, offering them economic opportunities and possibilities for upward mobility. The push factors inducing rural out-migration in developing countries are related mostly to declining opportunities in agriculture due to factors like surplus labour arising from scarcity of cultivable land, inequitable land distribution, land degradation, low agricultural productivity, negative effects of marcroeconomic and pricing policies on farming and the lack of other productive work opportunities.

As a result of migration, the global flow of remittances has been growing fast and steadily. From approximately USD 30 billion a year in the early 1990s, the amount of global remittances rose to an estimated USD 232 billion in 2005, with more than 70 percent (USD 167 billion) going to lower mid-income and low-income developing countries. But these sums are even larger if unrecorded flows through informal channels are included. In many countries, remittances surpass the total inflow of official development assistance and foreign direct investment and may constitute up to 20 per cent of a country's gross domestic product.

The analysis of remittance flows has tended to focus on flows between rich and poor countries, while internal remittances have received much less attention. Domestic flows of remittances are a source of income for a greater number of households than are overseas remittances. Though individual transaction values are lower, there are many more domestic migrants than international migrants, and thus their cumulative value is believed to be substantial. According to a report released by the Consultative Group to Assist the Poor (CGAP), the 95 million persons migrating primarily from rural to urban regions of China had sent home nearly USD 30 billion in 2005, which was more than the USD 22 billion that India – the largest recipient of international remittances - was expected to receive the same year. Similarly, in some West African countries, intraregional remittances (for example, remittances from Côte d'Ivoire to Burkina Faso) are also significant.

Effects of Migration on Rural Employment

The length of migration and the composition of the flow are critical variables influencing the effects of out-migration on rural areas, especially on employment. Out-migration with frequent returns to the community of origin –allows for a better deployment of labour, since those who are underemployed during the agricultural lean season can find work in town or in other areas. Migrants of this type tend to maintain their agricultural activities while taking advantage of opportunities available in other areas, thus increasing disposable income which can be invested in production or used for consumption.

Conversely, longer-term migration to cities or abroad usually means that migrants are unable to return home and engage in agricultural activities and employment during the farming season. Their absence may generate labour shortages. Labour shortage may contribute to a destabilization of traditional farming systems at household and community levels. In many rural areas, out-migration of young men and women has led to significant ageing of the rural labour force, with a negative effect on farm production and farm income. Another impact of migration on rural communities is the loss of innovative and better-educated community members. According to Skeldon, the loss of human capital can be compensated by the fact that the migrants may either return at a later stage or extend the resource base of their families through investments elsewhere. However, as noted by Mendola, the effects of the "brain drain" on rural development still remain devoid of evidence.

In some cases, remittances can compensate the negative impact of out-migration by allowing hired labour to replace the agricultural labour force lost. For instance, migration from the Bakel Region of Senegal to France has fostered the influx of Malian migrants into Senegal. In Southern Morocco, de Haas found that migrants usually entrusted land cultivation to other household members (women in particular), to sharecroppers or to hired labourers. This has resulted in improved wage levels and sharecropping conditions. According to research carried out in areas of high out-migration in China, total grain output declined by less than 2 per cent, while household disposable income increased by 16 per cent as a result of migration. However, the capacity of remittances to compensate the labour shortage caused by predominantly male out-migration depends on the amount of remittances received. Several studies in Africa and Asia found that these were often too low to allow for hiring labour.

Even with the arrival of remittances to rural areas and the growth of the local economy, those who remain behind do not always benefit. Newly created jobs are often primarily for men, while women tend to be stuck in traditional forms of employment. Often, women have to step in, doing more work and engaging themselves in traditionally male chores. For example, in some Central American and Caribbean countries certain agricultural activities have become female-dominated. In Haiti the number of females in the agricultural labour force increased from 30 per cent in 1980 to 37 per cent in 1990. Although the "feminization" of agriculture in these countries could be seen as a positive trend, with an improvement in women's status and autonomy, it is important to recognize that rural women are forced to continue to carry out household and family responsibilities in addition to the agricultural chores. As a result, their daily workload is increased. The same observation has been made in rural areas in Sub- Saharan Africa, where this situation rarely confers more power to women in the domestic sphere and in village decision making as women remain under the control of the lineage system during the migration of their husbands.

In some rural communities, out-migration can be seen as a means to reducing pressure on household consumption and on the land. In regions of high population density, out-migration of part of the population may be a way to alleviate underemployment in agriculture and protect the livelihoods of those farmers who stay behind. The remaining rural population may thus obtain access to more land and other resources which can make their farms economically viable.

Remittances and Rural Employment in Migrant-sending Areas

The increased financial inflows are opening up new possibilities for rural development. Short- and long-term migration (as well as remittances) is considered by most households to be a survival strategy, rather than an accumulation strategy, aimed at maintaining and diversifying household income in order to reduce risk in a context of economic constraints. Most research concludes that remittances are mainly used for consumption purposes, to cover health and education costs, to repay debts, and to build or repair houses. Only a small proportion is invested in production.

However, a clear distinction between investment and consumption may be difficult to establish. It has been argued that remittances spent on consumption can generate both direct and indirect benefits, with multiplier effects on local and regional development. In some isolated rural areas, most non-farm activities depend largely on migrant remittances. For example, in southeast Nigeria, migrants' investment in housing for retirement has given rise to a building boom, with construction work becoming more important than farming as a source of employment. Various case studies note the positive effects generated by house building on the local economy, as bricklayers and other workers use their wages for consumption or investment. Similar observations by Guest in rural Northeast Thailand indicate that the use of remittances from internal migration have had important multiplier effects on the local economy, since local purchasing power increases. Taylor showed that in some migrant-sending areas in Mexico the multiplier effects of remittances can be substantial for the local economy, particularly for the businesses that supply the products bought with remittances.

Although remittances are generally used for consumption, in some cases the additional income enables families to invest in local development and entrepreneurial endeavours. Higher income levels, greater income stability and future security ensured by remittances, as well as the migrants' skills acquired in urban areas or abroad, may stimulate households to invest in land and livestock, or in off-farm activities. In Thailand, the analysis by Guest demonstrated that a high proportion of households with urban migrants used remittances for inputs, such as buying fertilizer and paying wages. In rural Nepal, a study noted that one major impact of the increase in the remittance flow has been the creation of new wage labour and land-renting opportunities. Wage labour opportunities increased for landless and marginal farm households, while new land-renting possibilities provided scope to increase the scale of operation for those committed to farming.

The increasing financial capacity and entrepreneurial inclination of many migrants may gradually change the nature of peasant agriculture, moving from subsistence to more commercial farming. This may in turn create employment opportunities for other villagers. Cotula and Toulmin noted that Senegalese immigrants in France who have invested part of their savings in irrigated land in Senegal were employing hired labour and selling their produce, though on a very small scale. However, investing in agriculture is only one of the many possible uses of remittances.

There is also evidence of the use of remittances for investments in off-farm activities. Some authors relate that in sub-Saharan Africa an increasing number of migrants are investing in food processing and breweries, taxis and transport trucks, service stations and garages. This type of investment generally occurs when migrants have been successfully integrated in their place of migration, which in turn depends largely on their educational level and the income they can secure while they are away.

Migrant Networks

In addition to remittances in cash or in-kind, migrants have other ways of contributing to the development of their place of origin – through collective contributions of time and money, business networks, investments, and the transfer of skills, culture, knowledge and experience. For instance, migrant networks, either transnational or rural-urban, can form a bridgehead for local products or enterprises looking to market goods and services (for example, ethnic or "nostalgic" trade, rural tourism) or facilitate migrants' investment in their community of origin.

Through hometown associations (HTAs), migrants often provide collective financial support, skills and knowledge to development projects in their community of origin. Migrant groups as dissimilar as urban immigrants in Nigeria and Mexicans in the United States have supported health clinics, built schools, repaired roads and, more rarely, invested in small business enterprises in their home communities. However, in some cases, thanks to initiatives co-financed by governmental institutions (for example "3x1" matching funds programme in Mexico or *Co-développement* and *Cooperation Décentralisée* policies in France), some HTAs are becoming more involved in employment- and income-generating projects. Generally, these projects are managed by the community members and supervised by members of the HTAs and local non-governmental organizations.

The significant outflows of workers and inflow of remittances, as well as the continuous exchange of goods, ideas and cultural values, have changed the rural landscape economically, socially and demographically. The new rural space is characterized by the growth of small towns and medium-size cities with strong economic ties to the remaining "rural" inhabitants. In many countries, the economic activities generated by this new "rurality" provide the engine for the creation of rural non-agricultural employment, especially in trade, transport and a wide variety of services that have brought certain aspects of the urban quality of life closer to rural inhabitants. In rural Mexico, Taylor and Yuñez noted that village household income is diversified away from agriculture, largely as a result of families participating in labour markets outside the village through wage work in nearby towns, distant cities or migration abroad. The same study found that a large share of rural household demand for inputs, consumption and investment goods is supplied by towns which have proliferated in the last decade and which now account for most of the country's urban growth. Similar observations were made in South-East Nigeria by Okali et al., who noted that commuting into urban centres from nearby rural areas is made possible by a well-functioning and relatively cheap transport system. This has led to considerable occupational diversification for rural households and communities. However, this development has also brought negative effects as some traditional non-farm activities (for example, women's cloth-weaving) have suffered from increasing competition from imported goods.

Some researchers use the term "social remittances" to describe the diffusion of new and different social practices and transformations in migrant-sending areas: Positive examples include organizing social clubs, rebuilding schools and churches and beautifying common areas. Negative examples include criminality and the formation of street gangs. Nichols emphasizes the importance of agricultural innovations brought "back" by returning Mexican migrants from the United States. However, the potential of the skills and knowledge acquired by these migrants has not been yet properly explored and analysed.

Remittances ad Development: Issues and Complications

Remittances can alleviate household poverty and can sometimes have wider positive effects on communities through consumption, investments and savings. At the same time, they do not automatically generate development.

In certain contexts, strong ties with other labour markets may enhance a household's confidence in the continuation and stability of the income of migrants and thus reinforce dependency on remittances. However, remittance-dependent households and communities are vulnerable to the fluctuations of labour demand and economic crises in the migrant-receiving areas. This exposes remittance-recipient areas to unexpected economic disruptions. In other cases, remittance payments create a strong disincentive for domestic savings, leading to a depletion of the domestic resource base for investment.

Sharp contrasts between the standard of living of remittance-recipient households and non-recipient households may create new sub-class divisions and social tension. Inequalities are also exacerbated by the fact that it is not the poorest of the poor who migrate abroad, but rather the "relatively poor." In his study of rural communities in Pakistan, Adams shows that households receiving remittances belong to the wealthier classes, something which increases both income inequalities and land accumulation by the rich. Several researchers have stressed that the distributive effects of remittances depend on the distribution of income, wealth and land before migration.

The success of migrants in accumulating capital and skills is a necessary but not sufficient condition for them to invest productively in their place of origin. Other important factors come into play, including: the migrant's educational level; the living conditions at the destination; the intention of return; the characteristics of the migrant's household and her/his access to local assets; and the social, economic and ecological contexts in the home area.

Despite the positive experiences of many migrants, a large proportion of them continue to suffer abuse and exploitation at their destination – especially the most vulnerable groups of workers (women, undocumented migrants, trafficked persons). They may face forced labour, low wages, poor working conditions, absence of social protection and other forms of exploitation, which have negative consequences on the level of remittances they may send.

The use of migrants' resources in productive investment and employment generation also depends largely on the infrastructure and opportunities offered by their communities of origin. For example, in areas that lack communication infrastructure and access to financial institutions, the investment options for receiving families are very limited. Conversely, areas with good road and transport networks, with favourable conditions for agriculture, and that offer local non-farm employment opportunities are much more conducive to attract investment and employment generation. The same conclusion is drawn by Cotula and Toulmin, who note the increase in rural investment by the migrants' households or returnees in areas with irrigated land and good opportunities to invest in commercial farming. In places with unfavourable agricultural conditions and difficult access to urban markets, migrants largely prefer to invest in residential properties.

Migration in Search of Decent Work

A further 106 million will have joined the rural labour force in the developing world between 2005 and 2015, despite falling rates of overall population growth. What work will they fi nd, and where? And will it be what the International Labour Organization (ILO) calls 'decent work': that is, jobs that pay a living wage and offer reasonable and fair conditions? Will it be enough to allow rural people to escape poverty, when at the moment around 75% are poor? Finally, can work be found locally, or will increasing numbers have to migrate?

Currently, agriculture is still the single largest source of employment in rural areas, though non-farm activities are becoming increasingly important. These comprise a highly diverse range of activities: from manufacturing, usually artisan, to trading, to the provision of services of all kinds. Combined with farming, itself diverse, this produces a wide variety of occupations.

Despite the heterogeneity, some features of rural work are common across sectors and locations. Most rural workers are self-employed, whether it be on their own farms or in the small, often very small, enterprises typical of rural non-farm activities.

Hired workers are in the minority. A recent estimate put the number of farm workers at 450 million out of a total agricultural labour force of 1,100 million. When labour is hired it is often temporary and seasonal, particularly in farming and tourism and is usually informal and casual. Formal and permanent jobs in rural areas are rare, the main examples being teachers, health workers and police.

Evidence of this is scarce. Indeed, in some activities work is increasingly casual. The apple farms of South Africa's Western Cape, for example, have shed permanent staff in favour of contract labour. In India, planting and harvesting of most commercial crops in irrigated areas is done by labour gangs.

Employment patterns in agriculture seem to be divided sharply between two kinds of farming. For those crops and livestock that require ample areas of land, most of the labour force comes from farming household – albeit that the area used may vary considerably depending on access to machinery: from one or two hectares for those with hand tools, to hundreds of hectares for those with tractors and harvesters. Relatively little hired labour is used owing largely to the costs of supervising hired labour. But for activities that require little land, such as horticulture, floriculture, aquaculture, pigs and poultry, factory-style operations are both possible and economic. Economies of scale apply including those in hiring and supervising labour, so that the bulk of the work is carried out by paid employees.

Low Pay and Poor Conditions

Most rural work is poorly rewarded. For example, farming in much of Africa and Asia rarely generates more than US$750 per worker a year. From this must be deducted the cost of any purchased inputs. The remainder is shared between the workers and their dependents, leaving too little to escape dollar-a-day poverty.

Returns in many non-farm jobs are not much better, and sometimes worse. In Ghana in 2000, for example, estimates of returns per day were US$2.50 for carpentry and US$2.60 for charcoal-making, compared to US$3.90 for staple crops and US$1.60 for vegetable growing. Here then is the critical problem for rural employment: that so much effort leads only to poverty wages.

If the pay is low, the conditions are equally bad. Rural work, especially farming, is often arduous, sometimes monotonous, and frequently hazardous. The ILO reports 3–4 million people are affected by hazardous pesticides every year, with 40,000 deaths as a result; part of an annual toll of 170,000 deaths amongst agricultural workers. To make matters worse, given the informal conditions of most agricultural and rural work, few workers have insurance against the consequences of sickness, accidents, and unemployment.

In addition, farming is by the far the largest employer of child labour: 70% of the estimated 246 million working children are occupied in farming.

Some jobs, for example those where people are locked into labouring for others to pay off debts, amount to forced labour, if not outright slavery. Discrimination against female workers is common, with many being paid considerably less than male counterparts for the same job. In India in 1999/2000, female labourers earned on average just 72% of male rates in agriculture, and even less, 62%, in non-farm jobs.

Given these problems, it is not surprising that many rural workers migrate to try and find better paid jobs, often in urban areas or manufacturing industry. Export industries in Bangladesh and Vietnam, for example, attract cheap labour from under-developed rural areas. Here, workers may be offered a formal contract. But informal jobs in the service and construction sectors, with no contract or social security, also absorb large numbers of workers. Although hardly decent work, these jobs offer more days of work in a year and better wages than farm work. Poor working conditions do, however, involve elements of risk for the poor.

Many poor households in developing countries now combine farm and off-farm activities seasonally. What is especially striking is the increase in temporary and circular movements, ranging from trips that last several months to daily commuting for work. Dramatic improvements in communications and transport have created conditions for large-scale internal movement of people at unprecedented levels. In Andhra Pradesh, India, surveys show that 40% or more of villagers commute daily to urban centres. In China, one of the fastest growing economies in the world: rural-urban migrants increased from about 26 million in 1988 to 126 million in 2004. Most retain strong links with their rural families. Current projections suggest that between 12 and 13 million migrants will move to urban areas each year over the next couple of decades, and many will continue to circulate unless restrictions on settling in urban areas are relaxed.

Although domestic migrants far outnumber international ones, with greater potential to reduce poverty, lack of data means the importance of internal movements is not fully appreciated. While official statistics may show a slowing of permanent rural-urban migration, micro studies show increasing levels of circular migration.

For example, in Bangladesh, of those leaving their villages, one-tenth moved to other rural areas, just under one-quarter went to other countries, while two-thirds moved to urban areas. Dhaka, with its work opportunities in garments, rickshaws and domestic service, was the most common destination. Most people returned to their villages at the end of the working season.

Policies to Improve Rural Employment

Policies to improve rural employment can be divided into those affecting the demand and supply of labour, and those intervening directly in labour markets. On the *demand* side, the agenda is very much one of stimulating growth of private enterprise, be they farms or (usually small) rural businesses. Agricultural development can create large numbers of jobs in low income countries, as in the Asian Green Revolution. But since the 1990s, jobless growth has been seen in countries such as Egypt and India, where farming had used labour intensively. This results, in part, from a welcome increase in agricultural labour productivity. If there are to be additional jobs in farming, then most will probably arise in the more industrialised sectors - horticulture, flowers, fish farming, pigs, and poultry.

But if farming is not generating rural jobs, then the non-farm sector must do so. This prompts questions about how to promote rural activities other than farming, including to what extent they depend on vigorous growth of farming itself. Although in general the requirements for rural growth are well known - physical infrastructure, functioning economic institutions, a conducive investment climate, demand in urban areas - getting these in place in particular cases has often proved less than straightforward.

Many countries have programmes of public works. Whilst these can be an excellent way to provide social protection, create valuable infrastructure, and provide training to young workers, they are less successful in creating jobs. Even the largest examples do not always make much of a difference to overall demand for labour. For example an evaluation of two of India's largest rural employment generation schemes, the Jawaharlal Rozgar Yojana (JRY) and the Employment Assurance Scheme (EAS), by the Comptroller and Auditor General of India in the 1990s, found that the average number of days for which each employment seeker got work ranged between seven and 21 days under JRY and between nine and 18 days under EAS. On the other hand, the Maharashtra Employment Guarantee Scheme has been able to provide significant amounts of work, leading to increased wages in the rural economy.

In the past, cheap credit policies encouraged investment in machinery and reduced demand for labour. Such distortions are less common following policy reforms. Indeed, often the contrary may be the problem: the cost of capital is higher than it should be. Not that this is necessarily an advantage to labour – lack of investment lowers overall production, productivity, and ultimately reduces labour hiring.

On the *supply* side, too little vocational training is provided in rural areas, and even then the quality is often not good enough. Some recent innovations that bring together private enterprise and trainers, such as Brazil's National System for Rural Apprenticeship (SENAR), show some promise. Otherwise, most rural areas suffer from a marked deficit in health and education provision. Spurred in part by the Millennium Development Goals, some countries are making special efforts to correct this – as seen, for example, in Latin America, where cash transfers to the rural poor are offered on condition that children go to school and pre-schoolers attend clinics.

These programmes are also reducing child labour in rural areas – one of the few measures that has succeeded in doing so, since outright prohibition of child labour has rarely made much difference in rural areas. For middle income countries that can afford such programmes they hold great promise.

Until recently, most governments in the developing world have tried to reduce *migration*, or simply ignored it. Increasingly they are becoming aware of its potential. Priorities include: reducing the costs and risks faced by migrants; ensuring that entitlements to state services are portable; facilitating remittances; improving accountability and transparency in labour markets; and raising awareness of labourers' rights.

Governments are increasingly prepared to facilitate movement. For example, China has removed requirements for migrants to have permits to move to cities. Vietnam is also reviewing registration rules. In both countries, donor-funded programmes have started to cater to migrants, including informal movers. Mobile ration cards for 5,000 migrants are being piloted in small and major towns in Rajasthan, India; while in Madhya Pradesh, the UK Department for International Development is funding a comprehensive migrant support programme in eight tribal districts, which aims to provide information on opportunities and improve bargaining power by enhancing skills. Several NGOs, such as the Gramin Vikas Trust in Madhya Pradesh and Adhikar in Orissa, have migrant support programmes to improve the efficiency, safety and cost of remittance mechanisms.

There is, by and large, limited scope for successful *direct intervention* in rural labour markets – given that the bulk of work is self-employment or informal hiring that lies beyond the reach of most states. That said, in some cases, if the labour market is tightening and employers find it hard to get the staff they need, improved outcomes are possible.

Minimum wages can influence wage settlements, even in informal activities, since they signal acceptable levels of pay. Large companies with international reputations to protect and enhance do sign up to labour codes and implement them, as seen on Costa Rican banana farms (Smith 2006). And when trained labour is relatively scarce, unionisation can bring improvements to pay and conditions. A case in point is that of hired labourers on the irrigated farms of Petrolina-Juazeiro in North-East Brazil. A combination of shortage of trained workers, tutelage of newly-formed unions by an experienced federation of unions, the presence of ILO efforts to check child labour, and fear of loss of reputation by large companies operating export farms, enabled farm worker unions to negotiate higher rates of pay and better conditions. In India, actions by NGOs have also been effective. The All India Democratic Women's Association, has succeeded in raising wages in some locations through its evidence-based campaigns.

In many developing countries, workers in formal employment have long been protected from risks by insurance, and their old age provided for by pensions, both paid for by employers. To some extent the same applied to farm labourers attached or bonded to paternalistic employers. Fewer workers now benefit from these arrangements, as work is contracted out or made more casual. In some countries, especially in Latin America, this is prompting new thinking about providing social protection that is no longer linked to specific jobs. For the rural poor, this promises to provide them with benefits that they could never have obtained under previous systems. For example, South Africa extended pensions to all retired workers in 1996, irrespective of their race. The largest gainers from this move were the elderly in poor rural households.

Rural employment is inextricably bound up with the challenge of meeting the first Millennium Development Goal of reducing by half the proportion of people living on less than a dollar a day and the proportion of people who suffer from hunger. Ways to improve existing rural jobs and to create additional jobs for the more than 100 million new workers expected in the decade leading up to 2015 need to be found. Four things must be done:

1. *Increase growth* both in agriculture, since most rural workers earn their living from the land; and especially in the rural non-farm economy. Growth in agriculture will create some new jobs, primarily in the more industrial forms of farming, although the major contribution is most likely to be higher productivity and better returns to self-employed farmers. Growth in the non-farm economy will be critical to creating new jobs and, therefore, putting upward pressure on rural wages.
2. *Invest in rural people:* basic education, skills, health, and early nutrition. This not only improves people's job prospects, but also reduces unacceptable disparities between rural and urban people. Much can be done to remedy these disparities if public resources are allocated accordingly.
3. *Encourage migration* through provision of information, improved transport, making rights to public services and protection portable, and facilitating remittances. If some of the rural work force can find jobs in the cities as migrants or commuters, this will help tighten rural labour markets.

4. *Push for better labour standards* to end to child labour and to correct gender inequalities. As rural labour markets tighten, with rising productivity and wages, demanding this should become easier.
5. Finally, while much of this is a rural agenda, it also depends on thriving urban economies to generate markets for rural produce and services.

Migration and Rural Labour Markets

One of the most signifcant changes in the last half century is the increasing proportion of women migrating: today, they constitute half of the international migrant population, often migrating independently as the main economic providers for their families. Driven by economic, social and political forces as well as new challenges (such as environmental degradation, natural disasters or climate change impacts), migration can bring, both benefts and costs to the migrants themselves, their families, and their communities of origin and destination, depending on the migrants' profle and gender, and on labour market specifcities.

Over 214 million people resided outside their countries of origin in 2010 compared with 190 million in 2005, with an increased number of both origin and destination countries.

However, the bulk of rural migrants in the developing world are moving internally, into urban areas. During the last 50 years, 800 million people have migrated from rural to urban areas, a number that is steadily increasing. In Mexico for example, between 1995 and 2000, only 5 to 9% of the total migrants were international migrants.

Women constitute around 50% of the total international migrant population, but account for 60% or more of migrants from some countries (such as Indonesia and the Philippines). Women are more likely than men to migrate internally or just across borders.

Most destination countries have gender segregated labour markets, with migrant women concentrated in domestic and care-giving work, and men in construction, transport and trade.

Female migrants' wages are generally lower than male migrants' wages. In 2008, recent female migrants to the UK were 1.5 times more likely than male migrants to be paid less than the national minimum wage.

Remittances constitute the second largest flow of resources to developing countries (US$328 billion transferred in 2008), with formal transfers nearly tripling the value of Official Development Assistance (ODA) and accounting for up to 10% of GDP in some countries. 500 million people (8% of the world population) are estimated to depend, at least partly, on remittances. At household level, remittances can be very substantial, accounting for 30 to 70% of the household budget in Senegal for example.

500 million people (8% of the world population) are estimated to depend, at least partly, on remittances, with Latin America and the Caribbean receiving 25%, East Asia and the Pacific 24%, and Sub-Saharan Africa less than 5% of all international remittances.

Studies estimate that a 10% increase in per capita official international remittances in a country can lead to a 3.5% decline in the percentage of poor people living on less than US$1 a day.

Why is Action Needed?

The impacts of rural migration on local labour markets, the gender division of labour, and agricultural production and food security can be positive or negative, depending on: who migrates (individuals or families and their characteristics: age, gender, education, skills and assets); the reasons to migrate (better living conditions, family reunification, to escape conflict or environmental problems); the duration (permanent, temporary, circular); and the destination (internal rural-rural or rural-urban, intra-regional, international).

1. Rural Migration can Change Gender based Power Relations in Rural Households and Communities

Changes in gender roles and responsibilities triggered by the migration process can be positive or negative depending on who migrates. While these changes can lead to women's empowerment, they can also bring social and psychological problems.

Working abroad can increase migrants' social status and bargaining power. Enjoying greater social and economic independence, gender equality and welfare support in host countries, migrant women may be reluctant to return to their former roles and status in traditional patriarchal environments.

Migration can undermine the self-es teem and personal growth of those left behind, and threaten marital stability. Dependency on their wives' remit tances can be culturally diffcult for men (with some resorting to alcohol, drugs or domestic violence). Women can endure loneliness, social with drawal and reduced confdence when their husbands migrate. Children can suffer from lack of role models, disci pline or parental care and, especially if their mothers migrate, their educa tion and health may be jeopardized.

2. Migration has Gender-differentiated Impacts on Agricultural Labour Markets

In highly populated areas, seasona or permanent out-migration by either men or women can alleviate underemployment in agriculture, reduce pressure on land and other natural resources, and improve ivelihoods. Rural out-migration often leads to a reallocation of household agricultural labour, with women taking on male tasks or vice versa. While migration-induced labour shortages can increase gender-specifc work burdens and/or lead to lower production and greater food insecurity. Remittances from such migrations can partially compensate through on-farm nvestment, labour hiring, inputs use, or reduced credit constraints.

When a household can afford to hire labour with remittances but local labour is scarce, labourers from neighbouring areas or countries may come to fll the gap, with a specifc gender profle responding to the new demands. In Senegal, for example, Malian migrants (mostly male) substitute for Senegalese workers who have migrated to Europe or the Gulf. In the Philippines, female international migration generates internal migration of women to help with domestic or child care work in the sending communities.

Migrant remittances do not always lead to agricultural growth and employment, as they are often spent on housing and consumer goods rather than on agriculture. But such expenditures can generate local non-farm employment opportunities, creating a pathway out of agriculture into urban or rural non-farm activities.

3. Migrants' Remittances and New Skills can Improve Livelihoods and Stimulate Rural Development

Remittances can help poor rura families cope with agricultural risks and livelihood instability. With an appropriate enabling environment, they can foster productive investments in agriculture, reduce credit constraints (which particularly affect women) and stimulate off-farm businesses (e.g. rural women's handicrafts, trading, food processing activities), creating an income multiplier within the sending household similar to that created by public transfers.

If the increased income from remittances is spent on local products and services, this is likely to generate additiona employment in the sending area. Remittances of Mexican rural migrants in the US, increased the incomes of recipient families by 10%7 Non-migrant households also beneft from the "second round income effects'' of remittances: studies in South and South East Asia found that each migrant created, on average, three jobs through remittances.

Exposed to different social and economic systems in the host country, migrants often become social innovators, bringing back new ideas, skills and know-how and in some cases, new attitudes about gender equality. Policy makers can leverage these changes to elaborate new gender-equitable labour standards and legislation, and develop public and private partnerships to beneft local populations.

Gender differences in earnings, life cycle and family responsibilities, infuence the propensity to remit: Men tend to Internal migrant worker from the countryside coming to seek employment in town. Railway Station, Beijing, China. save or invest some of their wages whereas women usually dedicate remittances (which represent a higher percentage of women's incomes) to family needs.

Attitudes towards paid work in receivng communities also vary by gender. In Mexico, for example, women in rural families receiving remittances withdrew from paid work (mostly poorly paid informal sector work) to devote themselves to reproductive work, whereas their male counterparts shifted from formal jobs to start their own business (becoming risk takers).

Remittances generally have a positive impact on health and nutrition while the impact on education is mixed: school attendance improved in South Africa, Mexico and Guatemala, while performance and attendance declined in Albania, especially for girls and for rural areas which offer poor quality education. In Pakistan, if they can use remittances to hire labour, women recipients are more likely to send their children to school than non-migrant families.

When migratory flows to Spain first began, women remitted money to their husbands. Because they did not like the way the men managed the money, they then sent the money to their mothers or sisters who used it for basic consumption, or education, or health.

Businesses started by women with remittances were typically small and with a high failure rate due to women's heavy workload and time constraints and lack of access to finance, education and training.

The community benefited from reduced malnutrition and infant mortality, and improved amenities. However, migration was also seen as a cause of social problems such as family disintegration, low educational attainment, school abandonment, early pregnancy and increased drug use among children.

4. Migrants, Especially Women, are Often Face Discrimination

Women tend to migrate shorter distances, generally for informal, seasona jobs, since it is usually harder for them to leave their children or, for cultura reasons, to live away from their families, but also because migration may be too costly (expenses for transportation, ntermediaries, and resettlement).

Migrants can be very vulnerable until they fnd a job, learn the loca language, and become aware of their rights. If they cannot fnd a job, fall sick or receive very low wages, the risk of indebtedness and impoverishment is high, particularly if they bore heavy expenses to migrate. In such situations, women under economic pressure might be vulnerable to prostitution or traffcking.

Diffculties in obtaining work permits, particularly for women who migrate to join their husbands, may restrict migrants to lower paid informal work without social benefts.

While remittances generally reduce household vulnerability, providing better and more secure livelihoods, they can increase vulnerability if they are the main or only source of revenue and suddenly drop or stop, with the loss of the migrant's work, for example, due to health problems or an economic crises.

While the former can affect both men and women, economic crises tend to have mixed gender impacts on employment depending on the sector and skills involved, among other factors.

What are the Policy Options?

A combination of legal, policy and practical measures is required to provide viable alternatives to rural out-migration, ensure protection and welfare for migrants, encourage the best use of migrant earnings and learning by rural households and communities, and create viable and sustainable options for return and reintegration. While governments have a key responsibility for ensuring gender-sensitive migration policies, the engagement of concerned populations and their organizations, and the commitment of employers' and workers' organizations in both origin and destination countries, are also vital.

1. Address the Push Factors of Rural Out-migration with A Gender Sensitive Approach

Provide core public goods to mprove agricultural productivity and ncomes, reduce gender inequalities in access to productive resources, stimulate rural employment creation and entrepreneurship (with specifc incentives to encourage female employment), and lighten rural women's workloads (such as infrastructure to facilitate access to water, fuel, markets, education, training and health services).

Invest in education and vocationa training with equal opportunities for boys and girls to give them more employment options at home (and to strengthen work skills of potential migrants).

Invest in health services, ensure women's access to reproductive health, and train them to improve the health of their children and grandchildren, as healthier individuals are more productive and can better ensure their own and their families' livelihoods at home, or when they migrate.

- Infuence the gender patterns of migration through selective (prohibitive, permissive, or promotional) rules of exit that affect men and women migrants differently. Usually based on the status and roles of men and women within the family and the society, those rules can be implemented by labour-exporting countries to selectively encourage or prevent men or women from engaging in labour migration.

Address the specifc cases of forced migration in line with internationa conventions and guidelines, which nclude gender-specifc provisions for displaced and refugee women feeing natural and/or man-made disasters.

2.Develop Gender-sensitive Research on Rural Migration to Support Policy Design in Both Origin and Destination Countries/regions

Collect and analyze sex-disaggregated data on rural migrants and migration fows (short/long term, international/ internal, South-South or South-North).

Disaggregate remittance data by gender/ types of migration, to examine differences in remittance patterns (fows and use) and their role in poverty reduction and community development.

Assess the gender-differentiated impacts of migration on rural livelihoods and agricultural production, including:

— gender dynamics underlying migration decisions, especially the reasons for and the impacts of migration on areas/countries of origin and destination;

— the impacts of technology-led agricultural transformation on demand for/displacement of rural male, female and youth labour;

— the impacts of migrations on the agricultural and rural labour force, production and food security, and care and reproductive roles;

— the impacts of new skills, know-how and money acquired abroad on agricultural investment and farming systems.

3.Provide Tools and Legal Frameworks that Help Migrants, Especially Women, to Access Decent Work

Defne an entry status that allows both male and female migrants to equally access residency, social and employment rights in receiving countries. Because migrant women are often viewed as "dependent" (wife or daughter of an "independent" man with whom they migrate), they may face diffculties to obtain residence and work permits, limiting their access to legal and social rights, and leaving them in informal and precarious situations.

Promote female migrant associations, women's membership in mixed associations and migrants' membership in trade or workers' unions. This can facilitate access to information on the migration process (risks, immigration policies, working conditions and rights in the destination country/area), legal and social assistance, and health care.

Stimulate discussions between governments, social partners (employers and trade unions), civil society and migrant communities so that the contributions of migrants are recognized, their rights are protected, and positive social and economic changes in the local community can take place.

Introduce national labour and migration legislation that enshrines internationa standards for the legal protection of migrants (particularly women), and international labour standards to ensure decent work conditions for migrants and national workers alike. The ILO Multilateral Framework for Labour Migration provides a comprehensive, gender-sensitive guide to the principles, international standards, institutiona measures, and practical actions.

4. Maximize the Benefi ts of Migration, in Sending Areas, in Terms of Gender Equality and Development

Support female migrant associations in promoting gender equality back home through projects that encourage female migrants, upon return, to become change agents in local communities.

Create conditions for returnees, including women migrants who have gained independence, confi dence, and skills working abroad, to obtain employment and/or start-up entrepreneurial activities.

Provide information and incentives to optimize the use of remittances in rura areas of origin in ways that address gender-differentiated needs and ensure gender-equitable benefi ts. Strategies to enhance the contribution of migration to rural livelihoods, community welfare and development should:

— Ensure safe, effi cient and inexpensive remittance channels and facilitate access for men and women to fi nancial institutions;
— Develop special instruments and mechanisms that help women to have control over their remittances back home and to play a role in deciding how remittances are used;
— Encourage men and women migrants to engage in collective use of remittances for local rural development projects in communities of origin. The Asian Migration Centre in Hong Kong, for example, invites migrant workers to participate in group savings aiming at sustainable investments in their home countries. Migrant women, linking with their families left behind, local authorities and social institutions, can play an important role in designing gender sensitive projects which can improve the global welfare of their communities through investments in health, child care, or education.

References

Black, R., (2004) 'Migration and pro-poor policy in Africa', Development Research Centre on Migration, Globalisation and Poverty, University of Sussex, Working Paper C6, 28 p.

Deshingkar, P., (2004) 'Understanding the Implications of Migration for Pro-poor Agricultural Growth' Paper prepared for the DAC POVNET Agriculture Task Group Meeting, Helsinki, 17 – 18 June.

Guest, P., (2003) 'Bridging the gap: internal migration in Asia' Paper prepared for the Conference on African Migration in Comparative Perspective, Johannesburg, South Africa, 4-7 June.

International Labour Office (2004) 'Towards a fair deal for migrant workers in the global economy', International Labour Conference, 92nd Session, Geneva.

7

Gender Dimensions of Rural Employment

It examines the links between gender equality and rural employment for poverty reduction by constructing a gender analytical framework to interpret differentiated patterns and conditions of work across regions, socio-economic contexts and policy environments. The main objective of the study is to identify adequate policy responses to key gender-based constraints to the achievement of decent work for all. Decent work, as defined by the International Labour Organization (ILO), is employment that takes place under conditions of freedom, equity, security and dignity, in which rights are protected and adequate remuneration and social coverage are provided.

Gender norms and patterns are rigid, and very often put women in disadvantaged positions relative to men – including limiting women's equal access to decent work. But gender norms can and do change. Economic policies – at the macro, meso and micro levels – can be designed in ways that are transformative and that enhance gender equity.

The ability of paid employment to expand women's range of choices – hence contributing to closing persistent gender gaps in labour markets and within households – is related to the type of jobs women have access to, the level and regularity of their earnings, the opportunities for mobilizing and organizing, and the ways in which women's and men's productive and reproductive roles are coordinated and protected through policies. ILO statistics point to a large number of 'working poor' in many developing countries. This is worrying. The poverty reduction and empowerment potential of paid employment depends not just on the quantity of jobs that are created, but also on the quality of such jobs, including whether the rights, protection and voice of both female and male workers are respected.

Rural employment generation has been uneven across the world and in the last few decades appears to be frequently confined to irregular forms of work which do not always provide security of livelihoods and protection of labour rights. The flows of trade, capital, labour, technology and information across countries have accelerated. These processes of globalization provide a strong potential for a reduction in rural poverty, but they have risks and costs. Investments in agriculture also matter: an FAO study of investment trends in agriculture since the 1970s found that countries that reduced hunger more effectively were those with higher net investment rates per agricultural worker. The downside of globalization is most vividly illustrated during times of financial and economic crises, such as the current crisis. The costs of economic and financial liberalization are often borne disproportionately by the poor, and particularly by vulnerable women. This calls for a fuller understanding of key determinants of gender biases in rural labour markets and how the gendered structure of employment is evolving in response to the emerging trends.

The reasons for gender differences in rural employment and pay are many, and are often intertwined. Unequal access to decent work can be noted not only between women and men but also by ethnicity, age and education. Policies that can redress these inequalities include: measures to support education and training; policies to improve access to various markets (including land and credit); active labour market policies and labour legislation; policies to strengthen frameworks for rights; welfare policies; and broader macroeconomic reforms. To be effective, such policies need to be designed as a package of reinforcing measures, as emphasized in the ILO Decent Work Agenda. The decent work policy framework offers an integrated approach to pursuing the objectives of equitable and productive employment for women and men in rural areas. The approach addresses four pillars simultaneously:

(1) generating better jobs for both women and men through sustainable rural growth;
(2) extending the coverage of social protection to all categories of rural workers;
(3) closing the gap in labour standards for rural workers, paying particular attention to awareness of rights among government institutions,

employers' and workers' organizations and individual women and men workers, and to gender bias in enforcement; and

(4) fostering social dialogue by promoting rural institutions that equally represent women's and men's interests.

Importantly, any measure aiming at gender equality and poverty reduction must acknowledge that rural women do most of the work of caring for their children and families. The burden of combining productive and reproductive responsibilities inevitably affects their access to paid employment, often increases their stress levels and has an impact on power dynamics within households. These effects are not accounted for in conventional notions of decent work, which tend to focus only on paid employment outcomes. Policies need to be formulated in ways that address all dimensions of work life and do not disadvantage women because of their multiple productive and reproductive roles.

Institutional settings and economic structures vary a great deal between countries, and even between regions within a country. One of the goals is to identify under what contexts and circumstances some policy instruments are more effective than others. This will evidently vary also with the type of employment, whether waged employment or self-employment is concerned: for example, land reform is likely to be a more relevant enabling factor for own-account farmers than for waged workers, except in cases where agricultural workers themselves are beneficiaries of the land reform programme, as in Southern Africa.

Gender Patterns of Work

Rural employment includes farming, self-employment working in trade, small enterprises providing goods and services, wage labour in these and wage labour in agriculture. Some of this work involves long hours and is not sufficiently remunerated. Women, in particular, constitute a significant proportion of unpaid family workers. For example, unpaid work on family agricultural enterprises accounts for 34 percent of women's informal employment in India.

Women and men working in rural settings are often involved in multiple activities and different contractual arrangements simultaneously. They may need to change jobs, depending on the season, or may remain unemployed or underemployed for periods of time.

In rural contexts, the domestic sphere and market production appear to be more intertwined than in urban areas (and pressures on households to provide goods and services both for sale and for the home are stronger). Reproduction activities (such as caring for families), which are mostly on women's shoulders, constitute a heavier time burden because of poor infrastructure and lack of facilities and of institutional support. Necessity and survival are more prevalent driving factors than 'choice' in rural women's diversification strategies, as opposed to rural men's.

A wide range of data on many aspects (e.g. employment status, economic sectors, hours of paid and unpaid work, earnings, working conditions) and at many levels (e.g. household, district, region) are necessary to adequately understand the complexity of rural livelihoods and their gender patterns. Some of these data are not systematically collected or easily found in standard statistics. The researcher concerned with gender dimensions of rural work often has to patch together various sources and rely on a combination of specific case studies and anecdotal evidence.

Gender Structure of Rural Employment by Region

Agriculture continues to be the main source of rural employment for both women and men in sub-Saharan Africa, South Asia and Southeast Asia. In Latin America, rural female workers appear equally distributed between agricultural and non-agricultural sectors (with self-employment more prevalent in agriculture than in manufacturing and services), while rural men work mostly in agriculture, either as self-employed or wage workers. In the Middle East and North Africa (MENA) region, rural women work mostly as self-employed in agriculture and rural men work mostly as non-agricultural wage earners. Non-agricultural activities are the main source of employment for both men and women in Central Asia and Europe, where the majority of the rural population works as wage employees. In most regions, rural women seem more likely than rural men to be engaged in self-employment (and thus less likely to be wage earners).

The large number of rural women classified as either 'non-active or not reported' (up to 64 percent of the female population in South Asia, and above 50 percent both in Latin America and the MENA region) appears particularly dubious. It most likely reflects the fact that much of women's work in rural areas is informal or unpaid and thus still goes unrecorded. It is also quite odd that none of the figures in each column sum to 100, as one would expect.

In sub-Saharan Africa, where countries are still mostly agriculture-based (in the sense that agriculture contributes significantly to growth and the poor are mostly rural, as defined by the World Bank, 2007a), own-account farming is, not surprisingly, the most common form of employment for both sexes (about 56 percent and 54 percent of male and female adults, respectively, are agricultural self–employed). This is followed by non-agricultural wage work for men (9 percent) and non-agricultural self-employment for women (7 percent). African women are more likely than African men to be self-employed and to be working in the agricultural sector.

Gender differences in employment status appear to be more marked in South Asia, where only 13 percent of adult women are self-employed in agriculture compared with 33 percent of men, and less than 6 percent of rural women work in non-agricultural sectors compared with 27 percent of men. It is interesting to note that in South Asia, women appear somewhat equally distributed between wage work and self-employment (13 percent and 12 percent, respectively) within agriculture, whereas most men who work in agriculture are self-employed. Women in South Asia are relatively more engaged in agricultural wage employment than are women in any other region, most likely the result of women's weaker property rights in land and other assets than in most other regions, coupled with increasing landlessness.

South Asian women are also more likely to remain unpaid for work on their own family business than in any other region: ILO data for 2007 indicate that 59 percent of the total female labour force in South Asia works as contributing family workers, compared with 36 percent in Southeast Asia and the Pacific, 35 percent in sub-Saharan Africa and only 7 percent in Latin America. The corresponding shares for men are 18 percent in South Asia, 18 percent in sub-Saharan Africa and 4 percent in Latin America.

Women as own-account agricultural workers are a significant 38 percent of the rural female workforce in both the MENA region and East Asia and the Pacific, while they are only about 23 percent and 7 percent in Latin America and Europe and Central Asia, respectively. In the latter two regions, on average, agriculture constitutes a small share of gross domestic product (GDP) and poverty is no longer a rural phenomenon (i.e. in these regions most countries are 'urbanized' according to the World Bank's definition).

Non-agricultural employment appears to be less relevant for women than for men in the rural areas of most regions, and particularly in the MENA region, where only 7 percent of rural women work in non-farm activities compared with 40 percent of rural men. The only exception is Latin America, where the ratio of rural women's non-agricultural employment to agricultural employment is higher than the corresponding rural men's ratio.

In sum, overall, rural men appear to be more evenly distributed across sectors and forms of employment. The relationship between the distribution of rural female and male employment and a country's economic structure seems to be one in which a larger share of women tend to work in agriculture, even when agriculture is no longer a dominant sector (such as in transforming countries). Land availability and the structure of land rights in agricultural-based countries influence the form of employment to which rural women have access: a prevalence of wage labour and unpaid family contributions exist in South Asia – a land-scarce region – and (mostly smallholder) self-employment exists in sub-Saharan Africa – a land-abundant region. Latin America, which is the most urbanized of all developing regions (and has the most equal educational levels by gender), is the only region where the ratio of rural women's non-agricultural employment to agricultural employment is higher than the corresponding rural men's ratio.

Sub-Saharan Africa

Tanzania and Mozambique are agricultural-based countries, whereas South Africa is an urbanized country in which agriculture contributes a very small share of GDP but where poverty rates are hig her in rural are as than in urban are as (and inequality remains among the highest in the world). Agriculture is female-intensive in both Mozambique (60 percent of the agricultural labour force is female) and Tanzan ia (54 percent) but not in South Africa (34 percent). The data for Mozambique and Tanzania confirm African regional patterns in that agriculture in these countries is the main source of employment for both women and men. The productivity of agriculture is especially low in Mozambique, where agriculture contributes only 23 percent of GDP but provides employment to 78 percent of the labour force.

The share of the adult population working in agriculture is higher than regional averages, more so for the female population (81 percent of the female population works in agriculture compared with 55 percent for the corresponding share for the whole of sub-Saharan Africa).

South Asia

The share of the rural population in the total population in these countries is similar to the shares in Tanzania and Mozambique, but agricultural employment is smaller even through still significant (more than 50 percent of total employment) in both India and Bangladesh. Agriculture is a female-intensive activity in both India and Bangladesh, and in Bangladesh provides employment to more than 60 percent of the total female labour force (mostly in the form of rice production and poultry rearing). In Sri Lanka, agriculture appears to be less labour- and female-intensive than in the other two South Asian countries.

The share of the female adult population in both agriculture and non-agriculture work is higher than regional averages, and the share of female casual agricultural labour is especially significant (about 30 percent of the total female rural workforce). The male shares are more similar to regional patterns. Of note, in particular, is the high share of the rural male labour force working in non-agricultural activities relative to the high share of the rural female labour force working in agriculture, suggesting some 'feminization of agriculture'.

Table 1: Rural Employment by Gender and Employment Status, India 2005 (Percent of The Adult Population)

employment status	*Female*	*Male*
Agriculture	**83.2**	**66.5**
Self-employed	53.7	42.4
Regular/salaried	0.4	0.9
Casual labour	2 9.1	23.2
Non-agriculture	**16.8**	**33.5**
Self-employed	10.0	15.7
Regular/salaried	3.3	8.1
Casual labour	3.5	9.7
Total	**100.0**	**100.0**

Women contribute substantially to total productive work in male-headed households in Zimbabwe (about 40 percent of the total) but not in Ethiopia (where women's contribution can be less than 10 percent). In Zimbabwe, the vast majority of the work involves own farming (more than 90 percent of total activities), while in Uganda waged work/business constitutes between 26 percent and 29 percent of total work. The share of waged work/business in total employment is highest in Andhra Pradesh, India (more than 50 percent of the total). This could be expected, as Andhra Pradesh is a strong-performing state, classified as in between a 'transforming' and 'urbanized' economy. Farm work is mostly provided by men (except in Zimbabwe, where women are the main contributors), while livestock keeping is almost exclusively a children's activity in all the African countries. Children, more in general, seem to contribute significantly to household agricultural activities (up to seven hours per day in some regions). The share of paid work done by men relative to other family members is the highest across all African countries, and in particular in Ethiopia. In India, the share of paid work done by women, other relatives and children is higher than elsewhere and than the share done by men. This is a fascinating study, and more research of this kind would allow for more generalized understandings.

A few useful lessons can be drawn from this 'zooming in' section. First, disaggregated national-level surveys certainly allow for more nuances than international multi-country datasets, but their analysis is still significantly hampered by the lack of comprehensive and comparable statistics over time for a number of countries. Problems of definitions and irregularity in the collection of sex-disaggregated data need to be urgently addressed, particularly in least-developed countries (LDCs). Second, more innovative ways of collecting and reporting gender data need to be fostered, including by international organizations such as FAO and ILO. A gender perspective to rural livelihoods would require a better understanding of the division of tasks and complex decision making between members of the same household unit – not only between husbands and wives, but including children and other relatives of different age and social status. In other words, economists need to pay greater attention to the characteristics and circumstances of the women and men who are growing crops and producing goods, not in isolation, but in their relationship to each other. The study by Horrell *et al.*, offers a promising example in this regard. Their method could be extended to a wider range of household structures and settings.

The data presented so far offer only little hints as to the quality of employment opportunities available and the extent of gender-differentiated decent work deficits. Both farm and non-farm activities are very heterogeneous categories comprising both low- and high-return occupations with different entry requirements. For example, both land size and land quality matter for agricultural productivity, so it is essential to know whether landholding differs by gender in a country. Richer evidence on the quality of employment – not simply on its quantity and distribution – is needed in order to fully understand the relationship between employment and gender equality/poverty outcomes.

Gender and Decent Rural Work Deficits

Some of the factors that may push women into a disadvantaged economic position relative to men in terms of the returns to their labour are:

(a) employment (occupation and task) segmentation (women are disproportionately employed in low-quality jobs, including jobs in which their rights are not adequately respected and social protection is limited);

(b) the gender gap in earnings (partly as a consequence of high segmentation; women earn less for a given type of work than do men – usually for both wage employment and self-employment); and

(c) fewer hours of paid work but overall larger work burdens (due to competing demands of care responsibilities and non-market work, women spend less time on average in remunerated work, which lowers their total labour income and is likely to increase stress and fatigue).

Employment Segmentation and Working Conditions

There is evidence of gender-based labour market segmentation in both agricultural and non-agricultural sectors in most rural areas. Women tend to be clustered in fewer sectors than men and, in agriculture, tend to be mostly involved in subsistence production. This segmentation suggests that it may be more difficult for women than men to switch to better jobs in new sectors when new economic opportunities arise. Many rural workers, especially in agriculture, face difficulties and gaps in protection with regard to their basic rights. Women are likely to experience these problems in more severe ways than men, but unfortunately statistics on coverage and enforcement remain sparse.

Sectoral Differences and Working Conditions

As for the agricultural sectors, there seems to be a common pattern across regions in that women tend to be the main producers of food while men appear to be managing most of the commercial crops, although not without women's (often unpaid) contributions. Women also participate in commercial farming but within a rather rigid division of tasks. This rigidity in the gender division of tasks appears to be stronger in South Asia than in parts of Africa or Southeast Asia. It is important to note some sort of asymmetry in the dynamics regarding the gender division of crops: men may take over crops traditionally cultivated by women when these became more profitable (for example, in Zambia and the Gambia), but there seems to be no evidence of women taking over the management of crops previously controlled by men, except possibly in rare cases when the men in the household migrate.

In non-agricultural employment there is a similar pattern of marked concentration of the rural female labour force in only very few sectors relative to the male labour force. One of the most prevalent forms of rural non-agricultural employment for women in all regions, and particularly in Latin America, is domestic services. Domestic work, however, often pays below the agricultural wage rate (e.g. Brazil) and offers no social protection. Domestic workers are often migrants or belong to minority groups. Petty trade is a more prevalent activity for women in Africa, Latin America and some Southeast Asian countries than in South Asia. In South Asia, most female non-agricultural activities are home-based, reflecting prevailing strict norms of women's seclusion, particularly in parts of Afghanistan, Bangladesh and Pakistan. The location of their work (within private homes) makes it more difficult to enforce legislation. In sum, in most developing regions women appear to be overwhelmingly represented among the most vulnerable categories of workers, with no access to social security and limited potential to organize to ensure the enforcement of both international labour standards and national laws. In some cases, women providing unpaid contributions are often not even recognized as 'workers' and hence are seen as having no entitlement to workers' rights.

Rights and Social Dialogue

Despite the widespread commitment of many countries to respect and promote the principle of freedom of association, the effective recognition of the right to collective bargaining, the elimination of forced labour, the abolition of child labour and the elimination of all forms of discrimination in the workplace (including through ratification of a number of ILO Conventions particularly relevant to rural workers such as convention Nos. 11, 111, 129, 138, 141, 182, 184, and others), rural workers – and especially women and children – face both legal impediments and practical challenges in asserting their rights. According to a recent report of the ILO Committee of Experts on the Application of Conventions and Recommendations (CEACR), the problem of the exclusion of agricultural workers from relevant national laws and non-application of these in practice has been raised in 30 countries. Moreover, issues of violence, harassment, weak labour inspection mechanisms and non-recognition of trade unions concerning agricultural workers are quite common. For example, even where ILO provides technical assistance, many children continue to work in commercial agriculture, plantations, forestry and the informal sector. Also, despite the hazardous nature of the work and the high levels of risk, agriculture is often the least well-covered sector in the economy as far as national occupational safety and health regulations are concerned. There is an urgent need to document more fully whether all these problems affect rural female workers, both women and girls, more than male workers (as some evidence appears to suggest), and whether there are regional differences in the extent and intensity of these biases.

As for specific work categories where women are prevalent, the only ILO convention expressly targeted at home workers (Convention No. 177), for example, has been ratified by only a few developed countries. Legislative measures at the national level to provide basic labour rights for domestic workers remain limited to a handful of countries.

A recent study by the ILO shows that, globally, women's participation in institutions for social dialogue such as labour councils and advisory boards is still limited. By region, the average share of women participants is 35 percent in the Caribbean, 12 percent in Africa and 11 percent in both Asia and Latin America. The same review also finds that the institutions starting to include gender in social dialogue are about 57 percent in Asia, 33 percent in the Caribbean and in Africa, and 25 percent in Latin America (the scope of this inclusion varies considerably). However, the extent to which these institutions specifically represent the interests of rural workers is not indicated.

Trade unions in a number of countries are increasingly seeking to address the under-representation of women and their interests. The International Union of Food and Agricultural Workers (IUF), for example, has recently produced a gender-equality guide and aims to have all its committees composed of 40 percent women. There has also been an increase in the number of other more informal organizations promoting the rights of women workers, the best known of which is probably the Self-Employed Women's Association (SEWA) in India. However, these encouraging initiatives are still limited. Further research and action are much needed to foster institutional arrangements conducive to the effective and comprehensive realization of labour standards in rural areas for both women and men.

Gender Gaps in Earnings

Gender-disaggregated data on earnings from agriculture are very difficult to find. Most of the available, but still limited, evidence refers to wage work either in off-farm or non-farm activities. This partly reflects the fact that calculating labour earnings for self-employment is especially problematic because it requires undertaking complex calculations to separate the proportion of total self-employment income between labour income and income attributable to returns from other assets. Moreover, under-reporting is a more acute problem for self-employment earnings than for wages. This is an area where improvement in statistics is especially needed. The Rural Income Generating Activities (RIGA) dataset used in Hertz *et al.* although a promising effort, is no exception to these problems.

Women are generally paid less than men. However, what is interesting is the extent of this gender pay gap, and the variations across countries and occupations. Gender gaps seem to be lower in some of the NTAE activities in Mexico and Senegal. Gender wage gaps vary even within a sector in a country – for example, in Mexico, women's daily earnings are almost the same as men's daily earnings in avocado production, but only 78 percent of men's earnings in mango production. Differences in daily earnings may reflect gender differences in hours worked as well as differences in remuneration, which is why information on hourly wages is usually preferable (but more rarely available). Gaps appear to be largest for earnings from agricultural self-employment both in Africa (Ghana) and Latin America (Costa Rica and El Salvador). The sharpest gender differences in all forms of earnings are found in Afghanistan and Pakistan.

A Longer Working Day for Women

Women work longer hours than men in most developing countries when both paid and unpaid work are taken into consideration. However, much of their work remains undervalued because it is unpaid and confined to the domestic sphere. Women often spend less time on average in paid market work than men, whereas they are largely responsible for water and fuel collection, food preparation, household chores, child care and care of the sick and elderly.

Confirming patterns found in other developing countries, men appear to be working longer hours than women as far as the UN System of National Accounts (SNA) work is concerned. The difference in time spent farming and tending to the livestock is largest in Ethiopia, where men work double the time as women (eight hours per day for men compared with about four hours for women). In Zimbabwe, women and men spend on average the same time on agricultural work (about six hours). The pattern is reversed for housework: in all countries women work much more than men. In Ethiopia, in particular, women spend on average six hours on housework each day, while men do not do any of it.

The average time spent on agricultural work also varies by employment status. In Brazil, El Salvador, Kenya and South Africa, weekly hours of work in agriculture tend to be lower on average for the self-employed and for contributing family workers, both females and males, than for wage workers. In Brazil and El Salvador, the gender gap in hours worked is more pronounced among the self-employed, in the sense that women in this category appear to work significantly fewer hours than men relative to other categories of workers.

Rural Employment, Gender and Poverty

Remunerative employment is one of the most important channels through which the living standards of poor women and men can be improved. Many rural workers remain poor because they receive low earnings and live and work in precarious conditions, are vulnerable to health and other shocks and have little access to risk-coping mechanisms such as insurance or social assistance; in other words, they only have access to 'indecent' work. ILO data show that in 2007 the overall working poverty rate was 58 percent in sub-Saharan Africa, 47 percent in South Asia, about 16 percent in Southeast Asia and 7 percent in Latin America. Rates may be even higher in rural areas but unfortunately data are not easily available to confirm this point. Working poverty rates are determined at the level of the household. Hence, it is important to complement this information with analysis of employment dynamics, which focus on the individual. A full gendered picture can only be gained by intersecting the household structure with the employment structure.

In most countries, women tend to be more vulnerable workers than men because they face many biases in both rural labour markets and within households, and therefore have fewer opportunities than male workers to diversify into better-quality employment. In some family settings, they may also have weaker claims over what they earn.

The linkages between employment, poverty and gender inequality are complex and require an understanding of how household dynamics and labour market processes interact. The relationship between poverty and women's employment runs in both directions. Poverty can push women into employment – the so-called 'distress sale of labour' – often in informal and poorly paid jobs (a vicious circle). On the other hand, women's employment income often makes a critical difference in the poverty status of their households. However, this does not necessarily mean that the individual situation of the woman concerned improves at the same time, because household income may not be distributed according to the amount of time each member contributes to its generation. Attention should be given to separating out individual from average household well-being impacts, which may differ because of unequal distribution of rights, resources and time between women and men. Policies for rural employment and development must give due consideration to women's bargaining position in the household and in the labour market. Poverty is linked to weaker incorporation in both.

Poverty can push women into employment, often in informal jobs. In most developing countries, women often seek wage employment in response to economic crises and difficult family circumstances, such as separation and widowhood. Agricultural casual wage work often appears to be the only available employment option for poor rural women (more than for poor rural men). Being crowded in a limited number of occupations and lacking start-up assets, poor women enter the bargaining process with their employers in a weak position. Vulnerability may force them to sell their labour well below market rates. Measures to support the full enforcement of labour standards, to protect women's rights over their own financial assets and to assist them in mobilizing for a fair remuneration of their contributions, as envisaged in the Decent Work Agenda, thus become crucial.

Whitehead offers examples from West and East Africa. Evidence from Southern Africa corroborates these patterns. In Mozambique, a high share of female wage labourers are single heads of households. In-depth interviews indicate that women who are widows or divorced have greater difficulties in accessing decent jobs. Their weak bargaining position means that they often have to accept irregular wages and receive few, if any, benefits. In Zimbabwe, casual female wage labourers were hired for shorter periods of time than casual male labourers. They earned less than men and were more likely to be paid on a daily rather than on a monthly basis. Households headed by female casual workers were among the poorest households. Their children were more likely to be underweight (in 40 percent of the cases compared with 26 percent for other households).

Adams' study is rather dated, though, and would need to be revisited, especially in light of the crisis Zimbabwe has experienced in the last years. A study of South Africa from the mid-1990s shows that women working in the export fruit farming sector who had children were largely seasonal workers and 70 percent of them had experienced food shortages at least one time in the 12 months preceding the interviews. The situation has evolved in South Africa too, in terms of both economic developments and legislation, and an update of this analysis would be very useful.

Women's employment income can make a critical difference in the poverty status of their households. A much quoted study for Ghana and Uganda shows that poverty rates for female-headed households engaged in non-farm activities declined faster than poverty rates for other households. In Ghana, for instance, female-headed households combining both farm and non-farm work experienced a 37 percent decline in poverty compared with a 14 percent decline for male-headed households with similar characteristics over the 1987–1992 period. The study finds that women in Ghana are more involved in non-farm activities than in farming, while the reverse holds for Uganda. In both countries, high shares of non-farm employment performed by women are associated with higher overall household income. This would suggest that the ability of women to diversify out of agriculture may provide an effective pathway out of poverty, but these findings should be taken with caution as the time period over which changes were analysed is rather short (and the study dated).

A study of Vietnam offers similar findings. Rural women's ability to diversify out of farming was more strongly associated with household well-being than that of men's. Diversification into off-farm activities, rather than diversity *per se*, explained higher levels of household income. The study also suggests that, despite women's longer hours of work in domestic and child care activities, marginal returns to their off-farm activities were similar to those of men.

All these findings are very context-specific, and sounder evidence is needed to substantiate these claims. Rural non-farm work can be very diverse and, as discussed in earlier paragraphs with regard to the case of Mozambique, female members of the poorest households may be lacking the resources to participate in the most profitable activities.

As for the impact on other household members, substantial evidence (outlined in Salazar and Quisumbing, 2009 but also in earlier anthropological literature) shows that women's access to economic resources increases the share of household expenditures devoted to collective goods benefiting all household members (in particular the well-being of children) than income earned by men, who tend to use it more often to meet personal needs. However, the impact of women's access to paid labour more specifically is more mixed because of the presence of two opposite effects: a positive effect due to an increase in household income associated with mothers' paid work, and a negative effect due to a possible decline in the time devoted to housework and child care. These considerations suggest that attention needs to be paid to the type of employment obtained by women and the intensity of their work.

When household income increases as a result of women taking up paid employment, this does not necessarily mean that the individual situation of the woman concerned improves at the same time. For instance, a study of Kenya shows that increased participation of women in sugar production brought about significant income gains in overall household income and food consumption. However, women's direct control over income from the new cash crop was much less than that of men. Increases in women's own income were associated with decreases in their body mass index, because additional work and greater energy intensity of activities exceeded the concurrent increase in their caloric intake.

Emerging Trends

The flows of trade, capital, labour, technology and information across countries have accelerated in recent decades, but not all countries are benefiting in the same way. The gendered structure of employment is evolving in response to these processes of globalization.

Some of the dynamics likely to influence rural families, their livelihood strategies and gender relations are:

(a) greater economic vulnerability of smallholders to global market forces as international trade in high-value non-traditional agricultural products is increasing and increasingly dominated by large agribusiness, inputs into commercial agriculture often become more expensive and food becomes less efficient to produce; but also greater off-farm employment opportunities generated by NTAEs;

(b) increased migration which, if mostly undertaken by men, would leave women in rural areas with the main responsibility of providing for their families and, if undertaken by women, may also contribute to alter conventional gender roles and responsibilities within rural communities;

(c) the HIV/AIDS pandemic, leading to labour shortages and heavier care burdens in rural areas;

(d) climate change; and

(e) the recent food, fuel and financial crises, which are affecting different groups of countries in different ways and are expected to cause increases in working poverty and vulnerable employment worldwide.

International Trade

Trade expansion and liberalization can affect rural employment, food security and poverty in multiple ways: directly, through either agricultural export growth effects or import displacement effects (or both), and indirectly, through changes in other trade-related activities such as processing and packaging of agricultural exports. The resulting gender-differentiated employment effects vary depending on the socio-economic structure of the country concerned – in particular on which crops women produce relative to men, and the extent of gender discrimination and segmentation of rural labour markets.

Rural women and men can be involved in the production of goods traded in global markets either as farmers, wage workers or intermediaries (processing or selling products) at any node of the value chain. Commercial agriculture can include both staple crops and high value products. High-value agriculture involves a wide range of products such as vegetables, fruits, shrimps, nuts, poultry and non-food products such as cut flowers. The list continues to expand as new uses or added values are found for traditional products. A great variety of institutional arrangements characterizes production for export across regions, countries and even within a sector or value chain.

Fresh fruits and vegetables are among the fastest growing of all traded agricultural exports. Their production is heavily concentrated among a few middle-income countries in Latin America: Argentina, Chile and Mexico. Chile, Costa Rica, Ecuador and Mexico account for 43 percent of developing-country exports of fresh fruit while Argentina, Chile, Mexico and Syria provide 67 percent of fresh vegetables. Guatemala and Kenya are the main world producers of green peas.

Global value chains could offer in principle an opportunity for generating quality employment for rural women and men, but they can also be channels for transferring costs and risks to the weakest nodes, especially to women. As far as producers are concerned, emerging trends seem to indicate that small farmers are often not in a position to compete in overseas markets (while frequently having to compete with foreign food imports in the domestic market). They face a particular set of constraints relating to land tenure systems, poor infrastructure, lack of credit, and lack of access to technology and other resources. These constraints are gender-intensified.

Poor farmers in many developing countries are increasingly abandoning or selling farms, leading to land concentration in the hands of a few large commercial enterprises, including foreign companies. For example, in the early 2000s many small dairy farmers in Brazil abandoned the sector, while in Guatemala a farmer cooperative experienced a severe reduction of tomato producers.

Medium-sized and large-scale commercial farms are in a better position to take advantage of the expansion of agricultural traded goods, but these are mostly owned and managed by men. In Mozambique, Samoa and other sub-Saharan African countries, further evidence can be found that independent female producers experience more constraints in accessing international markets than male producers, and that women traders are often confined to local markets.

Even if not directly involved, women often increase the amount of time they contribute to their husbands' commercial crops, leading to higher female unpaid work burdens. In spite of their significant contribution to family crops as unpaid labour, women often have no control over the income generated from their work, as studies on NTAEs in India, Kenya and Senegal show. The effects of the expansion of agricultural exports vary evidently also with the gender intensity of the crops involved, but this may itself be endogenous. There is evidence, for example, that even when a crop is traditionally female-intensive, commercializing it causes men to enter the sector and take over production. This was the case for groundnuts in Zambia, rice in The Gambia and leafy vegetables in Uganda.

Poor households, and particularly poor women, seem to be benefiting from incorporation into international trade more through labour markets (i.e. increased employment opportunities on estate farms or packing houses) than through product markets. Wage employment in non-traditional agro-export production has emerged as a significant source of employment for rural women, particularly in Latin America, in countries such as Brazil, Chile, Colombia, Ecuador, Mexico and Peru as well as in some sub-Saharan African countries such as Kenya, South Africa, Uganda, Zambia and Zimbabwe and, more recently, Ethiopia. However, NTAE sectors remain small and employ a relatively small share of the rural labour force.

In NTAEs, women wage workers appear to be working in more precarious positions than men. For instance, in South Africa, women are 69 percent of temporary workers, and in Tanzania, women comprise 85 percent of the casual workers planting, harvesting and grading on flower farms, while men occupy managerial positions. In Bangladesh, exporters of shrimp (mostly men) realize more profits than fry catchers. Women fry catchers and sorters earn about 64 percent of what men earn and are found in the most insecure nodes of the shrimp chain. Working conditions in packing plants in the lemon sector in Northern Argentina remain rather poor, particularly for women, despite increasing pressures to comply with better standards for business owners.

Women's wages in NTAEs tend to be lower than men's, but often higher than the agricultural wage they could earn in other non-export-oriented sectors. Recent studies focusing on bean and tomato production in Senegal and banana production in Ghana show that permanent female workers employed in these sectors receive the same treatment as permanent male workers. However, a much smaller share of female workers than male workers has permanent status in these sectors. Further research on ways in which women could be included more equitably in NTAE employment is of great policy relevance.

Migration

Migration from rural areas is increasingly becoming an important livelihood strategy. Migration involves moving to another area of the country or another country on a long-term or short-term basis. Migration often occurs because of lack of economic opportunities, land shortages and poor infrastructure in rural areas, perceived better employment prospects elsewhere and improved communication. Although attention has focused on those who migrate, less attention has been given to those left behind, many of whom are women and children in most regions.

The effect of migration on the employment opportunities and well-being of those who stay behind is ambiguous. Out-migration of labour from agriculture might reduce crop production and undermine food security. On the other hand, remittances may facilitate on-farm investment or relieve credit constraints that prevented farmers from purchasing key inputs. An important policy question is thus whether remittances support production enough to compensate for the reduced availability of male or female labour and can improve intra-household welfare (through better education of children, a decline in women's workload and so on). For instance, does out-migration increase the incidence of female-headed households? And, as some evidence from Africa seems to suggest, are these female-headed households more able to engage in decent and productive work relative to other female-headed households with no migrants among their family members? Significant gaps in knowledge remain with relation to the effects of migration on rural employment opportunities and gender roles.

Gendered Employment Effects

Although data are sparse and trends are not well documented, migration patterns seem to have gender characteristics, with men migrating more frequently than women, especially internationally. A few countries in Asia provide exceptions to this pattern. In Sri Lanka and in the Philippines, female migrants are about 74 percent and 55 percent of total outflows, respectively. It appears that the number of women migrating as independent workers is steadily increasing in other countries as well.

Data on rural-urban migration from the 1970s show higher shares of men relative to women in most of sub-Saharan Africa and South Asia but higher shares of women relative to men in Southeast Asia (particularly in the Philippines, Thailand and Indonesia) and Latin America. These trends appear to have continued in recent decades.

Female and male migrant workers tend to cluster in different occupations. Women often work as domestic workers, nurses and sex workers, or find employment in export-oriented garment factories in urban areas (evidence of this can be found in Bangladesh, China, Malaysia and Nicaragua. In other cases, they migrate to other rural areas to take up jobs in NTAEs. Male migrants work in construction, transport and trading and tend to travel further away from their homes than female migrants. The experience of migration for work tends to be more short-lived for women than for men in some countries, as at times marriage brings an end to it, as documented, for example, for China.

Wages of female migrants appear on average to be lower than wages of male migrants. There is variation in the share of earnings that migrants send back home and in the use of remittances – these too seem to be gender-differentiated: paying for the education of younger siblings is a more important priority for female migrants, for instance, in Bangladesh, the Philippines and Thailand. But the evidence is mixed on this point. For example, a recent study of rural Mexico finds that households with female migrants spend less on education than similar households with no female migrants among their members.

Few studies document how migration affects the livelihood strategies of the household members left behind. The impact seems to vary depending on whether the family member who migrates is female or male, on the duration of migration and the type of employment. For example, rural women who migrate as seasonal casual labourers to work in agribusiness are found to be unable to contribute to improve their family's well-being and/or enhance their personal situation in India and Zimbabwe.

When men migrate, the household members left behind must either hire labour or substitute for male labour. Scattered evidence from sub-Saharan Africa suggests that male out-migration may intensify women's workload in agriculture and contribute to women taking up traditionally male farming tasks. In South Africa, for example, when men migrate, women must also clear the land for planting, and in Malawi 45 percent of the women interviewed were performing tasks once handled by men. These women were already over-burdened and remittances were too low to hire labour.

A comparative study of Southeast Asia shows that, in Northeast Thailand, as a result of male migration, a higher proportion of family members contributed to rice production, but more labour was also hired. In the Philippines, the proportion of hired labour was higher than family labour, and hired female labourers substituted for wives' labour. In North Vietnam, rice farming was dominated by female family labour, particularly in households with migrants. In all such cases, remittances were used to pay for farm inputs and/or hiring of labour, thus maintaining productivity. In the Philippines and Thailand, the absence of principal males and sons did not increase women's workload because female household members used remittances for hiring labour for land preparation, spraying of chemicals and other heavy tasks. In Vietnam, wives appear to have taken on additional responsibilities such as fertilizer and pesticide application and land preparation, which are typically male tasks. Some of the female farmers shifted their roles from unpaid family labourers to managers.

In rural China, as agriculture becomes less important than non-farming activities as a source of income and men increasingly migrate to urban areas, women undertake most of the farming activities, including management. However, they still have less decision-making power than men within households and their community.

In areas where sociocultural gender norms are very rigid, women withdraw from agricultural work or other types of rural employment as a result of male migration, reinforcing the gender division of labour between productive and reproductive spheres. Evidence of this is found in in rural Armenia and in Guatemala and in parts of South Asia.

In rural Mexico, male international migration, and hence higher remittances, appears to have been associated with gender-differentiated labour supply behaviour among those who stay behind. Women in families receiving remittances withdraw from paid work – mostly from poorly paid occupations in the informal sector, whereas men who remain in rural areas appear to shift from formal-sector jobs to the informal sector. A reason for this behaviour is hard to find. A more recent study finds that women who stay behind appear to have ambiguous feelings about their situation, enjoying greater independence in decision making in some instances, but also feeling further overburdened with family responsibilities. The effects of female migration on subsistence production and food security as well as on rural labour markets are documented even less than the effects of male migration. As for the impact of women's migration on subsistence production, a recent study finds that neither female nor male migration has any effect on the propensity to produce staple crops in rural Mexico, but that non-staple crop production responds negatively only to male migration.

If women migrate, their husbands often find it difficult to take on responsibility for child care and household work. For example, Toltstokorova reports frequent cases of anti-social behaviour among (mainly unemployed) husbands and adult sons in Ukraine. It is usually other female household members left behind, particularly old relatives, who take on more unpaid work in addition to their own, following female international migration, as documented in studies of rural China, Vietnam and the Philippines. In the Philippines, some female household members were able to move from unpaid subsistence agricultural work to running small businesses (e.g. Sari-sari stores) thanks to remittances from their female relatives.

HIV/AIDS

In 2007, 33 million people were estimated to be living with HIV in the whole world. Sub-Saharan Afric a accounts for 67 percent of people with HIV and for 75 percent of AIDS-related deaths. Countries especially affected include: South Africa, Botswana, Lesotho, Namibia, Swaziland, Zambia and Zimbabwe. Women account for nearly 60 percent of HIV infections in sub-Saharan Africa. HIV infection rates in rural areas are hard to measure and likely to go unreported. While early outbreaks of the disease occurred predominantly in urban areas, the majority of people living with HIV/AIDS are now in rural areas, as a result of many male migrant workers with AIDS symptoms returning to their villages.

HIV/AIDS affects rural households and rural employment in multiple ways. Many rural households appear to experience labour shortages for farm work, with serious implications for agricultural production and food security. The extent to which HIV/AIDS-affected households may diversify into non-farm jobs is not known. HIV/AIDS also has significant indirect effects on rural employment through restrictions on female labour availability, as women's productive time is diverted to taking care of the sick.

All these changes appear to be markedly gender-differentiated. Adult men may often be the first to be affected in a household and the first to die. When men are sick, women may attempt to maintain farm production by taking over farm tasks previously performed by their husbands. In Zambia, for example, wives with sick husbands or those recently widowed took over male tasks (e.g. ploughing) while retaining responsibility for all domestic activities and nursing sick household members. Occasionally, women received help from relatives but in most cases they hired male labourers to prepare rice fields in exchange for home-produced beer. In many cases, however, cash crops are abandoned when adult males fall sick or die. Widows may come under pressure to leave the fields to their husband's family. This severely restricts women's ability to work as independent farmers and to meet household food needs through their own production.

When women are sick, men may not be available to take over female tasks in farm production (such as weeding). For example, in Zambia, most male-headed households either sought help from other adult female relatives or, more frequently, relied on their children's work.

As for the impact of HIV/AIDS on the care burden, there is ample evidence that women disproportionately carry the burden which adds to already heavy workloads. Having to care for their sick relatives reduces women's capacity to engage in paid work, in both farm and non-farm activities. A few studies document the negative impact of increased care-giving responsibilities on women's agricultural labour supply. In Bukoba district, Tanzania, women spent 60 percent less time on agricultural activities if their husbands were ill. In Ethiopia, women in AIDS-affected households spend between 12 and 16 hours per week on agricultural activities. This compares with 34 hours for women in non-AIDS-affected households. In Southern Zambia women had to withdraw from agricultural work altogether.

The impact of HIV/AIDS on women's and men's rural non-farm activities is little investigated. In response to HIV/AIDS and declining agricultural production, rural households may seek non-farm employment opportunities. However, because women are overburdened, they may no longer have time for non-farm activities, such as artisan crafts, market gardening and food processing, that previously contributed to the family budget. They may be forced instead to enter the worst forms of paid work in order to feed their families or raise money for medicines. Sparse evidence suggests that some women in HIV/AIDS-affected households resort to commercial sex.

The HIV/AIDS epidemic also significantly affects children's work. Some plantations in Zimbabwe hired children in place of their dead parents to help them survive. It has also been reported that bonded and forced labour of children is on the increase on South African farms, where children inherit family obligations when their parents die. Moreover, AIDS-affected households often take children away from school, especially girls, so they can take care of sick family members and younger siblings.

Female-headed households affected by HIV are likely to be more vulnerable to poverty than male-headed households. For example, in the northern province of Zambia, female-headed households were found to have about three times as many orphans as male-headed households, owned fewer physical assets and fewer small ruminants, had the lowest average land available per person and suffered from shortages of labour.

Feminization of Agriculture

Since the 1990s, a number of studies on have been pointing to the 'feminization of agriculture', attributing it partly to the trends described in the previous sections. The term 'feminization of agriculture' can mean different things and should be used with care. It refers broadly to women's increasing presence (or visibility) in the agricultural labour force, whether as agricultural wage workers, independent produc ers or u nremuner ated fa mily workers. O t hers u se t he term to indicate deterioration in the quality of agricultural work. Evidently, the forms and conditions under which women are incorporated in agricultural employment matter for gender equality and poverty outcomes – feminization of casual agricultural labour is not the same as feminization of farm management. It also matters whether an increase in the share of women in the agricultural labour force relative to men is because more women are becoming economically active in agriculture or because fewer men are working in the sector.

Extra caution should also be used in interpreting higher rural female participation rates as true 'feminization', as these higher rates may be simply a reflection of women's contribution to agriculture starting to be better counted in standard statistics. The evidence is patchy and anecdotal in most countries and regions. Statistics over time are rarely available, making the task of answering this question even harder.

It is important to understand the processes behind the numbers. Asking about the factors leading to gender-differentiated changes in rural employment is a more fruitful policy question than simply quantifying the extent of such changes. Different contexts will require different types of interventions. What the earlier sections show is that the level of influence and strength of different drivers vary by region and sub-region and that there may be intersecting processes and tensions between offsetting effects. The HIV/AIDS epidemic has a much stronger negative impact in Southern Africa than in any other region. Migration seems a more significant phenomenon in Southeast Asia and Latin America (where the diversification of the rural economy appears more advanced, at least in some regions, and where women seem to be taking on farm management responsibilities in some cases) than in South Asia or sub-Saharan Africa. International trade seems to be affecting most regions, but each region and country in different ways, depending on the socio-economic and institutional structures of the countries concerned. For example, the increased demand for female labour in the agricultural wage labour market as a result of expanding non-traditional agricultural exports is affecting Latin America the most, and to a lesser extent some countries in India and sub-Saharan Africa.

New Challenges

Other processes and events, such as climate change and the recent global food, fuel and financial crises, pose significant new challenges to the achievement of poverty reduction and gender equality in the rural world. These processes are not sufficiently documented yet to permit any sound assessment. Thus only a few tentative considerations can be made.

Climate Change

One effect of climate change relevant to rural employment is related to the risk of declining farm yields. The resulting gender-differentiated impact will depend on multiple factors, including which crops women produce, as well as their ability to adapt and respond.

Female farmers' ability to develop effective coping strategies might be limited compared with male farmers because of their more restricted access to productive resources such as technology, knowledge and inputs. There is, however, some evidence that some women are adapting to the changing climate by shifting cultivation to flood- and drought-resistant crops, crops that can be harvested before the flood season or varieties of rice that will grow high enough to remain above the water when the floods come. Climate change might worsen the conditions of wage agricultural labourers if, in response to it, large producers expand informal employment and increase the use of pesticides. Climate change might also increase women's unpaid workload, further reducing their opportunities for paid employment, in areas affected by desertification where time required for water collection might increase.

Both mitigation and adaptation policies are likely to have gender-differentiated effects on employment that need to be better understood. For instance, environmental labelling, if discouraging the purchase of fruit and vegetables from developing countries, may have negative employment effects on female-intensive non-traditional agricultural export industries. Climate policies can contribute to rising demand for educated and qualified workers through promoting environmentally sound technologies. However, because of women's lower levels of education in many countries, women are less likely to benefit from such demand unless the relevant training is made available to them.

Financial, Food and Fuel Crises

The financial crisis, which started in 2008 in developed countries, is already having an impact on developing countries through reduced trade flows, declining commodity prices, tightening of credit markets for both private and public sectors, lower remittances flows, declining foreign direct investment and official development assistance, and, more broadly, greater uncertainty. Not all developing countries are being affected in the same way and through the same channels. It is predicted that some of the Asian countries (except China and India) and most sub-Saharan African countries will be hit the hardest, whereas Latin America seems the region best equipped institutionally to cope with the downturn. The financial crisis arrived at a time when many people in developing countries were already facing hardship because of the food and fuel crises. While the prices of food and fuel have declined since mid-2008, they nonetheless remain higher than in 2007 and have not dropped in all locations, indicating that those crises are not over either.

The effects of the three crises are likely to offset each other in some cases but to reinforce each other in other cases. The vulnerability to food, fuel and financial shocks is likely to vary widely across developing economies, depending on the extent of their integration with the global markets through trade and capital flows, their shares of food and energy imports and their within-country inequality. Policy responses to protect and extend decent work for both women and men in these circumstances must recognize the heterogeneity of effects across and within regions.

There is no clear evidence to date as to whether employment in rural areas is being more negatively affected than employment in urban areas, as this is context-specific and depends on a range of factors and pre-conditions. Nor is it possible to know conclusively whether rural job losses will be greater among women than among men. In a recent analysis of overall trends in developed economies, the ILO identifies three groups of countries: a group in which the employment impact of the crisis does not seem to be visible as yet (e.g. the Netherlands and Poland); a group experiencing job losses but where gender effects are ambiguous (e.g. Australia and Canada); and a third group displaying a rapid deterioration of labour market conditions, with higher unemployment rates for males than for females.

The employment effects of the crisis in the rural developing world will be contingent on the particular economic structures of different countries and on the sectors in which women and men work. For example, in countries where export sectors are female-intensive, rural women will disproportionately bear the loss of jobs. There may also be differences in impact between employment related to food such as vegetables and work opportunities in sectors producing luxury goods such as flowers, the demand for which can be expected to decline faster. In countries where minerals are key exports or where the construction sector is large, men will suffer the most (these sectors are often male-dominated). Male and female migration from rural areas to the cities, or to other countries, may also be affected differently, depending on the sectors in which workers are employed (for example, depending on whether, in receiving areas, the demand for construction workers, which is mostly a male job, will decline more than the demand for domestic workers, generally a female occupation). Rural women micro-entrepreneurs could also experience negative impacts from restrictions on the availability of credit since they tend to be the majority of microfinance clients.

It is plausible to predict that in most countries women will be expected to assume the primary responsibility for acting as safety nets of last resort and for ensuring that their families will survive. Rural women's unpaid work burdens are likely to further intensify, especially in low-income households, imposing significant costs and limiting further their ability to participate on decent terms in the paid labour market. It is possible that rural women, more than rural men, will be increasingly offered precarious employment with low prospects and that their children's health as well as their own health will deteriorate. During Mexico's 1995 crisis, for example, infant mortality rates increased most in the areas where women's work participation increased, with girls being affected the most. Moreover female workers, being on average less educated, may be less prepared for more remunerative employment involving the use of the new technology needed to ensure a 'green' recovery. Sound evidence for developing countries is still patchy but seems to confirm some of these predictions.

The only available accounts to date either rely mostly on newspaper reports or draw on small qualitative studies. In China, recent reports mention that 20 million migrant workers have already returned to their home villages and it is likely they will end up in marginal occupations in rural areas, but the gender dimension of these patterns is not fully highlighted. In India, a sample survey carried out by the Ministry of Labour and Employment shows that about a half a million workers have lost their jobs during October-December 2008 and most of them are contract workers. In Indonesia, the Philippines and Thailand, jobs have been declining mostly in manufacturing, including in factories that employ large shares of female workers (e.g. toy factories in Indonesia. In Bangladesh, however, there are yet no signs of declining orders in the ready-made garments export industry and, rather, the role of this country as a producer of cheap garments using cheap labour seems to be reinforced. More jobs are said to be available for women, but they are found in the unlicensed sweatshops that sub-contract work, pay irregularly and treat workers unfairly. This signals a rise in vulnerable employment rather than in open unemployment in this country, especially among female workers.

The gathering and sale of vegetables discarded by the wholesale vegetable market is another emerging activity. In Kenya, women explained that their work burden had increased dramatically, and that now they would have to leave home earlier and seek work washing clothes or selling charcoal, vegetables and food by the roadside. Other accounts point to an increase in activities of dubious legality. In many African countries most farmers described greater uncertainty and an inability to produce more in response to higher food prices.

These findings underline the importance of social protection strategies designed to especially support poor rural women in their effort to provide for their families. They also underscore the need for a stronger policy commitment to investment in agriculture and specific attention to marginal and landless female farmers so that they are not excluded from the possible benefits arising from the supply response to the current crises.

Changing Patterns of Gender Inequalities

Rural women and men experience work and employment differently also by age, ethnicity, social status and roles in their households. Patterns vary across countries and socio-economic settings and are changing in response to increased international trade, migration and other emerging trends. However, some of the broad structures identified by Ester Boserup in her seminal work on women's role in economic development in the 1970s seem to still be discernible in current regional configurations.

Boserup distinguished between a 'male farming system' and a 'female farming system'. The 'male farming system' was characterized by high incidence of landlessness, high levels of agricultural wage labour, inheritance through male lines and a low presence of women in the fields due to strict norms of female seclusion resulting in women concentrating mainly on tasks within the homestead. The 'female farming system' was characterized by family farming, low levels of wage labour, bilateral inheritance practices, communal ownership of land with usufruct rights for female members and high percentages of agricultural female family labourers. Women in this latter system played a major role in food production, had greater freedom of movement and were active in trade and commerce. Patterns similar to those of the 'male system' can still be found in the MENA region, in parts of South Asia (especially Pakistan, Afghanistan and Bangladesh) and even in some regions of Latin America. Except for Latin America, women in these countries still participate in trading in limited ways. Some characteristics of the 'female farming system' can be observed in sub-Saharan Africa but also in many countries of Southeast Asia.

Globalization is playing a role in transforming these gender patterns of rural work. Both female and male workers are now present in larger numbers in the traded, more market-oriented sectors of the rural economy, and rural women's contributions seem to have gained greater visibility both in policy-making and research. But the extent to which different groups of workers are incorporated into the global economy and participate in the new processes varies. Even if it is difficult to tell because of limited statistics, women seem to be participating in the general movement out of agriculture – but at a slower pace than men. Migration and involvement in profitable non-farm activities appear more prevalent among rural male workers. Smallholders, which include many female farmers, have been facing hardship and greater vulnerability. Rural wage employment in large corporate farming is emerging as an important source of employment for rural women, especially in Latin America, but the evidence about working conditions and pay in these new sectors is mixed. An unchanging aspect of the gender division of labour across regions is the division of domestic responsibilities: women are taking up a larger share of agricultural production and paid work but also continue to be the main providers of well-being to their family members. There are clearly many gender-related constraints still at work in rural labour markets. These pose some challenges to the achievement of decent work for women and men in the new global environment.

Burden of Unpaid Work

The division of domestic labour, giving women the main responsibility for household chores, care provision and other unpaid work to support their families and communities, is one of the major examples of a gender-specific constraint. Women effectively act as a safety net of last resort to ensure their family's well-being, even in the absence of adequate social provision by state and local institutions. This unpaid work has important economic functions that are rarely recognized and valued: it is key to food security and to maintaining adequate levels of productivity among the rural labour force.

The responsibility for children, in particular, may also constitute a reason for employers (unwilling to share the costs of care provision) to discriminate against married female workers in their hiring. Family responsibilities may also limit women's ability to participate actively in workers' cooperatives and other organizations and to mobilize for their rights.

There are many forms of unpaid work that rural women (more than rural men) engage in, and it is useful to distinguish them for policy purposes:

(a) Women (and children) in the rural areas of most regions spend long hours collecting water and fuel. There is scope for addressing this constraint through well-targeted interventions in physical infrastructure, which may be achieved through public investment and a variety of interventions, including, but not only, 'gender-aware' labour-intensive public works programmes.

(b) Women also spend much of their day caring for their children, assisting other family members who are ill or disabled, preparing food and cleaning. This would call for public financing of child care services, support for day care centres, health clinics, strengthening of community services for the elderly and other forms of social protection. Better physical infrastructure (e.g. rural electrification) and improved food preparation tools, as well as home- or community-based cottage industry food-processing technologies, could also help in reducing the drudgery of some tasks such as cooking and cleaning.

(c) Women often work on the family farm or help in small business enterprises without receiving remuneration as a result of unequal power relations within households that severely limit their ability to make claims over their contributions. Policies to address this problem may include strengthening women's legal rights, supporting the formation of self-help groups (SHGs) and ensuring greater visibility through participation in the public life of the rural communities where women live.

There seems to be little variation in gender imbalances in domestic responsibilities across regions – in all countries from sub-Saharan Africa, to Latin America, to Asia, women carry out the bulk of unpaid work. But there are differences between women in different stages of the life cycle (e.g. women with infants and young children usually face the heaviest burden relative to both older women and younger unmarried women), between locations (e.g. female farmers living in remote areas have to spend longer hours collecting water or processing food than women living in areas better endowed with infrastructure) and socio-economic status (e.g. better-off women can afford to pay for housework help and, if they are involved in paid work, they are also likely to be in forms of employment that provide child support).

Water and Fuel Collection

The burden of water and fuel collection is likely to reduce the amount of time women can spend in paid work and to increase the probability that they will be involved in more informal forms of employment. In South African poor rural households, for example, the time that women who must fetch water and fuel spend in paid employment is only 25 percent of the time that women who do not engage in water and fuel collection spend in it. In Tanzania, time spent fetching water and fuel appears to be a significant constraint on women's participation in off-farm self-employment. A simple simulation exercise using the recently released Tanzanian time-use data suggests that investing in water-related infrastructure could free up many female working hours in a year. If the freed-up hours were converted into paid employment, this would be equivalent to a million new full-time jobs for women and an increase in income corresponding to about 6 percent of the total cash earnings for the entire population in a year. During the dryer summer months, women participating in a microenterprise project run by the Self-Employed Women' s Association (SEWA) in Gujarat, India must reduce the time they spend on paid activities because of the need to spend longer hours collecting water.

Child Care

A generalization that can be made is that rural female workers with children are more likely to be self-employed (in agriculture or other sectors) or to work from home than single women. This type of work can be easily reconciled with reproductive responsibilities. Self-employment offers a more flexible work schedule (women in this category appear on average to spend fewer hours in paid work.

W hen women wit h children are ver y poor, t hough, they may lack even the most ba sic star t-up assets and hence are forced to take up casual wage work under very disadvantageous terms. Examples of female workers with young children who engage as seasonal workers in the most insecure forms of employment, with no child care support or maternity leave, can be found in some NTAE sectors: for example, in South Africa, where many female migrants live with their children in informal settlements close to the workplace; and in the Dominican Republic. In both cases, some of the children were still undernourished because their mothers' earnings were too low. In Punjab, Indian women working as wage labourers on contract farming in horticulture often bring their infants and children with them because they lack access to child care services.

Both the age and the gender of children matter in terms of their mothers' ability to choose from alternative options of remunerated work. An interesting, if dated, study from Guatemala, for example, shows that older women are more able to engage in marketing activities that require them to be mobile and travel long distances than young women with infants. Independent agricultural activities are only undertaken by women with adult sons who can provide them with access to land.

Time constraints can be even harder to overcome for women heads of household. In Uganda, child care burdens coupled with poor infrastructure (lack of piped water and cooking stoves) significantly compromised the ability of women heads of household to expand and/or diversify production. In the districts of Masindi and Mukono, when asked about the reasons for their lack of success in expanding agricultural production, men identified transport, marketing constraints and lack of credit, whereas women mentioned the time needed to look after their families, food preparation and the work on their husbands' gardens.

Child care is also a problem for many of the women working in employment guarantee schemes, especially for mothers of infants. A recent social audit of the National Rural Employment Guarantee Act in Tamil Nadu, India indicates that about 70 percent of the women interviewed had no child care facilities at the worksite despite the provision of the NREGA that 'in the event that there are at least five children under the age of six at the worksite, one of the female workers should be deputed to look after them and she should be paid the same wage as other NREGA workers'. About 50 percent of the women left their children at home and most of them were being dissuaded from bringing them to work.

The negative impact of child care on women's participation in public works – especially for women with children in the pre-school age group – was noted in other earlier studies such as Quisumbing and Yohannes for a Food for Work programme in Ethiopia, and Dejardin for a number of projects in other sub-Saharan African countries.

Caring obligations also often reduce the length of female wage workers' total years in employment, with negative consequences for their earnings and pension entitlements.

Young women with no children usually seem to have more chances than women with children to enter better paid jobs, in particular non-agricultural wage employment. Women with relatively grown-up daughters can rely on them for help with domestic chores if they take up paid employment. Evidence across countries and sectors suggests that a significant number of older children, especially girls, look after younger siblings while their mothers work.

Unpaid Family Labour on Farms

The main occupation of a high proportion of rural women, especially in South Asia and North Africa, is that of 'unpaid agricultural family worker'. This is a very vulnerable category of work, the involvement in which often implies limited claims over what is produced and restricted access to more decent forms of employment. Evidence from West Africa reviewed in Dey Abbas shows that women's obligation to work on their husbands' fields means they are often unable to undertake important operations on their own plots in time, with negative consequences for their own crops' productivity. Women contributing unpaid labour to their husbands' production of vegetable exports in Guatemala had to reduce their involvement in activities such as craft production, small livestock raising and storekeeping, all of which were sources of independent income for them. Many other similar cases are known to exist but are not sufficiently documented in economic analyses of agricultural employment, except for specific case studies within the intra-household resource allocation literature. Children, both girls and boys, also often work for no pay (or under very exploitative conditions) for their family or other plots. This work exposes them to health hazards and can severely compromise their education and future employment prospects.

Effects on Komen's Participation in Training and Extension Services

A survey of women farmers in central Thailand found that women involved in rice production as a result of male migration lacked basic skills in pest and disease diagnosis, pesticides and application methods. Despite the negative consequences that this lack of knowledge had for their health, most of these female farmers were not willing to participate in training courses because of conflicting caring and housework commitments. A USAID Integrated Agriculture Training Programme (IATP) in Papua New Guinea had only limited success because it failed to consider women's family responsibilities. The training courses were arranged away from the village for three full days and women found it particularly difficult to travel and arrange for alternative forms of child care.

Emerging Challenges

The burden of unpaid care work has been increasing in rural sub-Saharan Africa because of the HIV/AIDS epidemic. For example, because of the need to nurse HIV-affected household members, women devoted less time to agricultural work and child care in Ethiopia and in Zambia and had to switch to less labour-intensive crops in Uganda.

Increasing female migration is also likely to contribute to heavier housework burdens for the female household members remaining in rural areas, in particular if children are left behind. These other female members may be mothers, sisters, older daughters or grandmothers who may be negatively affected in terms of their own employment options or in their opportunities for education. Young single women with fewer reproductive responsibilities are more likely to migrate further away from home in search of better job opportunities. This has been observed in Bangladesh, China, Malaysia and other Asian and Latin American countries.

Already weak essential public social services in most rural areas of developing countries are likely to worsen with the current economic crisis and thus increase the care-giving burden of rural women at the household level.

Policy Responses

Physical Infrastructure and Home-based Technology Investment

Public investment in roads, rural electrification and improvements in water and sanitation infrastructure can significantly contribute to reducing rural women's unpaid work and generate many other benefits such as better health for women and their families. Cereal mills, other equipment for food processing, pressure cookers, refrigerators and other affordable and appropriate home-based technologies can also significantly help reduce the time and energy rural women must invest in food preparation and improve food availability and incomes from food sales off-season.

However, women do not always gain from improved energy services. In a mountainous village in rural China, following the introduction of electricity, some women moved part of their domestic activities to the evening and worked longer in the field during the day – the only substantial time-saving for them occurring in pig feeding. In the village there was a general increase in resting time, but this was much larger for men than for women. This points to the need to address the gender division of domestic labour with an integrated approach that combines improvements in physical infrastructure with awareness-generating programmes.

An example of a successful initiative in the area of water infrastructure is provided by SEWA's water campaign in Gujarat. The project was about improving access to safe and reliable drinking water and involved, among others, training women to repair hand pumps. Women's collective action was a crucial ingredient of the success. Women were initially reluctant to participate because water infrastructure was regarded as male territory and men were expressing hostility by refusing to drink water from a source built by women or to work on water structures that women managed. SEWA's district-level functionaries and village women leaders facilitated a process of mobilization through meetings, solidarity group formation and capacity building, and acted as interface between the local women and the water board. As a result, workloads from collecting water were reduced, enabling women to devote more time to remunerated employment or to rest. More reliable and safer water provision also led to a reduction of migration to nearby villages. From a general perspective, the project seems to have had a significant empowerment effect on women and on their willingness and ability to participate in the public domain, including involvement in *panchayat* (local council) meetings and formation of SHGs for savings.

Public Works

More roads and better water and electricity infrastructure can also be provided through government-supported public works. Well-designed employment guarantee programmes can simultaneously fulfil the two objectives of generating jobs for both women and men, and creating assets that reduce aspects of women's domestic workloads, with important gender redistributive implications. This is more likely to happen if women and communities are directly involved in the design of public works. In Peru, for example, women's direct participation in the design of a rural roads project ensured that greater priority was given to their needs. Upgrades included roads that connected communities and also many non-motorized transport tracks that were used mostly by women and ignored by other road programmes.

Public works that contribute to rural community welfare in a gender-equitable way do not have to be confined to physical infrastructure projects.

Care-providing public works programmes also could be an effective response to the upsurge in the need for care resulting from the HIV/AIDS pandemic, particularly in sub-Saharan Africa.

Child Care Services

Child care support for working women in rural areas can promote the ability of mothers to participate in economic activities and indirectly support their children's well-being. The provision of child care is of most immediate relevance to wage workers but it can also support women in self-employment by possibly enhancing their chances for better paid non-agricultural waged work. The most common form of child care in rural areas is still through family members, including older siblings looking after younger ones. Other forms of child care are still rather poor and scattered. Child care can be provided through a variety of arrangements: government-funded day care centres, services by voluntary organizations or informal baby-sitting services. Publicly funded child care facilities relative to market-based child care services have the potential to reach a wider range of workers, including the most disadvantaged.

Some innovative projects appear to be available to meet the demand for child care in rural contexts, particularly in India. Mobile Crèches is a voluntary organization that offers child care to women working in the construction sector. It has more than 300 centres and reaches about 200 000 children across India. It approaches builders in urban and rural construction sites, with a view to opening a centre there. Those who agree provide basic facilities. SEWA also provides child care and targets groups of migrant workers. For instance, it supports women in a district of West Gujarat where many of the poorest families work in salt extraction. The salt workers have to stay in the proximity of their workplace, near the coastal desert terrains, up to eight months in a year. The children have to follow their parents, with often negative implications for their education and overall development.

It is also important to encourage men to take on family responsibilities. An interesting project trying to achieve this objective is promoted by the Sonke Gender Justice Network in South Africa, which uses innovative methods to support men's involvement in the care of children, particularly in rural areas affected by HIV/AIDS. Sonke combines advocacy with participatory workshops in specific villages aimed at generating awareness on a variety of issues including health, sexuality, gender and violence.

Health Insurance

Coverage of public social security schemes, including health insurance, tends to be limited in rural areas. Even where, as in many Latin American and Caribbean countries, contributory social security systems are gradually being extended to agricultural wage workers, most seasonal and migrant workers remain excluded. Lack of health insurance may aggravate the load of unpaid care at moments when families are especially vulnerable. Health insurance schemes for informal workers implemented by civil society organizations can offer effective alternatives when public social security schemes are lacking. SEWA in India, for example, supports an innovative scheme providing about 100 000 women workers, in both urban and rural areas, with health insurance, including a maternity component and life and asset insurance. However, some of SEWA's poorest members cannot afford the premiums, which have to be set at a rate that ensures financial viability.

Rural Women, Education and Employment

Human capital gains through education can be a crucial factor in strengthening rural women's position in the labour process (sometimes labour is the main factor of production over which women have some control); can help diversify rural family incomes through non-farm earnings; may improve the stability and quality of non-farm employment by allowing access to vocational training; increase women's access to labour markets beyond their locality (such as through migration); and increase women's ability, through resources and information, to claim their rights. A crucial interrupter of female education is marriage and/or child-bearing. In turn, these can limit women's labour market access due to discriminatory practices, and therefore reduce incentives to invest in female education. Gender biases in both the demand and supply sides of education need to be addressed.

Education is likely to be positively associated with participation in high-productivity rural employment. This is, for example, suggested by a regression analysis including sub-Saharan African countries, Asian countries (Bangladesh, Indonesia, Nepal, Tajikistan and Vietnam) and Latin American countries. The estimated effects are stronger as national incomes rise, and women appear to gain more than men from each additional year of education. A similar result is found by Abdulai and Delgado for Northern Ghana: years of schooling increase the likelihood of participation in non-farm work and of earning higher wages, more so for rural women than for rural men.

Education appears to increase women's chances to enter the formal rural labour market, particularly the wage sector, in three rural states of Mexico. Unfortunately, the study does not separate agricultural from non-agricultural activities. Education is found to have a positive effect particularly on the labour market participation of married women, who generally face more barriers to employment than single women. Secondary and post-secondary education increases the chance that they are in the salaried sector relative to self-employment. Another study on Mexican *ejidos* examines gender and generational differences in off-farm wage labour market participation. Men are much more likely to hold off-farm jobs than women, but mainly in unskilled positions. The few women who access off-farm employment are more likely to be in skilled or semi-skilled jobs. However, since the majority of the women in the study were single, it is unclear whether they would continue to work after marriage.

Most of the women who earned relatively high wages in stable employment on large state-run farms (including citrus plantations, coffee plantations and irrigated tomato and vegetable projects) in Mpumalanga, South Africa had completed more years of schooling than other female wage labourers interviewed, avoided early and frequent pregnancies and had more work experience. An intergenerational effect was also found: women whose mothers attended school had completed more years of school (about nine years) than the women whose mothers had not attended school. Conversely, children whose mothers worked as child labourers (and were unable to attend school regularly) were more likely to be child labourers themselves. The majority of the workers with stable jobs were South African. By contrast, migrant female workers from Mozambique were unable to access remunerative employment on state-run farms and had uncertain legal status within South Africa.

Education can help rural women, particularly the young and single ones, to access urban wage employment. The positive effect of education on rural-urban migration propensities appears to be stronger for men than for women in some countries, for example in Ecuador, but the evidence is mixed. Still, Katz finds that in Mexico, higher levels of education are found to enhance rural women's chances of migrating to the United States but to reduce men's chances. Evidence from China suggests that the probability that women with higher levels of education will fnd a job by migrating to the cities has risen over time.

The impact of education on women's rural labour market participation may depend on the specific sociocultural context. For example, in southern India, where increasing the opportunity of a good marriage is often the main reason for supporting girls' education, education can lead to a decline in female wage employment and reinforce women's traditional roles, as found in a village in Maharashtra.

Barriers to women's non-farm employment reduce the returns to women's education and dampen parental incentives to invest in girls' education. For example, the higher probability of women obtaining non-farm employment has gone hand in hand with higher educational attainment of girls in the Philippines. In contrast, Ghanaian women have more limited access to non-farm labour markets, which in turn likely discourages parents from investing in their daughters' schooling.

Returns to education are greater in non-farm employment. While education has a positive relation to farm yields, education is less relevant for agricultural family work and self-employment. However, it does have a direct effect on rural household well-being. In Africa, children of mothers who spent five years in primary education are 40 percent more likely to live beyond the age of five years.

An important issue relates to whether some kind of minimum level of achieved education is required to acquire training. A study shows that entry into technical education requires a minimum of eight or ten years of schooling in Bangladesh. Very few women thus became eligible for such technical training, which could improve access to better jobs. Training may actually reinforce occupational segregation based on gender. In both formal and non-formal education, boys and girls are often channelled into different subjects. This means girls are often 'directed' into subjects that are essentially extensions of women's household and reproductive tasks, such as sewing, food processing and nutrition

In terms of accessing agricultural technology, Quisumbing shows that education substantially improves yields, but high levels of schooling might not be the most important factor. Well-designed extension services that can be easily understood may be more, or equally, effective for women. In Kenya, women who had less education than men excelled in the uptake of soil fertility replenishment technologies as long as explanations were given in simple terms. The study suggests that women in the programme understood the technologies better than men but does not provide any detail of why this was the case. In Bangladesh, a local non-governmental organization (NGO) successfully taught illiterate women how to manage fishponds by giving them notebooks with illustrated instructions.

Relevant and quality extension services and training are limited for women farmers. In Vietnam, for example, women made up only 25 percent and 10 percent of participants in training programmes on animal husbandry and on crop cultivation, respectively. In Cambodia, women were only 10 percent of extension beneficiaries. In Senegal, according to the 1998/1999 census, male plot managers received three times more agricultural extension services than female plot managers. Reasons include that research and extension services tend to focus on the tasks that males specialize in; access to extension services often requires travelling long distances to district centres, taking several hours away from the family; and extension services are staffed overwhelmingly by men, raising cultural difficulties in engaging in face-to-face communication with women farmers.

Policy Responses

Policies for promoting greater gender equality in education with a view to improve access to decent rural jobs must combine measures that address both the content of education and more practical problems that girls face more often than boys in accessing schools and training services. The emphasis of education policies should evidently vary depending on whether the labour market of the area concerned is dominated by agricultural activities or non-agricultural activities.

Measures could include: better design of curricula so as to be more relevant to the technical knowledge required in agriculture; encouraging girls (for example through scholarships) to include technical subjects in their study plans and boys to join 'home economics' classes; more and better designed vocational training for women; gender training for teachers, including on issues related to sexual harassment; incentives for male and especially female teachers to work and remain in rural schools; building new schools and improving physical access to them, paying particular attention to suitable locations and means of transportation which are safe and women-friendly; and adapting school times to patterns of rural life (including the need of some children to participate in aspects of rural work in particular moments of the day, or seasonally).

Progresa (Programa de Educación, Salud y Alimentación) is a much-cited example of a cash transfer programme implemented in rural Mexico to assist poor families in meeting the financial and opportunity costs of their children's school attendance. This programme transfers cash directly to the children's mothers and provides higher stipends for girls than for boys. The assessment of whether PROGRESA has been successful in achieving its goals is mixed.

While evidence points to an increase in enrolment rates, both in primary and in secondary education, especially for girls, there is concern that the programme may have reinforced existing gender inequalities within households by intensifying mothers' caring responsibilities. Mothers must spend more time taking children for regular health checks, attending workshops on health and programme co-ordinators' meetings and contributing to community work through cleaning buildings or clearing rubbish as a requirement for obtaining the cash transfer. In sum, this programme seems in practice to target women because they are an effective way of reaching children, but it does not contribute to increase their own agency and power.

FAO, in collaboration with the World Food Programme and other partners, has supported the creation of Junior Farmer Field and Life Schools (JFFLS) for orphaned youth and children in countries where the prevalence of HIV is highest: Cameroon, Kenya, Malawi, Mozambique, Namibia, Sudan, Swaziland, Tanzania, Uganda, Zambia and Zimbabwe. The particularly valuable feature of this project is that it combines support to very vulnerable children, using innovative and holistic teaching methods.

The JFFLS training programmes target both boys and girls and help them to develop agricultural knowledge and livelihood skills they will need to sustain themselves and their families in the future. The programmes so far appear to have been successful, but further support with access to productive assets such as land or credit is crucial to ensure that the knowledge acquired through JFFLSs will enable students to benefit from decent jobs once they complete their training programmes. More in general, integrated programmes that link skills training to creating new income-generating activities have great potential.

Emergencies and Double Discrimination

Mobile school programmes in rural areas have the potential to benefit the most vulnerable girls within groups that have been displaced by armed conflict, or are forced by other disasters to lead a nomadic life. A successful example is provided by the Hanuniye project run by the Nomadic Health Care Programme in Wajir, Kenya. Its implementation strategy follows the so-called 'dugsi approach', which involves a mobile teacher living with the family or herding group. The attraction of this model is that it is compatible with daily mobility needs – with lessons designed to fit around household labour arrangements – as well as long-distance mobility.

What is even more notable is that the project appears to have successfully managed to reach both girls and boys equally. Administrative difficulties, combined with shortcomings in the design and maintenance of collapsible classrooms and the reluctance of some teachers to adapt to a nomadic lifestyle, have undermined the planned use of mobile schools in other cases, such as in Nigeria. Mobile schools should be seen only as a temporary solution.

Female children with disabilities tend to face double discrimination based on their gender and their disability. Sensitizing and training school teachers and programme administrators to recognize and deal with disabilities is essential. Special learning materials are also needed in some cases.

Weak enforcement of legislation is also another important problem that needs to be addressed to facilitate girls' access to education. Countries which are party to international human rights covenants have automatically signed and agreed to eliminate any form of discrimination on the basis of sex. However, these rights have not been extended to issues such as marriage, access to education and other aspects of family life in some rural communities where cultural norms are strongly gender-biased. Under sections 21 and 23 of the UN Convention on the Rights of the Child (CRC), it is illegal for a parent to marry off his or her daughter if she is under 18 years. However, early marriages are still common in many rural communities, where people may be unaware of laws and where extreme poverty sometimes leads families to treat marrying girls at an early age as a form of insurance. Early marriages often mean the end of the educational experience for the girls involved.

School Facilities

Long distances between school and home seem to be a common problem for access to education in many countries. Lack of good and safe roads appears to be a significant problem especially for girls. Girls fear being attacked and sexually harassed, and parents are equally concerned. To remove such barriers, schools need to be placed in adequate locations, where access will not be threatening for girls. Inadequacy of school infrastructure also contributes to low enrolment of girls. Appropriate facilities, such as clean and separate latrines for girls and protected buildings and playgrounds, are an important factor in creating a friendlier learning environment. The school building programme was implemented by the Indonesian government in collaboration with the World Bank and it is reported to be one of the fastest primary school construction programmes ever undertaken. It was designed explicitly to target children who had not previously been enrolled in schools. The number of schools to be constructed in each district was proportional to the number of children of primary school age not enrolled in school.

Land and Credit

Land is the prime productive asset in most rural areas of developing countries. Owning land, using land owned by others and securing waged farm work often depend on complex social and legal frameworks, many with gender dimensions. These institutional issues are key linkages to poverty and incomes because of how they govern the allocation of labour and the distribution of the products from land. The specifics vary from place to place, but globally there is a marked bias against women's control of land as a productive resource.

A key characteristic is that women seldom own the land that they cultivate. While this is perhaps widely recognized, what is noteworthy is how substantial the gender gap is. In all countries for which data are available, women are less likely to own land, and own less amounts of land when they do own it. In Congo and Tanzania, for example, the female share of landowners was 25 percent, and in Benin, where 11 percent of landowners are female, the average size of women's holdings is about 1 hectare, compared with 2 hectares for men's holdings. In Pakistan, women own less t ha n 3 percent of plot s, even though 67 percent of sur veyed villages repor ted a wom a n's r ight to inherit land. In India, according to the 2000/2001 Agricultural Census (which provides information only on operational holdings and not on land ownership), only 12 percent of holdings covering 9 percent of the total area are operated by women. Even in Indian states that appear to have some progressive gender indicators, when it comes to land, female shares remain low: in Kerala, women operated only 21 percent of the holdings. In Latin America, the female share of landowners ranged from 11 percent in Brazil to 27 percent in Paraguay.

Women's control over land reflects deep-rooted land tenure norms and laws. These vary considerably and are difficult to generalize. Sub-Saharan Africa has the most diverse arrangements.

A major reason why generalization is difficult – and previewing the policy discussion – is the gap between social/legal norms and actual practice, which varies from place to place. An example is Muslim Africa, viz. the coastal eastern region, Northern Nigeria, Northern Sudan, Chad and the area from the Sahelian countries to Senegal. Islamic law entitles a daughter to inherit land amounting to half of what sons inherit (due to the view that a woman is provided for, whereas a man must provide). Also in some areas a woman can inherit one-eighth of her husband's land. While Muslim norms have been favourable relative to those in other parts of Africa such as the cocoa-producing regions of West Africa, many Islamic communities force women to surrender or sell inherited land to male relatives.

Under house-property systems, women have greater control of land or livestock, but formal ownership is often not given. Thus women's claims depend substantially on their status as daughters and wives, and may be weakened by claims by male relatives. Divorced women and widows are particularly vulnerable, especially in areas with high prevalence of HIV/ AIDS

Inheritance norms constitute the main access to land. In South Asia this has been traditionally patrilineal. The significant exception is Sri Lanka, where both sons and daughters can inherit, widows can inherit all of the deceased husband's property in the absence of descendants, and married women have the right to acquire and dispose of their individually owned property.

Across Southeast Asia in Cambodia, Indonesia, Laos and Vietnam, under both customary and formal law, men and women have equal rights to land. Parents usually decide which children will inherit what property. Traditionally, the youngest daughter remains home to care for elderly parents, even after marriage, and thereby inherits the family homestead. In China, too, women and men have equal rights to land, but in practice it is more difficult for rural women to exercise these rights than it is for rural men or urban women. Women in the countryside often lose their access to the family's land after marriage because they move to their husband's village. But if they divorce, or their husbands die, it is impossible for them to claim their share of land in their husbands' villages. As a result, rural women are becoming landless, especially upon divorce.

Even in Latin America, with perhaps the most favourable legal framework, inheritance has been historically skewed towards men, in part because agriculture is defined as a male activity and in part because legal headship status confers male privilege in marriage.

Lack of land significantly limits women's access to credit, water and grazing rights, and thereby constrains options for self-employment in agriculture and social protection in times of shocks. In Kenya and Senegal, for example, women are excluded from contract farming in high-value products because they lack statutory rights over land, have limited access to irrigation and infrastructure and have weaker claims over family labour. In India, the absence of land titles significantly limits women farmers' access to institutional credit.

The lack of secure tenure limits women's land use and cropping choices. In Guatemala, women's independent – but not joint – ownership of land was found to be a significant predictor of women's participation in non-traditional agro-export production. Joint ownership appeared to have a less clear benefit. In Guatemala, Katz found that land ownership affected the degree of women's control over the benefits from agro-export production.

A man's control over family land strengthens his ability to command more of his wife's labour time in order to maximize his income. In Zambia, for example, men were able to increase maize production by demanding greater labour inputs from their wives, whereas women producers were not able to exert similar claims over their husbands' labour.

It is important to note that land is not always the most binding constraint. Whitehead argues that while land is a constraint to women's farming in some places, in other parts of sub-Saharan Africa there are other constraints that play a larger role, such as inadequate access to labour and other inputs. According to Ann Whitehead, the land constraint may be felt more heavily in places where agriculture is a more important source of livelihoods, where the gender bias in land ownership is more serious and where land scarcity is a severe problem. In India, where growing land scarcity has intensified male competition and created additional constraints to women's usufruct, trusteeship and ownership rights, women's access to land seems to have become more constrained. In India, the land question is also crucial because, as a result of male out-migration, women remain largely confined to agriculture and they are faced with the prime responsibility for farming, but without rights to the land they cultivate.

Even where land constraints are binding, it should be noted that this affects mainly farm-related employment and earnings, with education as the more important determining factor in non-farm employment.

While women's access to land is becoming more constrained in India, the reverse seems to be happening with regard to access to credit. The provision of microcredit in South Asia (as well as in Africa and Latin America, although perhaps with a more limited coverage in these latter regions) is often celebrated as a great achievement for women's empowerment. Credit and other financial services are basic requisites for increasing agricultural production and developing profitable enterprises, but many women small producers remain excluded from formal sources because of lack of collateral and financial skills and institutional and cultural biases against them.

Microcredit has indeed provided some options for rural women's self employment, but cannot be regarded as producing successful female entrepreneurs broadly. Women in some rural areas may now have good credit access, but usually to small amounts; it is mostly men who continue to benefit from larger loans and formal financial services. Because of the small size of their loans and the many other economic barriers they face, rural women are often trapped in low-value activities. In Sri Lanka, for example, Quisumbing and Pandolfelli report that average returns to capital are zero among female-owned enterprises but greater than 9 percent a month for male-owned enterprises. A study of a credit programme in Egypt in which equal numbers of male and female clients were interviewed finds women to be involved in only 28 of 96 different enterprises reported by clients. This evidence stresses the importance of complementing microcredit with initiatives that promote rural women's access to higher-value sectors and non-traditional businesses as well as of developing more inclusive formal financial services.

Policy Responses

Policy options to redress gender disparities in land rights may include: legal reforms and measures to ensure their implementation; joint titling programmes; and collective approaches. Policy initiatives for gender-equitable finance need to integrate credit provision with a range of other measures to protect women's rights over their own financial assets and to promote women's participation in higher-return economic activities. Measures cannot be limited to microcredit, however, but must involve the development of more inclusive and less gender-biased formal and informal financial systems.

Land Legislation

Across sub-Saharan Africa (e.g. Eritrea, Kenya, South Africa, Tanzania, Uganda and Zimbabwe), Asia (e.g. India, Kyrgyzstan and Tajikstan) and Latin America (e.g. Brazil, Colombia, Honduras and Nicaragua), governments have enacted legislation to guarantee women's property and inheritance rights. Tanzania's 1999 Land Law, for example, provides co-ownership of land to both spouses and prohibits village councils from discriminating against women. Uganda's 1998 Land Action and Condominium Law recognizes women's equal right to buy and own land and housing. Tajikistan's 2004 amendments to the Land Reform Act strengthen women's legal entitlements.

Unfortunately women and men's equal access to land continues to not be realized in practice. Statutory laws sometimes conflict with customary laws. In Namibia, for example, the Married Person Equality Act of 1996 states that, upon the death of a spouse, both men and women are entitled to assets accumulated through marriage. However, women continue to face persistent discrimination arising from customary laws, as indicated by the numerous cases of property grabbing by family members of the husbands who had died from AIDS-related causes. In South Africa, the implementation of the land reform programme has been rather weak because of a range of factors including: lack of clear lines of accountability of either policy-makers in the national government or implementers at the provincial level with regard to the enforcement of the Land Reform Gender Policy Document issued in 1997; limited authority of the Gender Unit within the Ministry and Department of Land Affairs; a rather inflexible programme design; and limited involvement of grassroots movements, which tend to be more vocal in urban areas.

Joint Titling

Joint titling is another option for redressing gender imbalances in access to land. In the early 1990s, five Latin American countries (Brazil, Colombia, Costa Rica, Honduras and Nicaragua) passed agrarian legislation for joint adjudication or titling of land to couples. Similar initiatives have been taken in Cambodia, India, Indonesia and Vietnam. Joint titling can help to guard against capricious actions by one spouse and protects against the dispossession of women through abandonment, separation or divorce.

Joint titling initiatives have produced mixed results. In Nicaragua, the number of women landowners has increased as a result of joint titling programmes. Law 209, which came into effect in 1995, stated that men and women had the equal right to receive land titles and established the option for couples to apply for joint title to land. The principle of joint titling was strengthened in 1997 by making it compulsory for families receiving titles for land distributed under state agrarian reforms to be issued in the names of both spouses. As a result of this legislation and the dissemination campaign and training initiatives accompanying it, the number of women with legal rights to land dramatically increased. This success is also due to the active lobbying of well-organized rural women.

Similar achievements are reported for Colombia, but not for other Latin American countries. In Honduras, for example, deeply rooted sociocultural norms and the weakness of rural women's organizations appear to have been the main factors limiting the success of the joint titling reform.

In Cambodia, a survey of 20 000 land titles issued since 2001, following new laws for joint titling, found that 78 percent were in the names of both women and men. However, women's rights to land may be denied in practice because of cultural and social factors. In principle, when land is jointly registered, both parties must sign to transfer land titles; in practice, however, this is not enforced, and women are vulnerable to losing their portion of control over such decisions and deferring to their husbands. Men often sell land without consent from their wives, and, as a result, women may also lose access to the proceeds of the sale. Women's low literacy is an important factor limiting their access to information about land issues, sales and rights.

Collective Approaches to Land Ownership

An effective policy intervention could include what Agarwal calls a "collective approach". This would involve providing groups of landless women with credit for leasing or purchasing land, and encouraging them to cultivate it jointly. While collective ownership and management can raise its own challenges, groups can help resolve many of the difficulties women face as individuals. Being part of a group helps in mobilizing funds for capital investment and exploiting economies of scale, and leads to labour sharing and cooperation in product marketing. This is a very innovative approach, examples of which can be found only on a small scale, for example in South Asia. The extent to which these types of programmes have been implemented elsewhere, and could be extended successfully to other contexts, deserves further analysis.

Integrated Approaches to Credit

Credit and savings systems must be designed to address women's gender-specific constraints. Some of the most successful examples are provided by organizations that combine credit delivery with other supporting activities. For instance, Pro Mujer in Peru operates an integrated credit and microenterprise training programme. It also offers training for women's health and family planning and facilitates access to health services. The Land Conservation and Smallholder Rehabilitation Project in Ghana, a poverty-targeted group-lending project sponsored by IFAD, included successful negotiations with landowners and male leaders to improve women's access to irrigated land. The Bangladesh Rural Advancement Committee in Bangladesh combines a joint-liability approach with legal assistance, health and education services. SEWA in India combines the provision of banking services with the formation of co-operatives to promote women's economic, social and political interests.

A good example of a design feature in savings that could facilitate women's control over their assets is offered by the case of the Opportunity International Bank in Malawi, which introduced biometric smart cards enabling illiterate customers with no official government identification to open and manage accounts by using their fingerprints. Quisumbing and Pandolfelli report that this innovative measure prevented the in-laws of a poor widow from accessing her bank account and hence protected her assets.

Unequal Access to Markets

Both domestic and international markets are gendered institutions. Unequal access to markets is another important source of gender disadvantage likely to undermine the achievement of decent rural employment. Gender-differentiated access to markets affects the ability of women and men to receive fair prices for their work and their produce, and to control the income they generate. It results from gender inequalities in access to resources such as capital, technology, information, education and land. All these constraints interact with each other and influence the bargaining power of the various actors participating in the production, processing and sale of goods.

Women in many countries have to deal with cultural biases about what are considered appropriate modes of transportation for them (many women travel on foot and transport headloads, and their control over intermediate means of transport such as draught animals, bicycles and carts is limited) and often face harassment by market or trade officials. Their time constraints prevent them from travelling long distances and seeking the best prices for their output. Men are more likely to be approached by agricultural companies or other chain actors wanting to do business. Women may also face barriers to membership in rural organizations and cooperatives, which may further inhibit a channel to facilitate market access. Even in West African rural markets, despite the fame of the 'market queens' and despite the greater mobility of women relative to some regions in South Asia, it seems that women rarely achieve upward economic mobility. The economic resources necessary for the spatial and social mobility to amass wholesale consignments, command transport and/or own processing facilities are often in the hands of men. These forms of inequality can be further exacerbated by gender-blind policies with respect to credit, land, transport, marketing schemes, training and unpaid care work.

Women increasingly supply national and international markets with both traditional and high-value produce but continue to face greater disadvantages than men. Barriers to participation in export markets are even higher because the constraints just described for domestic markets are compounded by problems of compliance with strict international food safety and phytosanitary standards. As a consequence, small-scale female producers find it especially difficult to become independently involved in international trade. Poor households, and particularly poor women, seem to be benefiting from incorporation into global value chains more through labour markets than through product markets.

Depending on the type of goods produced, the characteristics of the value chain and the institutional setting of the country, different policies are required to facilitate integration of rural women and men into national and international markets. A useful step for designing adequate interventions to promote better access of poor producers and workers to markets should involve undertaking a thorough gender-aware value-chain analysis so as to identify where measures to reduce inequalities can be taken and by whom.

Measures to support market access will vary depending on whether the women concerned are producers or wage workers. Policies aimed at producers should mostly include: initiatives to improve market contacts and information on prices, as well as market analysis to identify high-value market opportunities; strengthening of property rights; better access to credit; technical assistance; and support for institutional strengthening of women's groups and women's inclusion, influence and negotiating power in farmer associations and trade unions. Policies for wage workers should involve: extending labour legislation beyond permanent workers; measures to ensure better enforcement of labour laws; measures to create greater awareness of legal rights; and more training.

Policy Responses

Self-employed Small-scale Producers

Studies show that high-value chains usually exclude asset-poor farmers. Entry into high-value chains may require having the ability to invest in greenhouses, irrigation and packing sheds. Dolan and Sorby find that contract farmers are more likely than non-contract farmers to own land and other assets and to have access to irrigation. Few of the contract households reviewed in their study were headed by women: 6 percent in Guatemala and less than 1 percent in Kenya. Moreover, smallholders in general, and women in particular, are likely to be in a weak position in negotiating terms and prices with powerful buyers because of limited experience and low levels of education.

An important avenue for smallholders to gain access to value chains is through involvement in producer organizations or cooperatives. Being part of an organization increases the bargaining power of farmers and may also be preferred by the large companies contracting the work because it simplifies procedures. This calls for the promotion of innovative institutional mechanisms that enable women to join groups, lead groups and remain active members. Measures to strengthen and increase knowledge of women's property rights and contractual rights, including their entitlements to land and financial skills could also contribute to make their position relative to powerful actors in the chain stronger, and to increase their chances of obtaining loans to start cooperatives or enterprises.

Better access to information and communication technologies can be used successfully to find market contacts and information on prices – another important channel to strengthen smallholders' bargaining position. Mobile phones are increasingly used in many remote rural areas by women farmers to learn market prices for inputs and crops. In Senegal, the Grand Coast Fishing Operators Union, an organization of women who market fish, set up a website to promote their produce, monitor export markets and negotiate prices with overseas buyers before they arrive in the country. In Samoa, a local NGO, Women in Business Development Incorporated, provided technical support to 13 cooperatives to enable them to produce organic virgin coconut oil for export markets. Market contacts in Australia and New Zealand were made with the assistance of the Internet.

An initiative by the Mennonite Economic Development Associates (MEDA) and the Entrepreneurship Career Development Institute implemented in 2004–07 in Baluchistan, Punjab and Sindh (Pakistan) provides an interesting example of how women in conservative areas can be better linked with more lucrative markets. The project aimed at helping homebound women embroiderers in remote rural areas by strengthening their linkages with richer urban markets and adding value to their work by incorporating new designs. The project's activities were: a) recruitment and training of women sales agents to provide rural embroiderers with product development, access to quality input supplies and higher-value markets; b) linking of sales agents to buyers and designers; and c) capacity building for sales agents in product development and design. A particular strength of the project is its focus not only on inputs to the production process but also on the linkages between homebound female workers in isolated parts of the country and market outlets.

Although data on the gender dimensions of smallholder contract farming are still sparse (an important knowledge gap that future research should aim to fill), it is known that companies usually contract with men. In Kenya, for instance, Dolan found that more than 90 percent of export contracts were issued to male household members, who controlled the household labour allocation and payment arrangements. When training and extension services are offered with contracts, it is essential that male extension agents are trained to meet the specific needs of female farmers and more female extension workers are recruited. It is also important that gender-focused agricultural development assistance does not target exclusively women heads of households, thus overlooking the vast majority of women who reside in male-headed households.

Women Wage Workers

Women wage workers represent at least half of the employees of export-oriented high-value agriculture in many Latin American and sub-Saharan African countries. For example, women account for 79 percent of the workforce in floriculture in Zimbabwe and 90 percent of the poultry workers in Brazil.

Achieving more equitable poverty reduction through decent rural employment generation requires first of all that national labour legislations be extended beyond permanent workers. However, this is a necessary but not sufficient condition. Even when a piece of legislation is good, enforcement may be weak. Barrientos and Kritzinger suggest that an effective approach to secure decent work for women and men employed in global agriculture may involve enhancing synergy between regulatory and voluntary approaches. South Africa offers a good example of how this synergy can be achieved. It now has exemplary labour legislation, including the Employment Equity Act and the Basic Conditions of Employment Act, which also covers labour brokers. It also has a Wine Industry and Agriculture Ethical Trading Association (WIETA) which was set up to develop and monitor its own local code of labour practice based on ILO Conventions. WIETA members include trade unions, NGOs, producers, government and UK supermarkets. The inclusion of civil society organisations in WIETA has played an important role in ensuring that the conditions of casual women workers are addressed in social audits.

There are other successful cases in which labour laws have been extended to vulnerable workers, such as temporary workers in agriculture, domestic workers and HIV-affected workers. For example, a New Labour

Act covering temporary workers was issued in Ghana in 2002. Labour relations regulations were adopted in Zimbabwe in 1998, and laws protecting women plantation workers were introduced in Brazil in the mid-1990s. Unfortunately the problem of enforcement of labour standards remains severe in most cases.

Codes of conduct can be useful in supporting national legislation but have more limitations than labour laws because they are voluntary, not well-monitored and apply to just a small fraction of the workforce. The Uganda Code of Practice for the horticulture sector appears to have led to an improvement in working conditions for women in flower farms. All workers have a stable contract, are entitled to 60 days' paid maternity leave and have easy access to basic medical assistance. More research would be required to understand the success factors in this initiative.

Programmes to make female wage workers aware of their legal entitlements are also essential so that they can organize to demand them in an effective way. In Kenya, Tanzania, Uganda and Zambia, for example, Women Working Worldwide, a UK-based network organization, together with local trade unions, promoted rights awareness among 6 000 permanent and casual female workers. It appears that such training increased women's confidence and their ability to negotiate with employers, leading to greater women's unionization and creation of new women's committees. In Tanzania, farm managers were also trained on women workers' rights, resulting in a general improvement in worker-management relations and greater space for gender concerns in collective bargaining agreements.

Although the track record of women's participation in and leadership of trade unions is mostly poor, the case of the National Union of Plantation and Agricultural Workers (NUPAWU) in Uganda suggests that existing trade unions can play a relevant role in advancing women wage workers' rights, provided women are fully integrated in management and decision making.

When women face obstacles to participating in mixed (male-dominated) groups, women-based groups may be the only alternative to represent female workers and help them in mobilizing. SEWA in India offers the best example of organizing women in both rural and urban areas. SEWA combines different forms of organization strategies: trade union activism, cooperative formation and provision of services such as health care, child care, insurance and housing to its members. However, it is not clear how easily the SEWA model could be replicated elsewhere.

Opportunities for training and promotion are more common among technicians, management and administrative staff, who tend to be men. There are only a few examples of good practice in training. In Thailand, the Sun Valley poultry company offers an educational plan to assist (mainly female) employees to advance within the firm. Workers are also trained to perform multiple tasks to avoid repetitive-stress injuries. Health and safety training, together with information about workers' rights, is crucial to prevent health hazards at the workplace. In Uganda, for example, flower workers are provided with the opportunity of learning about fumigation and grading and how to tackle pests and diseases.

Policy Lessons

Pathways out of poverty vary for rural women and men depending on socio-economic structures and institutional settings. A different policy mix is required in each setting to generate decent jobs and facilitate women's and men's equal access to them. Some broad policies are needed across the board, but their design and implementation will have to be context-specific.

The World Bank's recent World Development Report on agriculture suggest that different groups of countries may follow different poverty reduction strategies. For instance, increasing the productivity of staple food production and enabling integration of landless labourers into dynamic agricultural export sectors are strategies most relevant for agriculture-based countries. A policy approach focused on encouraging workers' shift out of the agricultural sector into off-farm activities, possibly through secondary education and training, may be more appropriate for transforming and urbanized countries.

Measures to generate decent jobs must be designed in such a way as to reflect the complexity of gendered rural livelihoods. Policies to address rural poverty cannot be treated in isolation and hence it is also important to implement education, land and credit measures, as well as active labour market policies and social protection, in an integrated manner, understanding their interdependencies and fostering synergies. The evidence reviewed and suggests that:

- In all circumstances, countries and settings, there is an urgent need to better acknowledge the important economic functions of unpaid activities and to implement measures for reducing and redistributing the burden of housework. This would be an essential step for promoting gender-equitable poverty reduction in rural areas, since the burden of this work falls disproportionately on women. Unpaid work limits women's access to all forms of paid rural employment. A combined approach that addresses weaknesses in physical and social infrastructure and that strengthens women's ability to make claims over their contributions is required.

- Public works programmes can be effectively used to support gender equality in rural employment, especially if genuine efforts are made to involve beneficiaries in the design of programmes from the outset. A truly gender-aware employment guarantee scheme (EGS) is one that fulfils the two objectives of: (1) making it easier for women to participate on equal terms as men (e.g. by providing child care on-site); and (2) creating useful assets that reduce aspects of women's domestic workloads (e.g. piped water). Public works do not have to be confined to physical infrastructure projects but can also offer social services and care for the community. However, if care services are provided through EGSs, special attention should be paid to ensure the quality and regularity of such services. Some of the most promising public works initiatives (from a gender perspective) can be found in Argentina, India and South Africa. A better understanding of the key determinants of success is required. Participation in an EGS can be an effective first step out of poverty for rural women only if their employability effectively improves once the scheme ends. To date, the record on this aspect appears rather weak across countries. There may be the risk that EGSs reinforce women's subordinate position in the rural labour market. Finding ways to strengthen the skills-training component of these programmes and linkages with other segments of the labour market should therefore be a policy priority.
- Promoting female education in rural areas and trying to reduce gender educational gaps at primary and secondary levels is obviously important for a number of reasons in addition to the objective of improving access to decent employment. Greater attention should be paid to the type and quality of education, rather than to education per se. Formal education appears to be a more significant pathway out of poverty in transforming and urbanized countries (such as some Latin American and Southeast Asian countries), and in relation to non-agricultural work. Appropriately designed gender-aware extension services are more

important determinants of labour productivity in agriculture-based contexts, especially in Africa. In both formal and non-formal education, rural girls and boys are treated differently and often channelled into different subject areas, reinforcing gender labour-market segregation. This is another important bias that needs to be challenged through innovative teaching methods, training of teachers and similar initiatives.

- Rural non-agricultural employment is a potential income source and a possible pathway out of rural poverty, but it is important to understand better under what circumstances it can lead to greater gender equality. Rural non-agricultural employment on average pays better than agriculture. It tends to be dominated by small-scale manufacturing (such as processing of food and other agricultural products), commerce and various forms of services. In the urbanized countries of Latin America, rural non-agricultural employment appears to be more prevalent among women than men, but women tend to be in the lowest-paid and most vulnerable forms of work, such as domestic services. When this is the case, non-agricultural employment is evidently not a route out of rural poverty but rather can contribute to reinforcing gender inequalities and stereotypes. Policies must avoid simply shifting low-productive agricultural employment into low-productive non-agricultural employment. Education is a key determinant of access to high-productivity rural non-agricultural employment, especially for female workers. Promotion of rural non-agricultural employment is a more viable option in countries with well-developed markets for non-agricultural goods and services.
- Constraints in access to land, credit and technology are mutually interdependent. Lack of access to land is an important obstacle but not necessarily the most binding constraint for women's agricultural productivity, especially in land-abundant countries. In land-scarce countries, such as India, innovative approaches involving small integrated programmes that support landless women's collective purchase of land, together with credit mobilization and environmentally friendly farming practices, appear especially promising but implementation is still limited to a few cases.
- Non-traditional agricultural exports offer an opportunity for generating quality employment for rural women and men, but there are also risks, especially for women, who are often the weakest nodes in the supply

value chain. NTAEs are mostly developing in Latin America. Some NTAE production can be found in sub-Saharan Africa too, but it usually involves only a small share of the rural labour force. Rural women, and most smallholders in general, seem able to benefit from increased international trade more through the labour market than through the product market. The formation of farmers' organizations, trade unions and cooperatives should be encouraged among smallholders, and women's participation (still rather limited) in them must be supported. Promoting synergies between labour legislation and voluntary codes of conduct appears to be a promising approach for maximizing women's employment gains from wage work in non-traditional agricultural exports. South Africa offers a good example of how this can be successfully accomplished, but enforcement of labour standards, especially among female workers and migrant workers, appears to be very weak in most countries. It remains a serious obstacle to the achievement of decent work.

- The introduction of new technology, either in NTAE plants or in other rural sectors, including in response to the need to protect the environment, may constitute a potential risk for the job security of rural women unless concerted efforts are made to provide skill upgrading and to ensure that employers retain their female labour force and remain committed to investing in their training.

More specifically, it is essential that countries continue to ratify fundamental ILO Conventions and, even more vitally, that the gender-equitable implementation of relevant labour standards, including those related to social security, safety and health, is ensured. Rural workers, and in particular women workers, must be covered more fully under national laws and regulations as well as in practice. Further research and action are much needed to foster innovative approaches for the effective and comprehensive representation of rural women's interests in the institutions of social dialogue. Rural organizations that mobilize and represent women are essential to create awareness around rights and to give women greater voice and bargaining power relative to their employers and their family members. A range of organization strategies exist, but it is difficult to say what works best in each particular context.

References

Anriquez G. & Stloukal L. (2008). *Rural Population change in developing countries: nlessons for Policymaking.* Rome. FAO

García M. and Paiewonsky A. (2006). *Gender, Migration, Remittances and Development.* Santo Domingo.INSTRAW.

IFAD and FAO. (2008). *International migration, remittances and rural development.* Rome.

Tolstokorova, A. (2009). Multiple Marginalities: Gender dimension of rural poverty, unemployment and labour migration in Ukraine. Paper presented at the FAO-IFAD-ILO Workshop op.cit. Rome.

UNDP. (2005). *The Potential Role of Remittances in Achieving the Millennium Development Goals – An Exploration.* Background Note, Roundtable on Remittances and the MDGs, September. New York.

UN DESA. (2008). *Rural Women in a Changing World: Opportunities and Challenges,* Division for the Advancement of Women, October, pp. 20-23.

8

Rural Employment and Social Protection

Article 22 of the Universal Declaration of Human Rights of 1948 states that:

> Everyone, as a member of society, has the right to social security and is entitled to realization, through national effort and international co-operation and in accordance with the organization and resources of each State, of the economic, social and cultural rights indispensable for his dignity and the free development of his personality.

Expenditure on and coverage of social protection varies significantly between countries and regions. Whilst the majority of experience with social protection in developing countries remains short-term and under-resourced, this is changing. There is evidence of a rapidly emerging agenda for increased social protection that results from a number of factors including:

- Recognition that there is a need to move out of the vicious cycle of emergency appeals into longer-term policies with predictable resources to address chronic hunger and deprivation, particularly in Africa.
- Recognition that high levels of risk and vulnerability need to be managed more effectively in order to overcome the negative impacts on livelihoods, productivity and the capacity of households to develop high-return activities in the short to medium term.
- Recognition that reducing risk and vulnerability constitutes an investment in people with critical longer-term payoffs that can end the intergenerational transmission of poverty in the long term.

The outcome of these changes is an increasing commitment to new or extended social protection programmes. At national level, social protection has gained higher priority in the development and anti-poverty agenda in many countries. In Africa, the Livingstone Declaration, adopted in 2005, commits governments to put together costed national social transfer plans within two to three years that are integrated within national development plans and within national budgets. At international level, the conclusions on social security of the International Labour Conference in 2001 state that "of highest priority are policies and initiatives which can bring social security to those who are not covered by existing systems". These are mostly workers in the informal economy and in rural areas.

The challenge addressed is how to use social protection to tackle poverty and decent work deficits in rural areas in a way that improves development capabilities and access to jobs and opportunities and so provides a critical mechanism to promote social inclusion, especially in remunerative labour markets.

Work Deficits in Relation to Social Protection

In many developing countries, existing social protection coverage is very limited, particularly in rural areas. Rural areas are characterized by high poverty levels, high informality and self-employment, limited payment capacity for services and corresponding limited service provision – especially in health.

Many people, especially the poorest, rely on subsistence agriculture or casual wage labour, either in agriculture or other sectors. This renders them particularly vulnerable both to the risks associated with agriculture – from climatic shocks to more predictable seasonal variations in the availability of food and employment. Other critical sources of vulnerability result from the heavy dependence on physical assets, especially land. Landless people are often among the chronically poor, especially in South Asia. Among the rural chronically poor in India, casual labour was the largest single occupational group. Income insecurity in migrant and seasonal labour constitutes a key factor leading to a decent work deficit. Casual labour provides few opportunities for households to invest in developing skills and building assets, and unequal power relations with employers limit households' capacities to improve their security or working conditions.

Table 1: Public social protection and health expenditures in selected countries, 1998–2003

	Percentage of GDP		*Percentage of general government expenditure*	
Country	***1998***	***2003***	***1998***	***2003***
Bangladesh	N/A	1.16	N/A	N/A
Bolivia	8.16	8.62	26.47	23.91
Brazil	14.33	19.10	53.47	N/A
Chile	9.52	9.69	45.90	45.58
China, P.R: Mainland	1.26	4.52	12.43	24.27
Congo, Republic of the	N/A	1.16	N/A	4.63
Costa Rica	9.99	9.25	46.25	36.67
Dominican Republic	2.69	4.45	16.50	29.03
Germany	26.70	27.60	54.73	55.97
Ghana	–	1.50	N/A	5.25
India	1.60	1.50	5.70	1.50
Indonesia	1.41	1.41	6.98	7.23
Korea, Republic of	5.50	5.70	22.13	18.32
Lesotho	N/A	4.53	N/A	10.38
Mexico	5.00	6.80	23.09	27.80
Namibia	N/A	6.75	N/A	17.55
Nepal	1.38	1.65	7.99	10.17
Pakistan	0.35	0.29	1.62	1.54
Russian Federation	N/A	12.30	N/A	34.64
Senegal	0.16	4.46	12.93	19.65
South Africa	7.03	N/A	20.55	N/A
Thailand	2.44	4.16	10.75	23.02
Tunisia	7.61	8.65	23.96	26.96
Uganda	0.30	0.92	9.94	14.36
United States	14.80	16.20	42.61	44.21
Viet Nam	3.34	2.68	14.81	10.00
Zambia	N/A	1.14	N/A	4.82

N/A = not available

Source: ILO calculation based on data from ECLAC, ILO, IMF and OECD:

Inequalities in social relations also exclude people from access to resources and drive impoverishment. The customary basis of much risk management in rural areas often involves family networks or local religious or political power holders. The limited resources available render people without strong kinship or local ties – orphans, migrants, old people without children – vulnerable to shocks and stresses. Women in rural societies are often particularly constrained by the "complex set of rights and obligations reflecting social and religious norms [that] prevail within rural communities". They must often rely on male relatives for access rights to productive assets. This lack of independent rights clearly makes women without husbands, parents or children, or in any way estranged from their family, vulnerable to impoverishment, which may have significant negative implications for maternal and infant health.

Social identity (whether self-chosen or ascribed) may also be a source of vulnerability – for example, caste, ethnic or religious group membership – can be associated with social exclusion, inequality and poverty across much of the world, as is being a migrant or refugee. Disabled people are more likely to be poor, not only because of the difficulties presented by living and working with an impairment, but because of the social barriers (such as inaccessible public services, discrimination or simply low expectations) to their participation in everyday life on equal terms with others. Similarly, sufferers of certain illnesses, e.g., leprosy or HIV/AIDS, experience stigmatization. Such inequalities may be particularly durable in rural areas isolated from centres of dynamic social change.

During the last two decades, the HIV/AIDS epidemic has greatly increased vulnerability in rural areas, particularly in Africa. The impact of HIV/AIDS is manifold and includes reduced income, productivity, food security, lower nutritional status and increased discrimination. Some of the effects of the condition are intergenerational and can therefore increase vulnerability in the long term. In particular, HIV/AIDS, directly or indirectly, has life-threatening consequences for children when they themselves are infected or have lost one or both parents due to AIDS. Children affected and infected by HIV/AIDS have less access to education and health services and are more exposed to discrimination and to the worst forms of child labour.

Social exclusion is one important factor that explains the lack of social protection coverage in rural areas. It is a concept that is increasingly being used, albeit in a variety of ways, to describe how people are left out of, or prevented from participating in, processes that lead to growth, improved welfare and, ultimately, development. Social exclusion and poverty are not mutually exclusive. Poor people are often excluded, so understanding and tackling the issue has the potential to contribute in a significant way to poverty reduction. Focusing on social exclusion is valuable because it enables policy-makers and planners to:

- contextualize poverty in social systems and structures;
- understand how political and historical processes lead to chronic deprivation;
- focus on causality rather than simple correlations or characteristics;
- recognize the multi-dimensional nature of poverty; and
- target social identities whose holders are prone to social exclusion.

However, the concept of social exclusion has its own problems. First, it often provokes normative assumptions that exclusion is bad while inclusion is good, and therefore ignores the ways in which inclusion can be bad for poor people. Second, by failing to focus on poor people's agency, poor people are often portrayed as powerless victims. Third, given that "social exclusion" was coined to describe a condition in industrialized countries and describes minority groups, its export to countries where a very large portion of the population is poor or there are different (non-Western) cultural contexts, may be unhelpful or inappropriate. In developing countries, it may therefore be as appropriate to focus on "differential or adverse incorporation" where the terms on which people are included are also critical. An example is where poor people work for very low wages which trap them in poverty but where they contribute to the accumulation of wealth by others. Social exclusion and adverse incorporation are not mutually exclusive. For example, "the gendered situation of many poor women can be mdescribed in terms of the 'social exclusion' through 'discrimination' and, equally validly, in terms of their 'adverse incorporation' in 'exploitative' labour relations".

There are thus many reasons to extend the coverage of social protection in rural areas of the developing world. Risk and vulnerability mean that many people live in a state of perpetual insecurity: they are unable to take risks such as investing in developmental activities, and are reliant on those wealthier and more powerful for protection and security which may – or may not – be forthcoming. And when risks materialize, lack of social protection – in the form of cash or asset transfers, or access to health care – mean that their impact can often be devastating. But the combination of activities that constitute social protection have the potential to protect households, promote their livelihoods and also to overcome social exclusion or adverse incorporation in rural areas.

Strategic Responses to Address Work Deficits

How they may constitute an obstacle to the development of capabilities and the access to productive jobs and opportunities was also tackled.

Addressing Minimum Living Standards

Ill health and old age affect people's physical capacity to work, making many either unable to work, or unable to earn sufficient income to provide for themselves. Insurance markets are weak in rural areas, especially for old and chronically ill people: coverage of contributions-based pensions or sickness payments in rural areas is very low, due to both the lack of formal sector employment and widespread poverty. Some people benefit from assistance through social networks (family, neighbours, etc.), but informal or community-based transfers can be insecure, and those who lack such support also face chronic poverty, malnutrition and, possibly, early death.

Social pensions are one key measure to address this problem for older people. For example, Brazil's current rural social pension scheme "Previdencia rural" dates back to the 1991 Social Security Act and provides a non-contributory pension to men and women (aged 60 years and 55 years and over, respectively) who can demonstrate a decade or more of productive-sector work in a rural location. In 2002, there were around 6 million beneficiaries (out of a total of less than 8 million rural households) and the scheme costs about R$11 billion each year. The benefits are equivalent to a national minimum wage. Pension income has a significant impact on well-being in rural areas – especially when paid to women. Rural pensions are associated with increased school enrolment (resulting in improved access to jobs and employment for the next generation), improved status of old people in households and communities, investments in rural production and providing an insurance function.

There is a particular gender dimension to social pensions. On the one hand, women are more likely to do unpaid, domestic or care work than men, which may decrease their ability to claim earnings-related pensions. On the other hand, they live longer and are often eligible for pensions at an earlier age than men. Some evidence from social pensions in southern Africa suggests that this may improve the terms of women's incorporation within rural households. One recent study drawing on a ten-year evaluation notes that it "reaches rural areas" and that there are three times as many female beneficiaries as male. (Eligibility begins at age 60 for women and 65 for men.) A major outcome of the design of the pension has therefore been to effectively offer "unpaid workers … a guarantee of partial economic security in their elderly years, affording them an earned place in the household". Such effects may improve the terms of inclusion of older people in general, where "targeting income transfers on the elderly has the beneficial side effect of elevating their status from economic burdens to valuable family members".

Improving Access to and Utilization of Basic Services

The exclusion of many people in rural areas from adequate basic services has serious implications for poverty and vulnerability. In particular, it undermines human capital and prevents households from building the skills and capabilities that will enable them to move out of poverty. Supply and demand for services are both important: government resource constraints result in sparse coverage and there is limited real demand for services because poor people are unable to afford the costs. Various policy responses attempt to address these problems. Social health insurance programmes attempt to ensure that people both with and without the capacity to pay are covered, through subsidization of premiums. Education programmes include stipends for school attendance, particularly for girls.

Conditional cash transfers (CCTs) are another response to the problem of weak effective demand for public services. These are programmes whereby regular cash transfers are conditional on certain behaviours, usually the enrolment and attendance of children at school, and visits to clinics by the mothers of infants. They are now found in a large number of countries in Latin America. These are very large programmes with extensive budgets.

Evidence from Latin American programmes shows that CCTs can achieve the twin objectives of increasing and smoothing consumption and investing in human capital. Nevertheless, there is a danger that they emphasize some development objectives (long-term human capital through access to services) at the expense of others (food security, investment in higher-return livelihoods by poor households). In Brazil and Mexico, the programmes are so large that they have a significant influence on the composition and funding of rural development policy.

It also appears important that social protection programmes be politically popular among both politicians and citizens. In Latin America, strong public information systems, as well as monitoring and evaluation, have been critical. Supply-side subsidies to promote use of health and education services are in general less progressive than demand-side transfers. Historically, transfers have been less popular with governments than supply-side subsidies but the inclusion of conditions make the programmes more politically acceptable. Many governments are now expressing interest in transfers, and in linking these to skills development and microfinancial services to capture their development potential.

The gender dimension of CCT programmes, particularly in Latin America, is significant in terms of their potential to address social exclusion. *Oportunidades*, for example, pays its transfers to mothers rather than fathers. While there is some evidence that many women find this payment valuable for their self-esteem, the programme's potential to address the adverse incorporation of women is undermined both by some of its conditionalities (notably a requirement that female beneficiaries undertake unpaid community work, adding to their "triple burden"), and its very focus on women as those responsible for children and the domestic sphere. It seems in practice to target women more because they are an effective way of reaching children than to increase their power and agency. The designers of *Oportunidades* have incorporated some gender-related concerns, notably by paying a higher stipend for girls' educational attendance than boys': a bold and important move. But the cultural stereotype of "motherhood" has survived largely intact and there is little attempt to address the behaviour of men. Arguably, a programme that paid to the principal caregiver without stipulating gender (like the South African Child Support Grant – which is not conditional on recipient behaviours) would be as likely to transfer income to women, but would also send an important cultural message about men's potential domestic role.

Access to childcare is another component of social protection strategies and programmes that strengthens families' social and economic security, improves the quantity and quality of women's jobs, reducing their vulnerability to risk. In rural areas, where women account for a large part of the waged agricultural workforce, access to childcare remains very limited. Migration patterns have disrupted extended family networks and single-mother households have increased in numbers in many areas. As a result, working parents often have few informal supports for their childcare responsibilities to compensate for a lack of formal supports. But, where childcare arrangements have been introduced in rural social protection strategies, the outcomes have been encouraging. This is the case of the

Expanded Public Works Programme of South Africa that has made the reduction of unpaid care work one of its priorities, and the National Rural Employment Guarantee Programme of South Africa that recognized the importance of childcare for women's ability to participate in the programme by including crèches among other worksite facilities.

Improving Access to Health Care for All

Access to health care is critical in reducing vulnerability and increasing the capacity of households to access more remunerative jobs and opportunities. In most of the countries, several schemes aimed at providing social protection in health coexist. The key challenges are improving efficiency and coverage of the relevant schemes (national health services, national or social health insurances, community-based health insurance, etc.) and incorporating the various schemes, in one equitable and well-regulated pluralistic national system.

Social health programming in the Republic of Korea provides a good example of how limited coverage can be overcome even with relatively low levels of GDP. In 1963, the Government passed the Health Insurance Act in order to tackle problems of low levels of coverage (especially the density of health-care professionals) due in part to problems of collecting contributions from the large informal sector.

The Republic of Korea example shows how a universal health-insurance system can be achieved, even where there is a large informal sector, and that, while economic growth is an important factor, universal coverage can be realized even on low levels of GDP. Other critical lessons from the Republic of Korea include the emphasis on building functional structures rather than achieving coverage in the first 14 years of the programme and the importance of strong stewardship and promotion of social protection. This meant that social insurance was a key policy and political priority for a number of years. The Republic of Korea has also taken care to integrate insurance funds for those who are not wage earners (especially important for women engaged in unpaid work) into the National Health Insurance programme.

Community-based health insurance schemes (CBHI) have emerged in developing countries in the absence of adequate state mechanisms to guarantee access to health care. Such schemes are often initiated by civil society organizations (in particular cooperatives and mutuals) and are delivered through a diversity of organizational settings, mainly to cover the costs of medical care in case of sickness and, more rarely, maternity or disability. The development of CBHI is ongoing and has been characterized by a rapid proliferation of new schemes during the last decade, notably in Africa and in Asia. CBHI schemes have shown a strong potential to reach groups excluded from statutory social insurance, to mobilize supplementary resources (financial and human) which benefit the social protection sector as a whole, to contribute to the participation of civil society and to empower socio-occupational groups, including women. In some countries, they have had a major role in strengthening the commitment of governments to extend social protection.

However, most stand-alone, self-financed CBHI schemes have major limitations in terms of their ability to be sustainable and efficient mechanisms capable of reaching large segments of the excluded populations. Ongoing experience has shown that their impact and sustainability are strongly increased by developing functional linkages with extended and expanded national social insurance systems (for example by subsidizing premiums paid by low-income members or supporting microinsurance schemes with technical assistance and training).

Providing Employment for the Rural Poor

Weak rural labour markets are characterized by monopsonistic employers, oversupply of labour, and poor transport and communications infrastructure restricting movement of labour to stronger markets. As a result, wages in rural areas are depressed and people are trapped in poverty. Rural employment schemes have been used in several countries to address this problem. They aim to provide income opportunities and to strengthen rural labour markets both through raising demand for labour and using that labour to create physical or social infrastructure.

The India National Rural Employment Guarantee Act (NREGA) was passed in 2005 and is based on the earlier Maharashtra Rural Employment Guarantee Scheme (MEGS). A critical defining feature of NREGA is that, as an act, it confers statutory rights on beneficiaries, unlike a "scheme" that is prone to change according to expediency. NREGA makes available up to 100 days of employment per rural household per year on public works, at the prevailing minimum unskilled wage rate.

NREGA is one of the largest rights-based social protection initiatives in the world. The national budget for the financial year 2006-07 was approximately US$2.5 billion or 0.3 per cent of GDP. Official cost estimates of the scheme, once fully operational and reaching around 40 million households living below the poverty line, range from approximately 1.06-1.33 per cent of GDP. However, there are differing views on the affordability of the programme: better tax administration could mobilize funds but the tax/GDP ratio is currently declining.

When NREGA was passed, it was thought that the rights-based platform of the programme could make a significant difference to rural livelihood security and safeguard the right to work which forms part of India's Constitution. As the programme unfolds, serious questions are emerging about founding the programme on a "rights" perspective - particularly because poor, often illiterate, households, cannot easily turn rights into action. NREGA is intended to be self-targeting on the basis that only the poorest households will want to do manual work for low wages, but paying wages below the prevailing agricultural wage rate raises questions about the balance between social inclusion and social justice. At the same time, there are concerns that the types of productive activities that can be funded under NREGA are more beneficial to richer rather than poor households. In the case of NREGA, exclusion is heavily associated with the location of employment - women are less able to travel long distances to find work.

At present, within NREGA there are limited linkages between employment generation and human capital development. The linkages between employment guarantee schemes and economic growth are better understood by looking at the more substantial and monitored Maharashtra experience. The benefits of MEGS have largely been secondary and indirect rather than direct, but it is generally agreed that:

- MEGS has raised agricultural wages as labourers have become reluctant to accept less than the official minimum wage.
- MEGS provides insurance for rural workers against unemployment and stabilizes work for rural households by providing opportunities during the agricultural off-season.
- Assets created by MEGS may contribute to increasing agricultural productivity (though the benefits of this are regressive because asset locations have tended to favour better-off households).

- Despite concerns about exclusion, evidence suggests that MEGS has mobilized women and enhanced their independence.

Addressing the Multi-dimensional Factors of Extreme Poverty

Poverty, exclusion and adverse incorporation are multi-dimensional phenomena. Different factors – geographical isolation, vulnerability to disease, low social status – interlock to prevent people escaping poverty. Some social protection programmes are emerging which attempt to integrate and sequence multiple interventions across the economic, social and political spheres to help break these multidimensional poverty traps.

One example of a multidimensional social-assistance programme is the "Challenging the Frontiers of Poverty Reduction – Targeting the Ultra Poor" (TUP) programme of the large Bangladesh NGO, BRAC. This was launched in 2002, following BRAC staff's conclusion that their existing interventions – while valuable to many Bangladeshis living in poverty – were not reaching or helping the poorest people in rural Bangladesh. The TUP programme combines asset transfers (grants rather than loans) linked to livelihood skills training, health promotion and other social programmes with potentially transformative aspects. An example of the latter is legal advice on issues such as marriage and domestic violence law – particularly relevant as many of the "ultra poor" are women. Again, "graduation" is built in to the programme as a whole, with the aim being that participants eventually join a BRAC microcredit programme. BRAC's evaluation found that, on average, by 2005 participants' incomes had grown beyond those who were "not quite poor enough" to be selected for the programme in 2002, but that they were still poor. This is perhaps not surprising in a relatively short period of time. The participants made progress in several key areas related to vulnerability (notably livelihood assets, savings and health), and appeared more confident in their ability to withstand serious shocks or livelihood "crises", such as the serious illness of an income earner. An illustration of the ongoing challenges facing poor rural households is that there was some evidence that, now possessing new assets such as livestock, they had become vulnerable to a number of new risks (such as livestock death or illness).

Reducing Occupational Risks

In terms of fatalities, injuries and work-related ill health, agriculture is one of the three most dangerous occupations. Work is arduous, hours are long and workers and their families are exposed to a wide range of hazards, including poorly designed and unsafe tools and equipment, toxic chemicals, and animal and plant disease. The ILO estimates that up to 170,000 agricultural workers are killed each year and millions more are seriously injured in workplace accidents involving agricultural machinery, pesticides and other agrochemicals. In developing countries, in particular, the risk of serious injury is compounded by the lack of information available to rural workers on safe work practices and the lack of safety systems to prevent environmental spillover. The interaction of poor living and working conditions and the prevalence of endemic disease in many rural areas contribute to poor health, reduced work capacity, low productivity and shortened life expectancy, particularly for the most vulnerable groups. Improving safety and health is an integral part of social protection.

Special measures should be taken to protect the health of pregnant and nursing workers and their children from occupational hazards that are common in agriculture. Paragraph 6 of the Maternity Protection Recommendation, 2000 (No. 191), lists the main categories of concern, including arduous work involving the manual lifting, carrying, pushing or pulling of loads; work involving exposure to biological, chemical or physical agents which represent a reproductive health hazard; work requiring special equilibrium; and work involving physical strain due to prolonged periods of sitting or standing, or to extreme temperatures, or vibration. All of these characterize work in agriculture.

Social Protection and Social Inclusion

The examples above show how social protection can contribute to the broad objectives of maintaining minimum living standards, providing income support, providing employment opportunities and guarantees, improving access to services, including health and reducing occupational risks. They also demonstrate how social protection can contribute to social inclusion and favourable incorporation. Social protection can contribute to wider development objectives in a number of different ways.

Social protection can protect poor people from unacceptably low levels of income and consumption, which would exclude them temporarily or permanently from accessing health services, and their children from education. Ensuring access to health care to tackle illness or maintaining food security in subsistence farming households during the hungry months leading up to harvest prevents the distress sale of productive assets. This helps to maintain the productive capacity of farmers and enable them to avoid becoming trapped in a vicious cycle of impoverishment and falling productivity. Employment guarantee schemes provide income security and smooth consumption due to rural seasonality, and help to mitigate the conditions that produce adverse incorporation. Improved working conditions increase the well-being of workers, provide a greater equity between gender and enhance the productive capacity of the labour force. Protection can have important implications in the longer – as well as the immediate term. There is strong evidence that social pensions help households avoid malnutrition in children so that they are able to develop skills and become productive workers as adults.

Social protection can *prevent* or reduce risks. Programmes to enable safe work include education programmes and the provision of equipment to ensure the safe use of hazardous chemicals, investments in infrastructure to reduce the impact of weather-related risks and hazards. Such programmes can include adversely incorporated people who have few defences against hazards in the more regulated economic mainstream. These programmes can, if designed appropriately, also increase labour productivity.

Social protection can *promote* rural employment. Programmes that link skills development with protection (for example the BRAC programme in Bangladesh) can provide poor people with increased capacity and access to more skilled and more remunerative employment. There is evidence from Brazil, Lesotho and South Africa that social pensions result in increased financing for economic activities and investments in productive assets. Transfers are usually associated with school attendance or health care with positive impacts on long-term human capital development. There is anecdotal evidence of the effects of transfers on savings, assets and investments, but this needs further research.

When programme design and implementation are done well, there can be very positive effects. Targeting can promote the inclusion of, for example, women or minority ethnic groups to make programmes more progressive. Targeting can also be used to break down stereotypes or assumptions about the types of work that excluded groups can do – for example women doing work that is traditionally assumed to be men's work. In this way, social protection can promote agency or economic choice, transform social relations and thus combat adverse incorporation. On the other hand, if poorly designed, social transfers can maintain or introduce social exclusion – for example where eligible households are not included in programmes. The increasing international mobility of labour raises, in particular, the question of exclusion of migrants to social protection programmes and the need to improve the portability of long-term social security entitlements. Social transfers can also lead to adverse incorporation, for example when cash-for-work programmes provide very low wages that divert household labour away from working on their own land during critical times such as ploughing, planting or weeding. These examples show that the programme design is critical.

Challenges for Extending Social Protection

Evidence from the various social protection initiatives described here confirms the manifold arguments for introducing or expanding the coverage of social protection programmes. But there are also challenges associated with the extension of social protection. These include questions about the affordability of social protection, institutional and administrative capacity, the specific difficulties in extending programming in remote rural areas, and political commitments to address risk and vulnerability.

Financial Capacity, Affordability and "Fiscal Space"

Good practice from middle-income countries shows that core social protection, that is transfers for the poorest, contributory and solidarity schemes for better-off beneficiaries, is affordable but depends on effective administration and good governance. Economic growth is important but countries can move to universal formal coverage even on modest levels of GDP per capita. The political will for redistribution is a precondition for such extension.

In low-income countries, there are significant affordability challenges for extending social protection coverage. The countries in greatest need of social protection, those with high levels of rural poverty, food insecurity and inequality, are most often those with a limited resource or tax base.

The ILO has calculated the cost and affordability of basic social protection package scenarios in five countries in Asia and seven in Africa. Over time and depending on the size of the domestic budget compared to GDP, a core social protection package is affordable. But the burden on government budgets is significantly larger for poorer countries and requires external funding for some of them. The differences between scenarios (for example targeting the poorest 10 per cent of households versus offering universal coverage) demonstrate the difficult policy choices for governments of low-income countries. There is a potential trade-off in terms of cost and impacts on poverty reduction and economic growth between universal coverage and targeted transfers to a much smaller proportion of the population. The implications for budgeting and expenditure are complex. Most low-income countries will require long-term aid to afford even a basic social protection package, though countries experiencing growth may be able to raise their tax revenues rapidly, should their politics be favourable.

Institutional and Administrative Capacity

Social transfer programmes are often located in central government ministries responsible for social development. While such ministries may be champions of social protection and sources of expertise and knowledge on social exclusion issues, they are often politically weak in relation to other parts of government, especially finance ministries, where decisions about budgets for social protection are made.

Linkages between ministries and departments are also important. Where social protection focuses solely on objectives of protection, it can be implemented from a single ministry or department – usually a ministry of social development or social affairs. However, ensuring that programmes maximize their protection, prevention and development potential requires strong and functional linkages between ministries responsible for social development and sectoral ministries responsible for rural livelihoods and for health and education. There is often limited capacity to maintain these cross-sectoral linkages. Competition for budgets can result in a competitive rather than collaborative relationship between sectors.

Linkages are even more critical at local government level. In the poorest countries, and especially those that have decentralized or devolved government in recent decades, district development plans outline activities and allocate budgets for district-level activities. Social protection is rarely a part of these plans, funds and resources are limited and there is only reduced capacity and expertise to introduce social protection into district-level programming. Local governments are likely to get involved in targeting and coordinating the inputs of communities into targeting decisions.

Specific Difficulties in Rural areas

Poverty tends to be more widespread, deeper and more severe in rural areas that are: *remote:* far from the centres of economic and political activity, in terms of not only distance, but also time taken to get there; *low potential:* with few agricultural or natural resources (often dry lands and highlands); *less favoured:* politically disadvantaged areas; and *weakly integrated:* not well-connected, both physically and in terms of communication and markets. These characteristics make social protection more difficult to deliver because of lack of transport and communications infrastructure, lack of access to markets and weak integration into larger economies, especially in relation to labour opportunities, and poor provision of public services infrastructure. Lack of social status and political power compound all of the above. Where governments do not rely on such areas for political support, public investment in infrastructure and services to remedy these problems is unlikely.

Thus, even where large-scale social protection programmes are in place, implementing them in rural areas may present particular difficulties. The expansion of the South African Old Age Pension has been a notable success and innovations, such as mobile payment stations, have improved coverage. However, even in this case, the impact on poverty is weaker in rural than in urban areas.

The problems associated with delivering social protection in remote areas has implications for the types of instruments that are appropriate. Where public services are either scarcely available or of very poor quality, making transfers conditional on use of them may be at best impractical, and at worst a damaging constraint on beneficiaries' agency, their capacity to choose and to act.

Remote or isolated rural areas are also more likely to experience conflict and this presents particular difficulties to implementing social protection programmes. High levels of risk and vulnerability add to the cost of programmes, transporting cash becomes increasingly hazardous, as does any travel, and social infrastructure may be targeted by armed movements attempting to weaken government legitimacy.

Political Commitment

Where social protection deficits are most acute in remote rural areas, or areas associated with the political opposition, it may be that central government is either uninterested or reluctant to commit public expenditure to filling them.

More generally, fears that social protection programmes will create "dependency" among the poor or encourage laziness are often voiced by politicians, even in countries where a large part of the population suffer poverty. Evidence that transfers are primarily spent on basic necessities can help counter this; as can the use of conditionality to promote the use of transfers for investment in education and health. But attention to the wider discourse of development, and the role of the State in it, is important too. To an extent, people should be able to depend on the State: its purpose can be seen as enabling the mitigation of risk and the reduction of vulnerability among the population. Linking social protection to narratives of nation building, and a vision of development based on a broadly inclusive social contract, may help build political commitment.

Social protection can have a positive impact on several dimensions of decent work deficits and in reducing gaps between rural and urban areas and within rural areas themselves. Social protection coverage remains incomplete, however, and is particularly patchy in rural areas. The potential of social protection to contribute to poverty reduction by improving development capabilities, access to good jobs and opportunities in a way that promotes social inclusion is thus currently not being fully exploited in rural areas.

There are a number of challenges associated with extending coverage of social protection in order to maximize the potential of social protection to transform rural lives and livelihoods. Modelling work on affordability is helping policy dialogues to move beyond anecdotal evidence and assumptions about the financial burden of long-term social protection programmes. This work shows that providing a basic set of social security benefits is affordable in most countries but that it depends on changes in political attitudes towards redistribution. Nevertheless, in some poor countries, significant long-term aid will be required until non-contributory social benefits can be funded solely from tax revenues. There are also significant challenges associated with institutional capacity, political commitment and the relationships between rural constituents and their governments.

There is no single blueprint for social protection. Policy design should therefore focus on tackling problems rather than on individual instruments.

The options are diverse and policy-makers have choices. In Latin America the focus is on the long-term goals of human capital building through conditional cash transfers and social pensions. In South Asia and Africa, the focus is on shorter-term objectives – achieving food security, mainly through asset building and managing food price risks; and on a wide variety of social protection policies. In South Asia and Africa, policies having some social protection function are implemented at multiple levels – from household-targeted transfers to the management of food prices through national grain option contracts.

No social protection instrument provides a magic bullet and expectations of what social protection can achieve in a limited time frame must be realistic. There can be trade-offs, for example, between using a single, easily implementable instrument with clear and simple targeting, and a more complex system of instruments that requires greater implementation capacity but has greater impact on risk, vulnerability and poverty reduction. Where there are multiple instruments, getting the combinations and sequencing right (for example by combining household transfers with actions to enhance skills and capacity) is critical and requires good information on the dimensions of poverty and vulnerability. Many countries lack the information required to support good programming. Too often, decisions about social protection responses are instrument-driven (for example switching from food aid to cash transfers) rather than problem-driven (identifying the sources or causes of poverty, risk and vulnerability and tackling them).

A long-term commitment to funding programmes is required because the efficacy of social protection in reducing poverty and vulnerability depends on its predictability. A general lesson is that social protection, and more precisely social security, works best when it is government-owned or government-driven. The private sector and donor agencies have important roles to play but governments are best placed to bring certainty and predictability to the resourcing of social protection and to regulate the activities of the private sector. Social dialogue is also needed to ensure the effectiveness of initiatives aimed at extending social protection. As a result, the politics of social protection are as important as the economics in driving policy decisions and choices. However, in the poorest countries, or those with states that have limited capacity or willingness to implement social protection, there is likely to be a heavy dependence on donors. Other institutional relationships are important. In Africa and South Asia, the focus on food security and building assets means that there are strong linkages between social protection policies and wider policies, particularly in the agricultural sector. Functional linkages between institutions are critical – especially between government departments and ministries but also between governments and civil society.

References

Barrientos A. and Lloyd-Sherlock P. : *Non-contributory pensions and poverty prevention – A comparative study of Brazil and South Africa*, IDPM and HelpAge International: 19.

Mizunoya S. et al. (2006). "Costing of basic social protection benefits for selected Asian countries: First results of a modelling exercise" in *Issues in Social Protection*: Discussion Paper 17, Social Security Department, Geneva, ILO.

Pal K. et al. (2006). "Can low income countries afford basic social protection? First results of a modelling exercise" in *Issues in Social Protection*: Discussion Paper 13, Social Security Department, Geneva, ILO.

Sjoblom D. and Farrington J. (2007). "The India National Rural Employment Guarantee Act in relation to Agricultural Growth and Social Protection", in *ODI Social Protection Project Briefing Note 1.* London, Overseas Development Institute.

9

Rural Employment and Development in Globalized World

At a time when countries of the world are fast adopting to market oriented neo-liberal economic policies, the demands of the time are multi-faceted. If we can take them as urgent, important, and long-term: the urgent among them is poverty reduction; important among them is economic growth; and the long-term among them is sustainability of this model of development.

A country needs international trade relations and economic growth; Businesses need profits; and the poor need their basic necessities such as employment and fair wages, food security, health care, education for children, safe drinking water supply, and dignity in the way we steer development; the civil society institutions look for integrity in democratic practice.

The views differ depending upon vantage-points. The aspirations are varied. But still ultimately what is desirable is dignity in development; a world free of poverty and hunger; equity in distribution of economic growth; a society that is equitable and just with peace.

Economists, especially the neo-liberals, argue in favour of economic benefits to the country; Industrialists ponder over business prospects and profitability across countries and continents; environmentalists argue in terms of sustainability of resource use; development professionals raise questions of poverty reduction and equity. We seem to live in a time that is most interesting in human history. The basic argument in favour of globalization policies is that they lay strong grounds for capital formation, exchange of technology, knowledge generation and information dissemination, and above all communication connectivity. The flow of capital through Foreign Direct Investment (FDI) and Foreign Institutional Investment (FII), coupled with private participation in economic development and employment generation have resulted for the Indian economy to be agile, and spoken about in the world forums.

Global Interdependence

The countries of the world are interdependent than ever before in human history. Global challenges, Global oil price hike, global inflationary tendencies, global terrorism, global financial meltdown – there is nothing local these days. There is nothing independent these days. Countries of the world are interdependent. The new slogan is: Be Indian and Buy Global. Buy global – but we are not responsible because it is not within our control, nor within the control of anybody in the 'global assembly'. It is global because we are all connected but nobody is in-charge. The best example is the global financial meltdown that started on Wall Street that became the topic of discussion on all streets. The effect has been global but the wrath sure enough goes down to the local as well. From where does this growth model emerge is significant.

System of Natural Liberty

The current model of development, we pursue is what made Adam Smith (1723 – 1790) who after his death came to be recognised as father of modern economics or path finder of scientific economics, called 'System of Natural Liberty'. He believed that each individual should be allowed to pursue and advance his own interests. This system, he argued, would result in the greatest wealth for both the individual and the society. Indeed, the effort of the individual to serve himself would bring the greatest possible benefits for society as a whole and for other individuals.

In Adam Smith's opinion, government interrupted economic progress. In the system of natural liberty, there were only three proper functions of government: (a) establishing and preserving justice; (b) defending the nation; and (c) creating and preserving certain public institutions, which no individual or group is interested in creating and preserving e.g. roads, communications, and education. Today, our contemporary economists and policy makers have gone a step further expanding the natural liberty by providing even roads, communications, and education for individual contractors and private companies to maintain and earn profits from. The role of the government has been contracted to be even smaller than what Smith envisioned. However, Smith was aware of the tendency of businessmen to serve their own interests at the expense of the public.

Comparative Advantage

Similar ideas can be found in the propositions developed and promoted by David Ricardo (1772-1823), a classical economist again. Ricardo said that policies which limited trade in order to protect domestic producers would injure the nation that established them. Free trade was the road to economic health internationally as well as domestically. Ricardo was able to prove that it would benefit the economy. He showed that as long as it costs less to produce cloth in England than it does to produce wheat, compared with costs in other countries, it will benefit Englishmen to shift their resources to cloth manufacturers, export the product, and import wheat from other countries.

For example, suppose an Englishman must work one day to produce a yard of cloth and two days to produce a bushel of wheat. Then wheat requires twice as much as effort as cloth. Suppose also that a Frenchman works one day to produce each product. In this case, Englishmen should produce cloth (one day's labour), export it to France, trade it one-for-one for wheat, and import the French Wheat. In this way, Englishmen would get, for one day's labour, the wheat it would otherwise require them two day's to produce. The Frenchmen would also benefit. They could produce wheat, ship it England and trade one bushel for two yards of cloth, and ship the cloth to France. They would also receive products worth two days' effort for one day's actual work. Both countries would benefit from this division of labour and free exchange.

Analogy can be traced in the works of contemporary economists such as Jagdish Bhagwati also. Going back to classical liberalism, John Stuart Mill (1806 – 1873) developed concepts and theories that opposed to government ownership of natural resources because he wished to preserve the institutions of private property, but favoured a large tax on profits derived from their exploitation because those resources rightly belonged to all. A free-market economy will use all its resources, is the basic argument.

Tragedy of the Commons

One seminal work that seriously questioned this model of development or this idea of resource use is 'The Tragedy of the Commons' published in 1968 by a biologist called Garret Hardin. He proposed a hypothesis that seeks to explain why Common Property Resources(CPR), or better put, open access resources, are over-exploited, degraded and depleted. The logic of the tragedy is purely economic and can be stated as: unregulated access to a CPR creates a decision-making environment in which incremental private benefits to an individual from the increased use of the resource markedly exceed the incremental private costs associated with the increased use.

The readers can find that these concepts revolve around in our arguments and interpretations in the current work of empirical evidences collected on the workings of Liberalization, Privatization and Globalization (LPG) policies on the ground in the form of cases in various districts of Tamil Nadu. The basic tenor is finding out if the free-market oriented reformists policies facilitate development in favour of the poor, and their basic necessities such as food security, basic education, health care, drinking water service delivery, employment generation, information access etc or not; and recording the voices of the poor in this respect. In trying to conceptualise the field-based participatory learning with the poor rural communities, the arguments by various political economists and the advocates of decentralised development have been constantly referred to.

Reference to decentralization is very essential in the context of India, after the 73rd Constitutional amendment made the local self-governments the legitimate body to plan and implement rural development programmes drawing support from state machinery, and taking cue from various policies pertaining to development such as education policy, health policy, policy and Government Orders on rural drinking water supply, employment generation policy etc.

Understanding Development

Development is used differently in diverse contexts. Generally speaking development implies a change that is desirable. Society is dynamic, and so, what is desirable at a particular time, place and in a particular culture may not always be desirable at other places or at other times at the same place and in the same cultural milieu. Therefore, it is impossible to think of a universally acceptable definition of development. But a development index generically includes aspects such as: (i) Increase in real income per capita (economic growth); (ii) improvement in distribution of income (equity); (iii) political and economic freedom; and (iv) equitable access to resources, education, health care, employment opportunities and justice.

Sustainable Development

The idea of sustainable development has been defined in many ways, but the most familiar definition remains that given in the Brundtland Commission report, Our Common Future: 'development which meets the needs of the present without compromising the ability of future generations to meet their own needs'. Sustainable development strategies aims at ensuring a better quality of life for everyone, now and for the generations to come. This means meeting four objectives at the same time, at home and around the world: They are: (i) social progress that recognises the needs of everyone; (ii) effective protection of the environment; (iii) prudent use of natural resources; and (iv) maintenance of high and stable levels of economic growth and employment.

Another definition, from the Real World member Forum for the Future, sees sustainable development in this way: 'sustainable development is a dynamic process which enables all people to realise their potential and improve their quality of life in ways that simultaneously protect and enhance the Earth's life-support systems'. The starting point for definitions of sustainable development is the diagnosis of unsustainable trends in the economy, and in our exploitation of natural resources. The core concept behind this are that : (a) the main goal of economic development should be create conditions for people to enjoy a better quality of life, not simply the pursuit of quantitative growth in the economy; (b) the pursuit of development must include policies to eliminate poverty importantly; (c) all parts of the society must be involved in decision-making about the measures that will bring about the transition to sustainable economic and social systems over the coming decade.

These definitions underscore the need for society to ensure inter-generational equity in the sense that present level of consumption and well-being. Constancy of natural capital stock – including natural resource and the environment – is a necessary condition for sustainable development. More and faster production, and more and faster consumption would definitely lead to economic growth. At the same time in the process it naturally leads to faster environmental degradation and much faster depletion of resources required depriving the future generation of a kind of life that the current generation is living. That which would be much depleted is the open access resources or the commons.

Another adversity in a country like India where one fifth of the worlds poor live is, those who are not able to catch up (make use of the opportunity) because of lack of education, or due to inaccessibility to financial, information and knowledge resources might be left behind in lurch. This will create two camps, where one section of the people make use and reap the benefits, whereas another group would get further marginalised and impoverished. This disparity in distribution of benefits of economic growth shall naturally result in wider inequity in society than it existed before. So, ensuring social development, especially better quality education for the poor children, safe drinking water, better health care, local employment opportunities, access to information resources for the poor, access to institutional sources of finance as part of economic growth are imperative, and a practical necessity, if at all equity should be ensured. Studies conducted by the International Labour Organisation (ILO) at macro level especially on social development and on fairness globalization have come out with results that indicate deteriorating conditions of labour and especially women as a result of profit-orientation.

Development at the Grassroots

Another debate going on analogous to the debate on globalization and identifying ways to managing globalization is 'what constitutes development'. Is it economic growth rate per se as being repeatedly reported by the Government of India; Is it enabling the ultra-poor earn more than $ 1 a day, as being advocated by the World bank; Is it a combination of education, health and employment (Human Development) related indicators as is being advocated by the UN? As a counter weight to the national economic statistics approach to measuring poverty, the Physical Quality of Life Index (PQLI) has been developed. Various ways of putting together the index have been proposed as well. Viewed closely these – enhancing basic educational facilities or enabling the ultra-poor getting out of the poverty trap - are issues to be addressed at the grassroots level, which require disaggregating the problem rather than in aggregating. That is localising rather than globalizing. Localisation (or disaggregating) means working with local self-governments, and aggregating means promoting globalization ideas. In India both globalization and localisation exercise commenced almost simultaneously. A little background about it would be pertinent here.

Decentralization and Globalization

Two concepts have occupied development literature more than anything else in the past couple of decades. One is 'globalization' and the other is 'decentralization'. Some describe these concepts as one being complementary to the other while others describe them as being antithetical to each other. At face value, they represent two extreme poles. Neither of them is new. But both of them have taken a new incarnation in the past decade. In the context of India, both of them, obviously, have historical routes, and they have legitimate sanctions too.

Globalization, in its primary sense means expansion of economic transactions and the organisation of economic activities across the political boundaries of nation-states. So, it is not only a matter pertaining to market economy, but also to political democracy. Decentralization is the process of dispersing or delegating decision-making authority relatively away from a central authority closer to the point of service or action. One of the main features of decentralization is a bottom-to-top flow of decision effecting ideas. That is a devolving political, administrative, and fiscal powers and responsibilities from a higher level Central Government to the smallest institution at the grassroots level. Globalization advocates doing away the borders and boundaries in order to ensure efficiency; decentralization advocates breaking up in order to bring things up in an effectively manageable unit.

There are several commonalities between globalization and decentralization. One commonality is that both the ideas emerged in India during the period 1990 – 95. Globalization was really started out of compulsions of economic situations in India during the late 1980s. Soon after we started liberalisation, privatisation and globalization exercises, it was incidental that we started decentralization exercises also simultaneously. But, we were not aware at that time that these two concepts [globalization and decentralization] have relevance. These are two independent events, but took place more or less at the same time. Neither globalization nor decentralization is concept of Indian origin as indicated in the works of economic theorists of the past two Centuries.

The World Bank and IMF propagated the idea of free-market economy as a way to get on faster growth path. Similarly, from organisations like the World Bank again, there was an international pressure to take up decentralization. It was taken not merely out of compulsion, but out of necessity due to the conditions that prevailed here. During early 1990s, India was selling off most of its gold reserve. Now, we have grown to the stage of buying gold in order to enhance gold reserve level. Whereas the condition in 1990 was that we had to mortgage our gold stock in order to get foreign exchange and for importing the items we need.

To put it very appropriately one can say that globalisation was an Indian local compulsion. It was a little before that time, late Sri Rajiv Gandhiji discussed with District Collectors, and several officials at various levels and came out with the idea that Panchayati Raj is the answer. He tried to pass an amendment in the constitution to bring Panchayati Raj System. It did not pass parliamentary support. So, on one side the economic compulsion made us introduce globalization; and on another side the political compulsion made us introduce decentralization. Though these are international concepts, they came in India out of local compulsions. It was demand of the time.

As a theory these two are not based on any erroneous concepts. The concept of globalization is 'you produce only those things that you can produce at cheap production cost, so that you can make it available for the consumers at lowest possible price. You can sell it universally, and economise. Instead if everybody started producing irrespective of access to raw materials or skill and technology requirements, then it will end up costly, which the consumer has to bear unnecessarily. Wherever there is a place where you can produce something cheap, why not you take it and give it to other person instead of asking him to produce at a higher cost. Everybody should get access to goods and services at lowest possible price, is the idea of globalization. After all, the world is bigger than any country. So, instead of producing and consuming within a country, why not go for global production and distribution.

In principle globalization is a good concept. The same holds good for decentralization also. The basic tenet of decentralization is: why all powers should be centered at Central level in Delhi. Why can't we have some powers in Delhi, some in Chennai, some at the districts, and some at the village level. So, if it is drinking water, let the decisions pertaining to that take place at local level; if it is something relating to defence let that decision be taken at Central government level. It would be something like an activity mapping at various levels - each with certain responsibilities and powers.

Another significant commonality with globalization and decentralization is that we implemented neither globalization nor decentralization the way it was intended to become operational. How we carry out these two exercises made the difference. In states like Kerala decentralization is reported to be functioning better than many other states. In Tamil Nadu, it gives a mixed picture – in some places it is active, and in many places they are not active. Especially at District level, Panchayats in Tamil Nadu are very weak. In Kerala, the village Panchayats and district Panchayats are said to be strong, whereas the block Panchayat is said to be almost defunct with very little powers or activities.

The last similarity we need to know is that we cannot shy away from any of these two concepts – globalization and decentralization. Both the processes are irreversible. Both mean development. Decentralization is about local level planning and rural development administration, and globalization is about social development through economic growth. All over the world now, globalization has become an accepted principle. There is no point if we start talking now, that we should give up or try for a reverse gear. The same thing holds good for decentralization as well. For the next 25 to 30 years we are not definitely going to find an alternative to decentralization or Panchayati Raj System.

How we respond to these changes, and how to make ourselves happy given the situation we live in, that is the major question we need to find answer for. Globalization is not an end in itself. Similarly decentralization is also not an end in itself. It's a route; it is a process. The whole purpose of globalization or decentralization is to enable people lead a happy life. In Bhutan they have Happiness Index in place of the Human Development Index (HDI) we are talking about in India. After all, ultimately what everyone is searching for in life? Peace and happiness. So, whatever policy you make, you keep the poorest man in view: If this policy will be of some use to bring about happiness in the 'poorest man's life'. This is what we need to bear in mind, instead of raising ideology-based questions about any policy change – including that of globalization policies.

Given the trend, globalization and decentralization will make significant changes in India. They could be such as: (i) Our public health care system is still poor; (ii) Primary Education, we have not been as successful as we intend to become. If we can provide good quality education to all our children, they can withstand all that one argues as challenges in the globalized era. We need to have good health care system including safe water and proper sanitation system. We need to have access to good quality education for all our children. The third important thing is (iii) livelihood options. This is about employment, income, and food security of the families. One can empirically analyse if improvement is being made in these fronts, before arriving at any conclusion on the contribution of reform measures / privatization, liberalization and globalization in India.

Development Challenges

In order to do away the ideological positioning for or against globalization policies, it is good to have an understanding that trading and exchange of expertise, and technology have been taking place even in 9th and 10th Century. There are certain social aspects and certain commercial aspects that are vulnerable to extinction. Occupations that are vulnerable to competition will be thrown away, and it is there throughout history, and not after globalization. Perhaps, globalization has intensified it. Globalization is like evolution. Like with evolution there would be extinction, and there would be rebirth. How are we going to manage globalization is the basic question?

How globalization can influence the state as an institution is a vital question. When we mention state – we need to bear in mind it has three elements viz. the Central government (Union Government), the provincial government (State Government), and the local government (Panchayats). Discussing about these institutions is important because all these institutions are being touched by globalization. Even before globalization got on the fast-lane, there were threats. But they were all localised. But, now many of the threats are global in nature. It transcends across national borders very easily. Today's problems like global warming, deforestation, nuclear threat can wipe out humanity which has never happened in the past at a global scale. It has happened in some province or in some part of a province, but not at a global scale. This is the first and foremost difference between the current phase of globalization and the one we had in the past. The second difference is nowhere in the past communication has been so instantly possible as today. Both good news and bad news can travel at lightning speed. There was interesting report about mobile phones in India that 85 per cent of the mobile phones have a rechargevalue of less than Rs.10. Technology can be used for good, and for bad. Technology is value-neutral. It is what we make of it counts.

Globalization demands change. Change to an unprecedented level. It demands change in the way one thinks, does business, and requires reforming the way one has led his/her life so long. Opportunities come with challenges as well. The advocates of globalization argue that when change requires you to face life with new opportunities and challenges, if you look at only the challenges and forget to take notice of the opportunities, you cannot attain development. However, studies prove the disparities in income and opportunity structures, as fallout of liberalization and privatisation policies. The gaps in good versus poor jobs are easily seen in the expanding Indian economy.

The task lies in developing the economic base of the local communities. The task lies in building the local capacities to take cognisance of the kind of development taking place, and seize technological and informational opportunities to convert them as income possibilities. The task lies in making use of the liberalised trend in banking and micro financing institutions for enhancing the access one has had to financial sources for multiplication of prospects in small business ventures. How to make rural development as a 'community-determined process' is the challenge. How to stimulate local economic activity and employment is a task. It is also the duty of the intellectuals, researchers, academics and policy makers to come with ideas on how to make globalization work for the poor. So, the responsibility of the educated should be to think how best I can make use of globalization to benefit my village, and my family. This can create be a movement and creating ripples.

Globalization is never one way. People refer to Mahatma Gandhi and swadeshi to oppose globalization. Gandhiji said: 'Let the wind come from east, west, and north, but I shall refuse to be blown out of my roots'. That was resolute thinking. That was progressive thinking. People should not misquote great leaders of this nation. Facing globalization and making wise use of globalization is in the hands of everyone of us. Our traditionalist and conservative thinking should not stand in the way blocking progress the humanity makes. That part of it which makes people feel inferior or make them blank, passive, meek and submissive is what is dangerous about it.

In the name of rural development we are doing several good things in a sporadic way. But, they do not take place in a massive scale. The principal goal of local economic development is to stimulate local employment opportunities in sectors that improve the community using existing human, natural, and institutional resources. For example, the idea of Rural Business Hub was launched with a view to providing markets and publicity for produces / products from rural areas. It should also serve to 'value-add' these products. Khadi should not always remain that pale white. Khadi should be produced in colour prints also so as to suit the contemporary demands of the consumers. We should know how to put consumers mind in product development. It looks logical when the neo-liberals argue that only when there is competition, people would get good quality product at cheaper prices. This is the crux of free-market economy. Instead of thinking coca cola is hitting local soft drinks such as Nanari sarpath, or bottled beverages one should find ways to enhance one's business strategy through changes in quality, price, publicity and promotion measures to take the local soft drinks or cola to the level of coca cola.

That which should get down on business mode should be presented in business mode only. Business cannot be run like a charity house, although business has its social responsibility dimension. Unfortunately in India, even NGOs today are also getting into business mode. The influence of business has craftily entered the NGO sector as well. NGOs call their Annual Plan and Operational Plans as 'Business Plans'. They are adopting several business models in the guise of attaining sustainability of their 'businesses'. When they go to lend a poor SHG woman, they explain various 'loan and insurance products' they have. NGOs appoint 'Business Development Managers'. SHG loans have become 'products' now. Similar is the case with several of the advertisements in the media including in the Television channels, and their influence on local cultures and the way people think. This leads us to an important question frequently raised in the context of globalization that is the psychic war between local cultures, organisational cultures and market forces.

Culture and Markets

Globalization can be viewed as a psychic war. It is a war on your psyche. Once you threaten a society, which is really vulnerable in certain respects, that you do not have strength; that you do not have capacity to grow; that you do not have the capability to take hold of your own problems, it silently attacks on your psyche. This is creating a passivity or inferiority complex, and you carry on your business with the psyche operating in your favour. It is not the product. It is a whole psyche saying that Indian products do not match the world market, so you better change. So, the products are not the real issue. That psyche war or submissiveness to the ideas that whatever that comes from outside India is good and whatever is produced here is inferior, that is the major issue. How to face this cultural war is the real problem.

To cite an example, in India, we all face poverty-driven diseases such as malnutrition, anaemia, miscarriages and other tropical diseases such as malaria etc. Suddenly we got down to addressing life-style diseases – the diseases that come because of our life-style – HIV-AIDS, cardiac problems, diabetics, obesity etc. How did we get this change in perception? This is because people in developed countries think that these are the major health problems. Suddenly you drive all your resources into this. All your major tropical diseases such as TB, malaria, filaria are not looked at because the 'they say' that the life-style diseases are the major problems we are going to suffer from. In India we had, more or less, won the war on leprosy, we were working on curing TB. Nobody talks about population control now. China and India are not looked at as countries with creativity, ethical and ethnic beauty. They are seen as big marketplaces. You do not talk about population now. It does not any more pose a threat. Suddenly how these values change? People from outside India imposing values on us. This is a danger of multiple channels of information-reach and influencing without letting you realise that the way you need to think is being inculcated and formatted. You know that inner tranquillity is questioned. This becomes a country whose psyche and culture questioned.

Another important dimension to this problem is that it is the duty of the Panchayats to protect rural livelihoods including the services of the rural artisans. As far as rural artisans are concerned, we have lost the war. Artisans are no more the service sector for us. Artisans are basically cultural sector for us. But, in the name of economic efficiency we allow all their livelihood resources being robbed. They are very fast being ripped off their raw material bases. You no more wear cotton, our weavers are gone. You no more use pottery products, how can potters survive. Now you think you don't need them. Construction works are going on all over in all the states. There is a lot of possibility for pottery products being used in construction such as flooring, tiles, flower vases, etc. if we really want to support pottery. Pottery articles are organic and non-toxic, unlike Teflon coated materials. We can have our gas stove, but we can use pottery materials in the kitchen. It can be a movement. On the one side we are breaking the tradition and we are making no efforts to revive the tradition.

There is no such cultural revival taking place in India. Works on cultural revivals, which sustains traditional livelihoods, and which keeps the community together are very much needed at a time, when globalization is eroding the tradition and culture. Storing water in plastic pots is unhealthy, and it could earn toxicity as hours go by. Plastic pots are easy to carry and so they can be used for fetching water. But, when it comes to storing it is always good to store in mud pots. Now, we need to re-educate the people, showing the science behind certain cultural practices such as wearing khadi; why plastic bindi should not be used; why use flowers on head; why store water in earthen pots and so on. We need to understand the logic of all that had been coming with culture. We must find ways to scientifically put it across to people. Thus, we can save some of the traditional industries and artisans.

In order to protect the interest of the jute farmers and jute workers of Bangaladesh, that country came up with a policy: 'We have plenty of jute, no more plastics. Jute must be used as the primary material in any kind of packing'. That was the policy. Just one single policy all those involved in that sector have been protected, and they are selling at massive quantity. Such policy measures are necessary. Whatever policy that is pursued one must see if that helps the common ordinary man in the villages. Protecting the interest of the industrialists they can do it themselves. They do not need a state policy for survival. It is the poor who needs state policy for their survival and sustenance.

The Swinging State

In whose interest should a state act is a vital question. Act in the interest of the market or act in the interest of the poor, who are vulnerable to the vagaries of market conditions and the changing state policies to be able to accommodate global economic trends. As we have become part of the global economy now, keeping track of global economic trends, while at the same time taking domestic level action for economic growth are important objectives too. They cannot be brushed aside completely tilting towards ideologies that base local community-centeredness. Economic growth and social development are twin important objectives. One cannot be achieved without the other. Economic growth demands private investments too. This is a kind of balancing act that the state and policy makers have to do often times. They need to protect the interest of the poor, while at the same without losing private investment that would generate additional employment, contribute to global trade, and economic growth.

Humanising the State

One thing about globalization is one cannot clearly think about it, and say categorically this is what it is, and this is how it will behave. This is so, especially because the principles that operate are essentially based on market forces. Consequently, it happens people are either for or against it. You either support it or oppose it. Some trends are clear that indicate or provide evidence to come to a conclusion where it works how. One such evidence in several places where globalization has brought about in several countries is nation-state becomes weak. It is possible one may argue that India is an exception to this. Secondly, the power of labour shall become weak. The organised labour power would become weak. The unorganised state or informal economy grows; inequality becomes wider. It means rich people become richer, but the poor may not become poorer, instead the rich becoming richer might widen the gap between the rich and the poor. Collective action becomes difficult, as it triggers the individuals to run faster in the competitive world.

The importance is to the investor and knowledge-based worker. Traditional economic activities tend to get whipped out especially agro-based industries -for example in Kerala Coir has picked up, but handloom has fallen into a deep pit. Some consider that if globalization has to operate, the state needs to be kept weak, therefore, powers should be decentralized at various levels.

As far as decentralisation is concerned there are two types of decentralization. One is rolling back the state. That is there is no need for a government. The other is humanising the state. Instead of rolling back, how to humanise the state is a vital question. This is not rolling back the state. This is about humanising the state. It is government failure in many of the places that gives way for the market to emerge to fill that gap. The state is powerful but it is no good to interact with the state. It is often rule-based and not human-faced.

In globalization there are several good ideas, and potentials. For good governance one common definition given world-wide is: 'equity'. If we gave a thought about equity the poor may not have become poorer by income criterion. They become vulnerable as a result of the unprecedented changes taking place. It means they are exposed to unprecedented shocks, stress and risk. They become defenceless because of lack of means to cope without damaging loss. They become less powerful, because they were not prepared to face such damage, shock or stress. Consequently, they get excluded in the kind of development taking place. They are not able to make sense of the goings-on to fit them in, and get along. They get excluded. This process causes exclusion in gaining technological or economic benefits, not necessarily impoverishment. We should understand this distinction.

When we find the formal economy does not support the poor. We get down to informal economy such as SHGs. The government may slowly support it for political reasons. But, all said and done it is an informal economy. In Tamil Nadu as well as in Kerala, almost everyone has a mobile phone. The Kerala Government has removed 'mobile phone' as a proxy indicator of a person or family being below poverty line. Having been put out by the mainstream development of the economy, the poor get sidelined on the track of informal economy such as SHGs, government's rural employment programme etc. to earn a living and for survival. They get shelter into such social safety nets.

One argument we can positively present is that the social capital built up such as Panchayats, and SHGs are results of decentralization. The ethnic food, ethnic dress, traditional medicines or Indian System of medicine have all started finding important place because of the fear that globalization might wash away these. Panchayats are provided with computers to be able to retrieve any information the district administration is required to supply to the state government, any moment.

The thinking of formal linking of rural producers with urban markets, value-addition, quality consciousness and Rural Business Hub etc. are aspects we have started seriously thinking about as a result of globalization or these are cultures that globalization has brought about. These are aspects pertaining to local economic development and individual entrepreneurship. Earlier the thinking was the state should do every thing for the village. Now, after decentralization we have started thinking about local development, we claim Gram Sabha can decide what is important to a given Panchayat. For local economic development, how international contacts through NGOs can help is a positive thinking. We can also think of Panchayat level Investors Meet. Like the state government is facilitating the industrialists to commence business, the Panchayats can also invite investors to set up industries in their Panchayat area. But, the aspects pertaining to employment for local people, and environmental sustainability, and corrosion of local cultural sectors such as rural artisans should not become poorer, as a result.

REFERENCES

Brue, Mcconnel, (2007) *Essentials of Economics,* Tata McGraw Hill Publishing Company, New Delhi.

David Macarov, (2003). *What the Market Does to the People: Privatisation, Globalization and Poverty,* Clarity Press Inc. Atlanta and ZED Books, London.

Deepak Nayar (Ed.) 2002. *Governing Globalization: Issues and Institutions,* Oxford University Press, New Delhi.

Edward J Blakely & Ted K Bradshaw, (2003). *Planning Local Economic Development: Theory and Practice*, Vistaar Publications, New Delhi. Hardin, 1968. The Tragedy of the Commons

Jagdish Bhagwati, (2004). *In Defence of Globalization*, Oxford University Press, New Delhi.

10

Rurla Labour Standards

Many rural workers, especially in agriculture, experience severe difficulties and gaps in protection as regards freedom of association, forced labour, child labour, discrimination, wages, working time, occupational safety and health and social security. For example, 70 per cent of child labour is found in agriculture and bonded labour is prevalent in certain countries. The level of accidents and work-related illness in rural areas accounts for half the global total, with an average of 170,000 agricultural workers killed at work annually.

Rural workers often fall outside the scope of national labour laws. In a number of cases, they are explicitly excluded, either fully or partially, from the relevant laws, or, when they are covered under the law, they are excluded from protection in practice. Such exclusions are often due to their employment status (e.g., self-employed, smallhold farmers, casual and seasonal workers) or because they belong to vulnerable groups (e.g., women, migrant workers, indigenous peoples, lower castes) making them particularly susceptible to abuse. In addition, labour inspection is often non-existent or weak.

The labour protection gap is huge and hence the dimension of the decent work deficit for rural workers. This severe decent work deficit needs to be addressed if approaches to address rural employment and reduce poverty are to be successful. They provide an internationally recognized framework for governments in the implementation of decent work principles in all areas of labour, including in rural areas. The supervisory system plays a key role in ensuring that real progress is made towards decent work for all, as a means of obtaining information on the application of international labour standards, in guaranteeing their effective implementation and by providing a dialogue and reference framework supporting the efforts of member States to implement international labour standards. The Global Reports, published annually as part of the follow-up to the ILO Declaration on Fundamental Principles and Rights at Work, 1998, also provide valuable information on the implementation of fundamental principles and rights at work, including in rural areas.

Since its foundation in 1919, the ILO has been concerned with the protection of rural workers, especially in agriculture. In 1921, ten instruments were adopted to protect agricultural workers, covering freedom of association, minimum age, child labour, hours of work, social security, living conditions and vocational training. Since then, 19 new instruments have been adopted. The term "rural workers" is defined, by Article 2 of the Rural Workers' Organisations Convention, 1975 (No. 141), as "any person engaged in agriculture, handicrafts or a related occupation in a rural area, whether as a wage earner or, subject to the provisions of paragraph 2 of this Article, as a self-employed person such as a tenant, sharecropper or small owner–occupier." In addition to these specific instruments, many other ILO standards include rural workers in their scope of application.

Approximately 3.4 billion people live in rural areas, of which approximately 1 billion are employed in agriculture and 97 per cent live in developing countries. Poverty levels are often higher in rural areas. In addition, rural workers, in particular agricultural workers, are confronted with both legal and practical hurdles in attaining effective protection and decent work. The following sections will describe the most relevant instruments for rural workers, both specific and general, and provide details on their application.

Fundamental Principles and Rights at Work

The importance of the fundamental Conventions is today universally recognized. According to the 1998 Declaration, all ILO member States, even if they have not ratified the Conventions in question, have an obligation – arising from the very fact of membership of the Organization – to respect, to promote and to realize, in good faith and in accordance with the Constitution, the principles concerning the fundamental rights which are the subject of those Conventions, namely: freedom of association and the effective recognition of the right to collective bargaining; the elimination of all forms of forced or compulsory labour; the effective abolition of child labour; and the elimination of discrimination in respect of employment and occupation. These rights are even more important in that they are enabling rights, i.e. they create conditions to allow access to other rights.

Freedom of Association and Collective Bargaining

Freedom of association is a fundamental human right, which paves the way for improvements in social and labour conditions, for example, through collective bargaining. The Freedom of Association and Protection of the Right to Organise Convention, 1948 (No. 87), provides that workers and employers, "without distinction whatsoever", have the right to establish and join organizations of their own choosing. The Right to Organise and Collective Bargaining Convention, 1949 (No. 98), provides that workers are to enjoy adequate protection against acts of anti-union discrimination in respect of their employment.

Two other Conventions particularly relevant to rural workers are: the Right of Association (Agriculture) Convention, 1921 (No. 11), which provides that member States are "to secure to all those engaged in agriculture the same rights of association and combination as to industrial workers, and to repeal any statutory or other provisions restricting such rights in the case of those engaged in agriculture". This is the most highly ratified ILO Convention dealing specifically with agricultural workers.

The Rural Workers' Organisations Convention, 1975 (No. 141), provides that "all categories of rural workers, whether they are wage earners or self-employed, shall have the right to establish and ... join organisations, of their own choosing without previous authorisation". This Convention gives formal recognition to the importance of rural workers in the world and the urgency of associating them with economic and social development action if their conditions of work and life are to be permanently and efficiently improved. Member States who ratify the Convention have an obligation to adopt and carry out a policy of active encouragement in respect of these organizations. It also provides that an objective of national policy concerning rural development should be to facilitate the establishment and growth of strong and independent organizations of rural workers as an effective means of ensuring their participation, without discrimination, in economic and social development and the resulting benefits.

Despite universal recognition of the right to freedom of association, rural workers, especially in agriculture, face both legal impediments and practical challenges in asserting this right (as a result of poverty, informality, dependency on the employer who provides not only income but also housing and schooling, the large number of women workers in agriculture and the often atypical employment relationships, such as migrant, seasonal or casual workers). The need to promote trade unions, in general, and organizations in the rural sector, in particular, has been raised on several occasions by the Committee of Experts on the Application of Conventions and Recommendations (CEACR). In some cases, legislation or administrative obstacles impede the right of workers to establish and join trade unions, for example by prohibiting the establishment of more than one trade union to represent the same economic category; requiring a certain number of organizations to form federations and confederations; limiting the right of rural workers' organizations to choose their own organizational structure; and requiring that trade unions represent at least half the workforce of an enterprise or bargaining unit in order to gain recognition or bargain collectively.

Trade unions in this sector face similar problems as those faced by trade unions in other sectors (e.g., slowness and ineffectiveness of administrative and judicial procedures in cases concerning anti-union practices, impossibility of exercising the right to strike, lack of legislative protection of the right to establish and join trade unions, violence and harassment of union officials and unjustified dismissal of trade union members).

Another key element is the effective promotion of the right to organize and collective bargaining in this sector, by ensuring full and effective protection against anti- union discrimination. Collective bargaining is a very important tool in terms of enabling agricultural workers to obtain improvements in their terms and conditions of employment (e.g., with respect to occupational safety and health, wages, social security and maternity protection) so as to make decent work in this sector a reality and allow agricultural workers to break away from poverty. Taking into account the above difficulties and issues, the ILO has developed particular tripartite activities to promote freedom of association and collective bargaining in this sector.

Prevention of Forced Labour

Forced labour is prevalent in many rural areas, especially among migrant agricultural workers and victims of trafficking. The Forced Labour Convention, 1930 (No. 29), provides that all member States undertake to suppress the use of forced or compulsory labour in all its forms. In accordance with the Abolition of Forced Labour Convention, 1957 (No. 105), member States shall undertake to suppress and not to make use of any form of forced or compulsory labour, for example, as a method of mobilizing and using labour for purposes of economic development or for having participated in strikes. These core Conventions cover all workers from the exaction of forced labour. This broad protection is afforded regardless of the sector of activity (whether in the formal or informal economy) or the legal status of the worker.

The supervisory bodies have drawn attention to situations where slavery-like conditions are transmitted by birth to individuals who are compelled to work for their master without pay. In some cases, the CEACR has noted situations where non-respect of rights concerning payment of wages and working time has led to the imposition of practices of forced labour, such as debt bondage or the obligation to do overtime work under the threat of a penalty. Furthermore, in some countries, national laws still provide for the possibility of imposing work in the agricultural sector, for example in the form of compulsory cultivation, etc.

Elimination of Child Labour

While great progress has been made in many countries in reducing child labour, a number of factors make child labour in agriculture and rural areas particularly difficult to tackle. These include large numbers of working children (approximately 132 million girls and boys aged 5–14), starting work at a young age, the hazardous nature of agricultural work, a lack of regulations in the area, the invisibility of their work, the denial of education, the effects of poverty, and ingrained attitudes and perceptions about the roles of children in rural areas. The prevalence of child labour, especially in agriculture, undermines decent work and employment for adults and weakens rural labour markets as it maintains a cycle where household income for both farmers and waged workers is insufficient to meet the economic needs of their families.

Rural poverty also drives girls and boys to migrate to towns and cities where they often end up as urban child labourers, urban unemployed or underemployed, exchanging their rural poverty for urban poverty. Child labour undermines efforts to promote rural youth employment under decent conditions of work. Children who have reached the minimum legal age for employment in their country (14 years of age or higher) continue to work in exploitative and hazardous child labour with poor future job and economic prospects. It is now widely acknowledged that combating child labour also implies addressing the problem of ending poverty and promoting decent work for youth and adults.

The international legal framework for the elimination of child labour is provided by the Minimum Age Convention, 1973 (No. 138), and the Worst Forms of Child Labour Convention, 1999 (No. 182). Convention No. 138 provides that member States are to pursue a national policy designed to ensure the effective abolition of child labour and to progressively raise the minimum age for admission to employment or work to a level consistent with the fullest physical and mental development of young persons. Convention No. 138 allows for the exclusion of family and small-scale holdings, producing for local consumption and not regularly employing hired workers, from its application. Convention No. 182 calls on member States to prohibit and eliminate the worst forms of child labour and applies to all children under 18.

The CEACR stresses that the application of Convention No. 138 continues to give rise to serious difficulties. Even in countries where the ILO provides technical assistance, millions of children continue to work in the informal economy, commercial agriculture, plantations and forestry. There is also concern that where minimum age limits for agriculture exist, these are not enforced. With respect to Convention No. 182, many children in rural areas were found to be in the worst forms of child labour, especially hazardous child labour.

To eliminate child labour in rural areas, four main gaps need to be addressed. First, national legislation has to include legislation prohibiting hazardous child labour in accordance with Conventions Nos 138 and 182. Second, exclusions and exemptions in national labour laws for agricultural workers need to be eliminated. In addition, exemptions to the minimum age for working on family farms, or children working alongside their parents, deprives children of proper protection and, therefore, needs revision. Third, labour inspection in agriculture is often either non-existent or inherently weak. Building the capacity of labour inspectorates and their inspectors to deal with child labour in agriculture and to ensure decent youth employment is vital. Fourth, gaps in educational standards in rural areas should be remedied. Due to factors such as lack of schools, poor educational standards, and families being too poor to be able to send their children to school, there are often no viable alternatives for children other than to work under harsh and exploitative conditions in agriculture. Educational deficits carry on into adulthood as lack of literacy, poor educational levels, and low-skill levels block pathways out of rural poverty for many agricultural workers.

Equality of Opportunity and Treatment

Agricultural workers face discrimination on a number of levels, including often being excluded from relevant national laws. The Equal Remuneration Convention, 1951 (No. 100) provides that member States are to ensure the application to all workers of the principle of equal remuneration for men and women workers for work of equal value. Under the Discrimination (Employment and Occupation) Convention, 1958 (No. 111), member States undertake to declare and pursue a national policy designed to promote equality of opportunity and treatment.

The CEACR has stressed in a number of its comments the absence of legislation providing equality of treatment and equal remuneration for agricultural workers, which particularly affects women and workers belonging to disadvantaged groups. Even where there is legislation in force, agricultural workers may face discrimination (in particular women, indigenous workers, migrant workers and lower-caste workers), abusive or insalubrious working conditions, and are often paid lower wages. In many developing countries, export-oriented agriculture has become an important source of paid work for women in the last decade. In some countries, women still need the permission of their husbands to join agricultural cooperatives. It also noted, however, that progress has been made towards equality of treatment of women through the adoption of national laws, in some countries.

Tripartite Consultation

Tripartite dialogue is essential in order to ensure that all workers, including agricultural workers, have a voice in governance. The Tripartite Consultation (International Labour Standards) Convention, 1976 (No. 144), provides that member States are to introduce procedures which ensure effective consultations, with respect to labour matters with representatives of employers' and workers' organizations, who are freely chosen by their representative organizations. Its accompanying Recommendation (No. 152) suggests examples of consultation procedures. These procedures should include, inter alia, consultations on the preparation and implementation of legislative or other measures to give effect to Conventions and Recommendations. In addition, many of the Conventions in the area of agriculture also request that the government consult with representatives of workers and employers on the implementation of the Convention. The report form under article 22 of the Constitution concerning Convention No. 144 gives the example of representatives of persons working in the rural sector and informal economy as "persons affected", in addition to representatives of employers' and workers' organizations.

Labour Administration and Inspection

The Labour Administration Convention, 1978 (No. 150) is a key Convention for improving governance in rural areas and is dealt with.

Labour inspection is the most important tool governments have at their disposal to ensure compliance with labour laws and to identify gaps in national legislation. The CEACR has emphasized the need to develop labour inspection activities in agriculture, especially to protect young workers and tackle child labour.

The Labour Inspection (Agriculture) Convention, 1969 (No. 129), requires governments to establish a system of labour inspection in agriculture. Three main functions of labour inspection are identified: securing the enforcement of the legal provisions relating to conditions of work and protection of workers; providing technical information and advice to employers and workers on how best to comply with relevant legal provisions; and bringing to the attention of the competent authorities defects or abuses that are not specifically covered by the law and submitting proposals on how to improve laws and regulations. In this sense, labour inspection has a crucial and proactive role to play.

The CEACR also noted the reluctance of member States to extend labour inspection systems to the agricultural sector, due in part to administrative, technical and economic obstacles. This is evidenced in the difference in ratification rates between the Labour Inspection Convention,

1947 (No. 81) and Convention No. 129. Only a small proportion of agricultural enterprises are legally covered by labour inspection systems worldwide. In addition, in many developing countries, these enterprises are rarely visited in practice due to a lack of resources allocated to labour inspectorates. The influence of labour inspection is, in practice, mostly confined to formal activities in urban areas. The CEACR has stressed that the increase in ILO technical cooperation and assistance activities in the area of inspection, as well as in a certain number of international initiatives in which the ILO is involved, has demonstrated that, even if somewhat belated, collective awareness of the need to develop labour inspection systems in agriculture was increasingly noticeable and labour inspectors' duties, powers and prerogatives and their field of intervention have been substantially expanded in the agricultural sector in some countries.

Employment Policy and Promotion

Under the Employment Policy Convention, 1964 (No. 122), and linked Recommendations (Nos 122 and 169), ratifying member States shall declare and pursue, as a major goal, an active policy designed to promote full, productive and freely chosen employment. Priorities for the rural sector include developmental policies, rural development, and educational and skills training policies. Article 3 of Convention No. 122 is of particular relevance to rural workers because it requires governments to consult with representatives of employers and workers in order to take into account their views and experiences when formulating and implementing employment policies. The article 22 report form for the Convention specifies that consultations with representatives of other sectors of the economically active population such as those working in the rural sector and the informal economy should take place concerning employment policy measures.

The Employment Policy Recommendation, 1964 (No. 122), provides that special emphasis on a broadly based programme to promote productive employment in the rural sector should be incorporated within the framework of an integrated national policy. The promotion of rural employment is also present in the Employment Policy (Supplementary Provisions) Recommendation, 1984 (No. 169), which states that all member States might implement special public works programmes, such as rural infrastructure projects, in order to create and maintain employment, to raise income levels and to reduce poverty.

The Promotion of Cooperatives Recommendation, 2002 (No. 193) provides guidance on developing employment polices that encourage promotion and strengthening of the identity of cooperatives. The goal is, inter alia, to: create and develop income-generating activities and sustainable decent employment; develop human resource capacities and knowledge of the values, advantages and benefits of the cooperative movement through education and training; improve social and economic well-being, taking into account the need to eliminate all forms of discrimination; contribute to sustainable human development; establish and expand a viable and dynamic distinctive sector of the economy, which includes cooperatives, that responds to the social and economic needs of the community.

The CEACR also advocates rural employment promotion through its comments. Governments are regularly requested to provide information on the programmes implemented and their impact on employment promotion both in the aggregate and as they affect particular categories of workers such as women, young persons, older workers and those in the rural sector and on the need to implement an active employment policy in the rural sector.

Vocational Guidance and Training

Many rural workers are poorly trained and lack marketable skills. Addressing this gap by ensuring a skilled rural workforce is key to empowering people to escape from the poverty trap. The Human Resources Development Convention, 1975 (No. 142), provides that ratifying States shall adopt and develop comprehensive and coordinated policies and programmes of vocational guidance and vocational training, closely linked with employment, to meet the needs of both young persons and adults in all sectors of the economy and branches of economic activity. Recommendation No. 195 provides that member States should promote access to education, training and lifelong learning for rural workers.

As regards vocational rehabilitation, the Vocational Rehabilitation and Employment (Disabled Persons) Convention, 1983 (No. 159), expressly mentions the obligation to formulate and periodically review national policy with respect to all categories of disabled persons, especially in rural areas. Recommendation No. 168 advocates particular efforts to provide vocational rehabilitation services for disabled people in rural areas and in remote communities at the same level and on the same terms as those for urban areas, and provides an indicative list of measures to be taken.

The CEACR noted that the best results regarding vocational rehabilitation and employment services in rural areas and remote communities for persons with disabilities have been achieved through various models of community-based rehabilitation (CBR). These are said to rely largely on voluntary, community and family resources and are less costly than public rehabilitation institutions. In developing countries with a significant population that have been experimenting with various models of CBR, these programmes remain a valid way of serving people with disabilities in rural areas.

Wages

Wages in agriculture tend to be low, with many workers being paid below the national minimum wage. Wage setting is one of the most contentious rural labour issues, especially as payments are often delayed. The Minimum Wage Fixing Machinery (Agriculture) Convention, 1951 (No. 99) calls for the creation or maintenance of adequate machinery to fix minimum wage rates. The national competent authority may exclude from the scope of application of this Convention certain categories of agricultural workers, such as members of the farmer's family. Workers are to be guaranteed a minimum wage sufficient to meet their needs, but also to preserve the purchasing power of the wage. The Convention provides that the employers and workers concerned may participate in, or be consulted with regard to, the operation of the minimum wage-fixing machinery on a basis of complete equality. Guidelines for the fixing of minimum wages are found in the accompanying Minimum Wage-Fixing Machinery (Agriculture) Recommendation, 1951 (No. 89). Other relevant ILO standards are the Minimum Wage-Fixing Machinery Convention, 1928 (No. 26), and the Minimum Wage Fixing Convention, 1970 (No. 131).

The protection and timely payment of wages is dealt with by the Protection of Wages Convention, 1949 (No. 95), which applies to all workers, without qualification. It provides that wages are only payable in legal tender. The partial payment of wages in the form of allowances in kind may only be authorized in certain circumstances for certain occupations. Partial payment in kind is a practice that is often used in the agricultural sector. Where there is full payment in kind, with no cash remuneration, this poses serious problems for agricultural workers.

Over the years, the supervisory bodies have raised a number of problems concerning the application of these Conventions to rural workers, including non-payment or deferred payment of wages; exclusion of agricultural workers from national legislation; non-respect of periodic readjustment of minimum wage rates; the lack of adequate sanctions to deter abuse of the minimum wage system, where it exists; and the lack of statistics and data on workers covered by minimum wages in this sector. The CEACR has also commented for many years on practices resulting in ten of thousands of indigenous agricultural workers being in a situation of debt bondage, through the use of systems of advances on wages, stores located in camps which charge excessive rates compared to market prices, compulsory deductions from wages for savings schemes, payments in kind and the deferred payment of wages.

Working Time

Working time is one of the main gaps in the protection of agricultural workers, with many of them regularly working long hours, often from sunrise to sunset according to the seasons, weather and crops. These workers often exceed the prescribed limit for the number of hours worked and national laws often exclude agricultural workers from provisions concerning maximum working time.

Agricultural workers are not covered by the two main Conventions on hours of work or weekly rest. They are also excluded from the scope of application of the Night Work Convention, 1990 (No. 171). They are covered under the Forty-Hour Week Convention, 1935 (No. 47), which provides that each member State is to apply the principle of the 40-hour working week. This is only a global objective, however, and the text does not prescribe specific limits to working hours. The right to annual leave with pay for agricultural workers is recognized by the Holidays with Pay Convention (Revised), 1970 (No. 132), which provides that workers are entitled to annual paid holidays of no less than three weeks. The provisions of this Convention can be accepted separately with respect to agricultural workers, or employed persons in the other economic sectors. Ratifying member States also have the possibility to exclude, following consultation with the organizations of employers and workers concerned, limited categories of employed persons in respect of whose employment special problems arise of a substantial nature, relating to enforcement or to legislative or constitutional matters. In practice, agriculture is often excluded from the application of this Convention, an issue raised by the supervisory bodies in a number of cases.

Occupational Safety and Health

Agriculture is one of the three most dangerous occupations to work in, along with construction and mining. Despite the hazardous nature of the work, and the high levels of risk, agriculture is often excluded from coverage under national occupational safety and health regulations or is the least well covered sector of the economy.

The Safety and Health in Agriculture Convention, 2001 (No. 184), and its accompanying Recommendation No. 192 are particularly significant because for the first time in international law, agricultural workers are formally guaranteed the same rights and protection with regard to their health and safety as other categories of workers. They provide a framework for the development of national policies and mechanisms to ensure the participation of workers' and employers' organizations in that process. However, the Convention does not cover subsistence farming, industrial processes that use agricultural products as raw materials, and the industrial exploitation of forests. Furthermore, it allows member States to exclude certain agricultural undertakings or limited categories of workers from the application of this Convention or certain provisions thereof, when special problems of a substantial nature arise.

The Convention calls for the adoption of a national policy on safety and health in agriculture and the setting up of an appropriate system of inspection for agricultural workplaces and prescribes preventive and protective measures regarding machinery safety and ergonomics, handling and transport of materials, sound management of chemicals, animal handling and protection against biological risks, and the construction and maintenance of agricultural facilities. It provides that 18 years is the minimum age for employment in agriculture in dangerous jobs and 16 years for other farm jobs. Other provisions require that temporary and seasonal workers receive the same level of protection as permanent workers, and that the special needs of women agricultural workers in relation to pregnancy, breastfeeding and reproductive health are taken into account. The Convention also regulates working time arrangements and coverage against occupational injuries and diseases. The Recommendation provides further guidance on occupational safety and health surveillance and recommended preventive and protective measures in the areas regulated by the Convention. While it may be some time before this new instrument achieves wide ratification, it already provides comprehensive guidance to ILO member States and the social partners working to improve their national law and practice. This Convention and Recommendation are also important new reference texts for those working with voluntary initiatives, codes of conduct and social labelling schemes as occupational safety and health is the workplace issue most frequently addressed in codes of conduct.

Social Security

Agricultural workers remain among the least well protected with respect to access to health care, sickness and maternity benefits, workers' compensation, etc. Pension schemes in developing countries rarely apply to the rural population. International labour standards have always advocated equal social security coverage of agricultural and industrial workers. In 1921, the Workmen's Compensation (Agriculture) Convention, 1921 (No. 12) requested ratifying States to "extend to all agricultural wage earners its laws and regulations which provide for the compensation of workers for personal injury by accidents arising out of or in the course of their employment". The Social Insurance (Agriculture) Recommendation, 1921 (No. 17), adopted the same year generalized this principle to apply also to insurance systems against sickness, invalidity, old age and other similar social risks ensuring agricultural wage earners conditions equivalent to those prevailing in industrial and commercial occupations.

Maternity Protection

The Maternity Protection Convention, 2000 (No. 183), and its Recommendation No. 191 apply to "all employed women, including those in atypical forms of dependent work", hence it also applies to the agricultural sector. Although the Convention provides for the possibility for member States to exclude certain categories of workers from application of the Convention, this provision has so far not been used. Under the Convention, governments are to protect pregnant and breastfeeding women from health hazards and women are entitled to maternity leave and cash benefits as well as breaks for breastfeeding mothers. They are to be "guaranteed the right to return to the same position or an equivalent position paid at the same rate at the end of her maternity leave" and their employment is not to be terminated during her pregnancy or maternity leave. Convention No. 183 revised the Maternity Protection Convention (Revised), 1952 (No. 103). While the supervisory bodies have not commented yet on the application of the former with respect to agriculture, they often do so with respect to Convention No. 103. Problems raised include the exclusion or non-coverage of women in the agricultural sector with respect to maternity leave as well as the lack of statistical data on coverage in this sector.

Migrant Workers

Migrant workers who make up a large part of the agricultural labour force are particularly vulnerable to abuse. Protective instruments include the specific Migration for Employment Convention (Revised), 1949 (No. 97), and the Migrant Workers (Supplementary Provisions) Convention, 1975 (No. 143), and their accompanying Recommendations. Convention No. 97 aims to regulate the conditions in migration for employment, provides general provisions for protection and prohibits inequality of treatment between nationals and migrant workers lawfully in the country of employment.

Convention No. 143 and Recommendation No. 151 aim to address problems relating to irregular migration and provide a minimum level of protection of all migrants, independent of their status. Under Part I of Convention No. 143, ratifying States have a general obligation to respect the basic human rights of all migrant workers. Under Part II of the Convention, migrant workers who are lawfully in the country of employment are not only entitled to equal treatment (as provided for in Convention No. 97) but also to equality of opportunity, e.g., equality with regard to access to employment, trade union rights, cultural rights and individual and collective freedoms.

The Migrant Workers Equality of Treatment (Social Security) Convention, 1962 (No. 118) provides for the right to equality of treatment with regard to all nine branches of social security. For each of the nine branches that it accepts, a State party to the Convention undertakes to grant, within its territory to nationals of any other State that has ratified the Convention, equality of treatment with its own nationals. The provisions are thus reliant on reciprocity. One of the tools used by governments, and advocated for under the ILO instruments, is the use of model contracts and bilateral and multilateral agreements.

Indigenous and Tribal Peoples

Indigenous peoples are more likely than non-indigenous peoples to work in agriculture, and they face de facto discrimination in terms of conditions of employment. If they earn their livelihood as subsistence farmers, their main problems frequently arise from unequal access to land with respect to land title and ownership rights, credit, marketing facilities and resources. They are also often subject to forced dispossession of land for the creation of agricultural undertakings as well as logging and mining activities. In all such cases, official policies should make provision for measures to allow indigenous peoples access to resources, including the means to carry out the activities from which they earn their living.

The Indigenous and Tribal Peoples Convention, 1989 (No. 169), provides protection and rights for indigenous workers in seasonal and casual employment, including in agriculture. The Convention deals in Part II with the rights and ownership of land that has been traditionally occupied by indigenous peoples as well as safeguarding their rights to natural resources. Part III provides that they are to enjoy the protection afforded by national law and practice, as do other such workers in the same sectors, and that they are fully informed of their rights under labour legislation and of the means of redress available to them. Part IV addresses vocational training, handicrafts and rural industries, and advocates for the strengthening and promotion of rural industries, and traditional occupations as a tool in maintaining indigenous cultures, economic self-reliance and development.

Plantations

At the time the Plantations Convention, 1958 (No. 110) was adopted, plantations constituted an important economic sector for many countries in tropical and subtropical regions, and the poor living and working conditions of plantation workers were widely recognized. The principal objective of the Convention was to afford broader protection to those workers. Convention No. 110, supplemented by its Protocol of 1982, is a comprehensive instrument which deals, inter alia, with conditions of work, contracts of employment, collective bargaining, methods of wage payment, holidays with pay, weekly rest, maternity protection, accident compensation, freedom of association, labour inspection, housing and medical care. Ratifying States have the possibility of excluding this part from the application of the Convention. Its accompanying Recommendation No. 110

proposes a number of measures that governments should take to improve the conditions of plantation workers. Detailed guidance is offered in areas such as vocational training, systems of wage payment, equal pay for women doing work of equal value, hours of work, welfare, compensation for accidents and industrial diseases, and labour inspection.

Considering the comprehensive scope of this Convention, it is indeed disappointing that so few countries have ratified it.

Tenants and Sharecroppers

The Tenants and Share-croppers Recommendation, 1968 (No. 132), provides guidance to member Sates with respect to tenants, sharecroppers and similar categories of agricultural workers who do not receive a fixed wage. Social and economic policy should promote a progressive and continuing increase in the well-being of these workers and assure them the greatest possible degree of stability and security of work and livelihood. They should have the main responsibility for managing their holding and access to land. The development of organizations representing tenants, sharecroppers, etc., and those representing the interests of landowners should be encouraged.

Relevance and Impact of International Labour Standards

While there is no comprehensive instrument dealing with the rural sector, the ILO has a large number of instruments that apply to the rural sector, especially agriculture.

They provide an international legal framework for the protection of rural workers, especially agricultural workers. However, the high number of instruments in question may make it difficult to promote them. They are not necessarily easily identifiable, and this may cause problems in the perception of what protection international labour standards provide for the workers concerned. Another difficulty comes from the fact that, apart from the fundamental and a few other instruments including three of the priority Conventions and Conventions Nos 11 and 12, many of the relevant instruments are not very well ratified. The ratification rates of the up to date or interim status Conventions dealing specifically with agriculture are very uneven. They range from 122 ratifications for Convention No. 11 to eight ratifications for Convention No. 184. Furthermore, even if the possibility to exclude rural or agricultural workers from application of certain Conventions is rarely used by ratifying States, serious problems of application have been highlighted in a large number of countries by the supervisory bodies.

Globally, rural workers still form the largest workforce. While improvements have been made in the protection of agricultural workers in some countries, in many others, they are not covered by labour legislation and other regulations protecting workers. Furthermore, where laws do exist, lack of resources and political will to enforce the provisions as well as isolation, poor literacy, poverty and lack of organization, often prevent workers from fully asserting their rights. The labour protection gap for these workers remains huge.What are the options for the way forward to address and redress this enormous decent work deficit? The first would be national-level action. Member States could be called upon to review their legislation with a view to extending the coverage of protection to rural workers, including rural wage earners, and in particular to ensure that they enjoy the protection of fundamental principles and rights at work as contained in the Declaration on Fundamental Principles and Rights at Work. This would require better monitoring and enforcement of national legislation, including the extension of labour inspection. There is, however, no existing mechanism to monitor measures taken and evaluate progress made by countries.A second option could be to invite member States to remove any exclusion that may exist in national law concerning the application of the fundamental Conventions to rural workers. This could also include an invitation to them to consider ratifying the relevant up to date Conventions, in particular Conventions Nos 184 (occupational safety and health), 129 (labour inspection) and 122 (employment policy). It should be noted that in November 2007, the Governing Body decided that the promotion of priority Conventions, including Conventions Nos 122 and 129, should be strengthened. A third option could be to consider the advantages of consolidating all the relevant standards into a single instrument with a view to providing more effective protection for the world's 3.4 billion people living in rural areas. The Plantations Convention, 1958 (No. 110) and the Rural Workers' Organisations Convention, 1975 (No. 141) could also be examined more closely with a view to better determining the difficulties and impediments to ratification and implementation and to extend coverage to all rural workers. Considering the large number of people concerned and the huge gap in protection, the ILO would be responding in providing a framework that would bolster the efforts for employment creation as a way out of poverty for rural workers.

References

Chadha, G.K. (2001). "Impact of Economic Reforms on Rural Employment: No Smooth Sailing Anticipated." *Indian Jl. of Agricultural Economics, Vol.* 56, No.3, pp. 491-97.

Saith, A. (1991). "Development Strategies and the Rural Poor", *Journal of Peasant Studies* 17(2): 171-243.

Sen, Abhijit (2003). "Globalisation Growth and Inequality in South Asia- The Evidence from Rural India", in Jayati Ghosh and C. P. Chandrasekhar (eds), *Work and Well being in the Age of Finance*, New Delhi : Tulika Books.

Shah, Mihir (2004). "National Rural Employment Guarantee Act: A Historic Opportunity", *Economic and Political Weekly*, Vol. 39, No.49 (December 11): 5287-5290.

Uma Rani and Jeemol Unni (2004). "Unorganised and Organised Manufacturing in India- Potential for Employment Generating Growth" *Economic and Political Weekly*, Vol. 49, (October 9): 4568-4580.

UNDP,(2009). *The National Rural Employment Guarantee Act (NREGA) Design, Process and Impact,* Nreganet Series from UNDP, New Delhi.

11

Role of Rural Labour Administration Systems

Governments and the social partners play key governance roles in labour administration systems and institutions of social dialogue, which offer avenues for consensus building at national and sectoral levels. These need to be extended to rural areas, where they can provide one means of encouraging democratic governance in local economic development. Decentralization offers an opportunity for local actors to participate more fully in governance, but capacity needs to be strengthened, and the tripartite constituents need to reach out to work with other actors concerned with social and economic development. Poverty and poor governance increase the likelihood of violence and social unrest.

Importance of Governance

Governance broadly refers to the process of decision-making and the process through which those decisions are implemented. Governance issues arise within the government system as a whole as well as in its various parts, for example, in the determination of policy, or the functioning of the bureaucracy or of the judiciary. The setting of just rules and their unbiased application are among the key features of good governance, as are principles such as participation, fairness, decency, accountability, transparency and efficiency that provide the basis for governmental action.

Above all, governance is a political process in which legitimacy depends on people's perception that their voices have been heard, their needs recognized and their problems addressed. Freedom of association and the practice of social dialogue enable democratic participation in decision-making.

Governance is not limited to government, though government has a key role to play in overall governance. Political parties, economic interest groups, civil society organizations and major economic actors, such as corporate entities, all face governance issues as well. Governance in the world of work is a central concern of the ILO's tripartite constituents.

Never before has governance achieved such prominence in international public debate. MDG 8, with its aim of a global partnership for development, stressed a shared commitment to good governance, development and poverty reduction, both nationally and internationally. International financial institutions and major donors have begun to link loans and aid to governance issues, for example, those related to probity in the use of funds, transparency in decision-making, accountability to citizens, commitment to human rights and the fight against corruption. To this end, a number of national and multilateral development agencies and independent research institutions have developed governance assessment tools and indices. The World Bank's Worldwide Governance Indicators measure six dimensions of governance: voice and accountability; political stability; government effectiveness; regulatory quality; rule of law; and control of corruption. UNDP's Governance Indicators Project has carried out citizen surveys regarding parliamentary development, electoral systems, human rights, justice, decentralization and local government administrative reforms. The United Kingdom's Department for International Development (DFID) uses country governance assessments to evaluate governmental capability, accountability and responsiveness.

When the last general discussion on rural employment took place, many countries were governed by authoritarian regimes or were under single party rule. Today most governments proclaim adherence to democratic principles. Many have parliaments and heads of government chosen through an electoral process. Many have recognized the linkages between good governance and economic growth. Yet in most countries, democratic aspirations exceed actual performance and the deeper attributes of democratic systems have yet to be realized. Equity, inclusiveness, and respect for the rights of minorities and of the disadvantaged are just a few of these. Good governance is a work in progress.

Governance Issues in the World of Work

Governance issues permeate the world of work. Many are addressed through international labour standards, which highlight broad principles of good governance, particularly those expressed as fundamental principles and rights at work, such as freedom of association, institutional frameworks for good governance, for example those relating to labour administration and labour inspection, and processes of good governance, that emphasize tripartite consultation. Social inclusion and the rights of marginalized or vulnerable groups are the focus of numerous ILO instruments as well. Voice and representation through tripartism and social dialogue are inherent to their conception and implementation.

Labour market governance has been missing in the development strategies of many countries, yet the quality of labour market governance can be an important factor in determining whether countries are successful in increasing opportunities for full, productive and freely chosen employment and, more broadly, for decent work. Conversely, effective labour administration can strengthen compliance with national law and can thereby contribute to a stable business climate by encouraging investment and supporting markets. In order to do this, national governments and local authorities need to promote efficient bureaucracies that are corruption- and harassment free, are transparent and consistent in the application of rules and regulations, and that protect and enforce contractual obligations and respect the rights of workers and employers. Three key actors are central to effective and equitable labour market governance: a well-functioning system of labour administration and representative organizations of employers and workers.

A system of labour administration, as defined in the Labour Administration Convention, 1978, "covers all public administration bodies responsible for and/or engaged in labour administration – whether they are ministerial departments or public agencies, including parastatal and regional or local agencies or any other form of decentralized administration – and any institutional framework for the coordination of the activities of such bodies and for consultation with and participation by employers and workers and their organizations". Their role in setting the framework of governance in the world of work through policies, laws and regulations is clear. Article 6 of that Convention states that "the competent bodies within the system of labour administration shall ... be responsible for or contribute to the preparation, administration, coordination, checking and review of national labour policy, and be the instrument within the ambit of public administration for the preparation and implementation of laws and regulations giving effect thereto". Among the functions of the competent bodies figure the development of a national employment policy; the review of the situation of employed, unemployed and underemployed persons; the promotion of effective consultation and cooperation between public authorities and bodies and employers' and workers' organizations at national, regional and local levels as well as at the level of different sectors of economic activity; and at their request, the provision of technical advice to employers and workers and their organizations. Article 7 provides for the extension of the functions of the system of labour administration beyond the formal economy to include activities relating to the conditions of work and working life of workers who are not employed persons under the law, such as tenants who do not engage outside help, sharecroppers and similar categories of agricultural workers; self-employed workers who do not engage outside help, occupied in the informal economy; members of cooperatives and worker-managed undertakings; and persons working under systems established by communal customs or traditions.

The relevance of these provisions to any discussion of rural employment promotion and the challenges they pose to the tripartite constituents are evident. Key among them are: the need for explicit inclusion of rural issues within the national employment policy which takes into account the specific features of work in the rural economy; the need for a comprehensive framework of labour law that is sensitive to the most common forms of employment in the rural sector so that conditions of employment and work and issues of social protection are no longer dealt with in a legal limbo; and the institutional capacity of government and the social partners to engage in consultation and cooperation at the national, regional and local levels and to address conditions of work and working life of those who are not employees under the law.

In many developing countries, ministries of labour limit their realm of activities to waged workers, perhaps 10 per cent or less of the workforce, since the contract of employment is the main point of entry through which labour administrations act. Relatively few have extended the functions of labour administration to include activities relating to the conditions of work and working life in rural areas and in the informal economy, as foreseen in

Article 7 of Convention No. 150. This may be due to a number of factors: the lack of human and financial resources to adequately monitor developments throughout the labour force as a whole; lack of linkages between the ministry of labour and other ministries with responsibilities in rural development, such as the ministry of agriculture or ministry of commerce and industry; lack of knowledge and contact with rural institutions; and weak institutional presence at provincial and local levels.

The Labour Administration Recommendation, 1978 (No. 158), in Paragraph 26, directly addresses the key issues associated with the decentralization of services. It recommends that field services be appropriately arranged for their effective organization and operation and in particular that they meet the needs of the various areas, that they be provided with adequate staff, equipment and transport facilities and that they have sufficient and clear instructions to preclude the possibility of laws and regulations being differently interpreted in different areas.

Many countries recognize the importance of building social dialogue institutions and networks at national level to ensure that the voices of social partner organizations are heard when national policies are discussed, developed, implemented and reviewed. In many cases, however, government agencies that deliver key services in rural areas are absent from such national level social dialogue, as are representative organizations of rural employers and workers, farmers, water users, pastoralists, fishers and the like. Horizontal linkages within government are needed to ensure that all relevant agencies are included in policy discussions, but vertical linkages of consultation, communication and coordination are important as well. To the extent possible, social dialogue arrangements also need to be made at the regional, local and sectoral levels.

Many labour administrations are relatively weak and have little outreach beyond the national level. Many developing countries have inherited structures from the colonial past and have done little to reorganize their programmes, approaches and activities to achieve greater impact. Countries with a large share of the workforce living and working in rural areas may need to consider whether the goals, organizational structure, resource allocations and current working methods of their labour administration system enable them to deliver services that are essential for the welfare of rural workers and the self-employed. For example, in many countries, labour inspection is among the key services offered by ministries of labour, but inspection focuses almost solely on factory inspections, leaving aside most agricultural workplaces. Little has been done to develop collaboration with other government inspectorates responsible for work in rural areas, for example, health inspectorates or safety inspectors in rural electrification. In some cases, labour administration may not take account of rural issues, simply because there is no unit designated as responsible for such questions. Countries with administrative units responsible for women's issues or for child labour issues offer an example of how structural changes within the organization of work within a ministry can result in attention being paid to particular issues of concern. To improve the impact of their efforts, a number of countries have already embarked on the process of re-engineering their labour administration to promote decent work.

The establishment of the National Economic Development and Labour Council (NEDLAC) in South Africa provides an example of rethinking the interaction between government and constituents with a view to making economic decision-making more inclusive and promoting economic growth and social equity. NEDLAC brings together several departments of government, organized business, organized labour and organized community groups on a national level to discuss and try to reach consensus on social and economic policy issues through social dialogue. NEDLAC is funded through the Department of Labour, but the Departments of Trade and Industry, Finance and Public Works are also centrally involved and other departments attend meetings when an issue relevant to their portfolios is discussed. NEDLAC seeks constructive relationships with provincial governments and provincial economic and developments forums as well.

Institutions of Social Dialogue

Strong institutions of social dialogue can be a significant factor in promoting good governance in the world of work. In relation to labour market governance, social dialogue offers voice to those most affected by the issues under deliberation. Whether at workplace level or in national labour market institutions, such as tripartite labour advisory bodies, health and safety councils, productivity centres, or welfare funds, social dialogue can widen understanding of public policy-making processes and increase transparency and accountability in decision-making. A formal role for the social partners in tripartite bodies does not necessarily translate into real influence, however. Such bodies must exercise autonomy from the State and the social partners must be fully representative of the parties in the world of work. Where the social partners are weak or fragmented, such institutions play a minor role.

A number of enabling conditions must be present for social dialogue to take place. These include respect for the fundamental rights of freedom of association and collective bargaining; strong, independent and representative organizations of workers and employers with the technical capacity and the access to relevant information to participate in social dialogue; the political will and commitment to engage in social dialogue on the part of all parties; and appropriate institutional support. Governments are responsible for providing the enabling environment within which employers and workers can exercise their right to form and join organizations of their own choosing without fear of reprisal or intimidation and for establishing the legal, institutional and other frameworks that enable the parties to engage effectively.

The main goal of social dialogue is to promote consensus building and democratic involvement among the main stakeholders in the world of work – governments and employers' and workers' organizations. Successful social dialogue structures and processes have the potential to resolve important economic and social issues, encourage good governance, advance social and labour peace and stability and boost economic progress. For example, in a number of ILO member States governments, and employers' and workers' organizations have, through a process of social dialogue, been able to incorporate elements of the Decent Work Agenda into the PRSP process.

Collective Bargaining and Good Governance

Collective bargaining is one of the most widespread forms of social dialogue. In rural areas, collective agreements in the agricultural sector have an extremely important role to play in securing decent conditions of work and ensuring stable labour relations on plantations and commercial farms. They often set out agreed principles and processes of governance at the enterprise level. Many collective agreements incorporate relevant provisions of the labour code with regard to issues such as working time, overtime pay, leave and medical care, for example. This is important for two main reasons. First, because knowledge and enforcement of the law tend to be weak in rural areas, whereas the provisions of collective agreements are known to, and have been accepted by, the parties concerned, and second, because labour codes frequently treat the agricultural sector differently from other sectors with regard to these issues. Incorporation of legal provisions within the agreement clarifies the applicable law. The collective agreement constitutes a shared understanding of the rights and duties of employers and workers at the farm level. Since many large farms and plantations are in remote locations, infrequently visited by labour inspectors, this common understanding is of great importance.

An analysis of 23 recent collective bargaining agreements in agriculture from Africa revealed the importance of such agreements to ensure basic rights in the workplace as well as the setting out of procedures to ensure stable labour relations. All agreements included sections on wages, overtime and severance pay, occupational safety and health, and funeral costs and facilities. Twenty-two of the 23 agreements included sections on allowances (e.g., housing allowance), leave (e.g., annual leave, sick leave, maternity leave and compassionate leave) and medical care. Twenty-one agreements contained provisions related to the handling of conflict (e.g., warnings and termination of employment) and leave to attend to union business. Approximately three-quarters of the agreements contained clauses regarding the employment status of the worker (permanent, seasonal or casual), which demonstrates the importance of this question for workers' well-being, and a number set out a probationary period, time frame or process through which workers could move from less stable to more regular employment, for example, from seasonal to permanent status. Seventeen agreements contained provisions related to education, whether of workers themselves or of their children, and 18 included provisions related to incentives.

Role of Decentralized Rural Governance

Good governance at local levels refers to the quality, effectiveness and efficiency of local administration and public service delivery; the quality of local public policy and decision-making procedures and the manner in which power and authority are exercised. Local government – whether provincial, municipal or village councils or other forms of sub-national government authority – is the essential institutional building block towards sound local governance. But life must be instilled into institutions through mechanisms and procedures for management of local public affairs that are responsive to the needs of the local community, including business people, civil society organizations, and other stakeholders, such as user groups.

Good governance in rural areas can be facilitated by decentralization, the political restructuring that devolves administrative, and less commonly, fiscal, power to local-level administrative units. Decentralization can lead to more effective and efficient service delivery. Devolving resource allocation decisions to local leaders, it is thought, can improve the match between the services available from the public sector and the preferences of the local population. Because local officials have better knowledge of local conditions and are more accessible to their constituents, they may prove more responsive to local needs and desires and more accountable for their decisions. Decentralization is thought to be particularly beneficial for rural development in disadvantaged jurisdictions as it usually entails a net transfer of fiscal resources from richer to poorer areas and leads to an increase in the quantity and quality of expenditures in these areas.

Democratic local governance does not arise through a simple shift of power and responsibility from the centre to the local; it is rather a way of connecting the local into processes of national government and governance. The concept involves the vertical transfer of responsibilities and resources from central to local government, as well as the development of horizontal networks between local governments and local non-state actors. Local democratic governance needs efficient and effective national governance to provide direction, shape practices and regulate relationships.

Where successful, decentralization can contribute to more accessible, legitimate and accountable government; better service delivery; more balanced and sustainable village development; speedier resolution of local disputes; and greater empowerment of the most vulnerable and disadvantaged groups. Local government can also offer a training ground for political leadership and management of public affairs.

Building institutions of democratic governance is not easy, however, and decentralizing already weak institutions solves few problems. In countries wheredecentralization has been initiated, the devolution of responsibility has not always been accompanied by devolution of authority or the allocation of sufficient human and budgetary resources to provide the needed services to rural areas, particularly to remote, scattered localities. Decentralization without the necessary capacity building, both among local authorities and local stakeholders, may further weaken a government's ability to carry out its functions. Nor does decentralization solve the problem of capture of governmental processes by powerful elites, who in rural areas, may own or control access to land, water and other productive resources on which the wider population depends.

Territorial Approaches

Nonetheless, as globalization advances, so does localization. Territorial approaches to development, sometimes referred to as local economic development (LED), have been adopted by many governments and are increasingly supported by a growing number of international organizations. In part, they have emerged in response to the disappointing results obtained from traditional top-down, supply-side development strategies. The concentration of decision-making in urban areas, particularly the capital, the non-inclusion of representative rural organizations in policy-making processes and the sheer physical distance – not to mention the economic and social differences – that separates urban decision-makers from the rural milieu have often skewed national policies, programmes and resource allocations to the detriment of rural areas.

Territorial-based strategies present a number of potential social and economic benefits, in that they allow local people and institutions to adopt a more proactive stance with regard to their own future. The active involvement of a variety of stakeholders not only helps to develop a stronger local civil society, but can also contribute to making local institutions more transparent and accountable. LED calls for innovative thinking to work out development strategies based on the distinct economic and social assets of the region, province, municipality or district concerned. The development plans that result commonly focus on such areas as the improvement of local enterprise competitiveness and exports, the stimulation of entrepreneurship, the promotion of micro-enterprises, SMEs and cooperatives, the attraction of inward investment, the improvement of skills and knowledge, the reduction of social exclusion, and the improvement of infrastructure.

The basic elements which define LED initiatives include the participation of local actors, a proactive attitude of local government, the existence of local leadership teams, public–private cooperation, and coordination among institutions for local economic development. Local authorities have become key partners in such processes.

Nonetheless, local and regional governments generally face a difficult development environment. Lack of a supportive national policy framework, funding and government capacity can limit the ability of sub-national institutions to develop and implement successful strategies, especially in those areas where capacity constraints are greatest. Notwithstanding the trend towards decentralization which can give impetus to territorial approaches, the nation State's economic, political, and legal systems remain in most cases the framework in which economic and social activities at the local level take place. For example, in countries with adverse macroeconomic framework conditions, the amount of growth and employment that can be generated through territorial development approaches is limited. The link between national and local or regional policies and the funding to implement these policies are crucial for any successful territorial development strategy.

The increasing reliance on territorial strategies highlights the need for good governance at all governmental levels. Whereas traditional development strategies have relied mostly on national systems and on the capabilities of central government officials, today the design and implementation of development strategies are no longer a purely national concern. The success of territorial strategies depends, to a large degree, on the existence of appropriate local and regional institutional systems and on the availability of the necessary frameworks and skill levels at all government levels.

Cost of Poor Governance

Globalization lays bare poor governance, exposing institutional weaknesses, and the sometimes tenuous control that some governments exercise in their national territory. Poverty and poor governance raise the likelihood that social unrest and armed conflict will affect a country. Indeed, it has been estimated that almost 40 per cent of the States ranked as low on the Human Development Index were affected by armed conflict during the ten-year period 1997–2006 whereas less than 2 per cent of those rated as high human development States were so affected.

Armed civil conflict disproportionately affects those living in rural areas, where people live from the land, competition for natural resources is intense and the capacity for governance can be weak. In some cases, the near-absence of the State is exploited by major economic players – plantations, logging and mining companies – as well as guerrilla and paramilitary groups, drugs and weapons dealers, and rival political or ethnic interests. In some, national armies and security forces contribute to the general lawlessness by engaging in rape, pillage and extrajudicial killings, while armed insurgents prey on rural populations and forcefully induct children into their ranks. In a number of countries, assassinations, abductions, torture, intimidation, looting and burning of homes and crops, and threats of further violence have led to forced displacement of the rural civilian population, forced land sales or abandonment of land. Violence against trade union organizers and representatives of rural workers is exercised with impunity.

Armed conflict has been called one of the four traps that keep the world's poorest countries poor and keep the world's "bottom billion" confined to a life of poverty in stagnant or shrinking economies. The average annual cost of conflict in Africa, for example, has been estimated at 15 per cent of GDP, or roughly one-and-a-half times the average African spending on health and education combined, a tremendous economic burden with dramatic social consequences. Conflict-ridden countries in that region have 50 per cent more infant deaths, 15 per cent more undernourished people, life expectancy reduced by five years, 20 per cent more adult illiteracy, two and a half times fewer doctors per patient and 12.4 per cent less food per person compared to their regional neighbours living in peace.

It may be in the breach that the key principles of governance are the most keenly recognized. For example, the Comprehensive Peace Agreement concluded between the Government of Nepal and the Communist Party of Nepal (Maoist) in 2006 after ten years of civil strife refers in its preamble to "the popular mandate in favour of democracy, peace and progress" and "commitments to a competitive, multiparty democratic system, civil liberties, fundamental rights, human rights, complete press freedom and all other democratic norms and values including the concept of the rule of law". Among the policy areas cited are those to establish the rights of all citizens to education, health, shelter, employment and food security, as well as those to provide land and socio-economic security to communities such as landless squatters, bonded labourers, tillers, bonded domestics, bonded cattle-tenders and other such groups.

Similarly, the Agreement on Social and Economic Aspects and the Agrarian Situation, which in 1996 put an end to 36 years of civil war in Guatemala, spelled out the principles of democratization and participatory development, notably consensus-building and participation at the local level, and of social development, relating to education and training, health, social security, housing and work. It described in some length the "essential and unavoidable" need to solve the problems of agrarian reform and rural development "in order to address the situation of the majority population, which live in rural areas and is most affected by poverty, extreme poverty, injustice and the weakness of State institutions". The Agreement affirmed the State's fundamental and vital role "as the guide for national development, as a legislator, as a source of public investment and provider of services and as a promoter of social cooperation and conflict resolution". It was seen as essential that the State "increase and refocus its efforts and its resources towards rural areas" and that it "promote agrarian modernization in a sustained manner, in the direction of greater justice and greater efficiency".

Such agreements between former adversaries affirm common principles of governance on which peace and social justice can be built. These key principles are given life, however, through processes of empowerment and the strengthening of institutions for voice and representation. The lessons drawn by those who have endured the bitter experience of civil conflict can offer insights into the steps needed to build more responsive institutions and participatory processes of governance, that contribute to addressing national development challenges in an integrated, rather than piecemeal manner.

Building New Partnerships

Since decent work deficits are often traceable to good governance deficits, it is important that the interests of rural populations are represented in the formulation and implementation of laws, policies and programmes that affect them. Increasing the participation of small- and medium-business operators, rural workers and small farmers in these processes, and strengthening the social partner organizations that represent them contribute to good governance.

Good governance requires representation and participation at several levels and in many forums in order to achieve a degree of policy coherence and communication between one level and another. National organizations of employers and workers need to ensure that their rural affiliates are included in the national-level tripartite consultation and dialogue processes that focus on rural issues and that the results of policy discussions are disseminated to their local affiliates. Central organizations are also well placed to militate for the placement of issues of concern on the national policy agenda, either separately or as part of a more general discussion of nationwide interest, for example, by ensuring that rural employment issues figure within any national debate on employment policy. One of the key challenges for the social partners is to increase their outreach and engagement in rural areas, as this can involve building new partnerships and alliances both at national and local levels.

There are numerous examples of the social partners working together with civil society institutions and organizations, such as cooperatives, economic producer organizations, and other community-based rural organizations that share the same values and objectives and pursue them in a constructive manner. Collaboration proceeds most smoothly when all parties respect the roles and responsibilities of others, particularly concerning questions of representation.

One of the key questions that agricultural trade unions have addressed over the past 15years, especially in the light of the impacts of globalization and structural adjustment policies, has been how to strengthen relationships between trade unions representing waged workers and small farmers' organizations. Building networks and alliances is considered key to ensuring the participation of these groups and organizations in national decision-making processes, and in achieving sustainable agriculture and rural development. Whilst there are many issues of common concern around which the two types of groups can unite, the relationships and interaction between them can also pose dilemmas, for example, when small farmers are employers or, in the process of land reform, when their interests may differ and livelihoods are at stake.

To build links and alliances between trade unions and small farmers' organizations, the IUF started a Land and Freedom Project in 1998 to ensure the common defence of legal rights, improved access to land, and greater influence on local, national, regional and international policies, and to counter the concentration of power of multinational enterprises in the agricultural sector. It has developed models to help trade unions and small farmers to work more closely together, and to adapt trade union structures, rules and training programmes with a view to recruiting small farmers as members.

Mobilization at the grassroots level has led to the emergence of a wide variety of community-based organizations in rural areas, which are unlike traditional workplace-based trade unions. In some cases, trade unions have chosen to work alongside or in close collaboration with such local organizations when their primary aim is to promote and defend workers' rights and this has led to more broad-based organizations in rural areas. For example, the Confederation of Mexican Workers (CTM) has broadened its base by bringing together within its purview a wide range of organizations, such as cooperatives, production associations, social interest enterprises, agricultural credit associations, agrarian communities and small businesses.

Peasant organizations – including national peasant organizations and coalitions, peasant women's organizations, landless peoples' movements, family-farm coalitions, and agricultural labour associations – can also play an important role in rural areas. Such organizations often work on issues such as gender equality and social justice in fair economic relations; the preservation of land, water, seeds and other natural resources; food sovereignty; and sustainable agricultural production by small- and medium-sized producers. Many advocate a model of peasant or family-farm agriculture based on sustainable production with local resources and in harmony with local culture and traditions.

Confederaçäo Nacional dos Trabalhadores na Agricultura (CONTAG) in Brazil is the world's largest national organization representing both agricultural wage earners and self-employed farmers. CONTAG has some 9 million members, approximately 3 million waged workers and 6 million smallholders. Such unions usually have separate organizational and political structures for dealing with the dual types of membership. Sometimes the relationship between the two types of members is not easy, especially where small farmer members, who form the base of CONTAG, also employ waged labour. CONTAG recognizes the need to discuss and, to the extent possible, reconcile the different realities and needs of the two groups. With regard to wages, for example, when small farmer members hire in labour during planting or harvesting, the waged worker is covered by the collective agreement established for the particular crop in that locality or state. In the event that there is no collective agreement, the reference wage should not be lower than the national minimum wage.

The General Agricultural Workers' Union (GAWU) in Ghana was one of the first agricultural unions to address the problem of the decline in union membership in rural areas by establishing partnerships with other community-based organizations working locally. Its strategy was to open its membership to all rural workers – both wage earners and the self-employed – so as to extend the role of trade unions beyond the worker–employer relationship. It also pursued broader goals such as agrarian reform and rural development. GAWU has played a rural development role through different interventions, such as support services targeted at the self-employed, group enterprise promotion, transfer of improved technology and techniques, economic support services and social and community development activities. GAWU has also worked to sensitize local religious leaders and teachers on rural employment issues at the local level. For example, in 2004, GAWU co-sponsored with the ILO a workshop on the elimination of hazardous child labour in agriculture, which brought together men and women farmers from eight of the country's ten regions. Many of them were elected representatives or councillors in local assemblies, and some were chiefs.

Employers' organizations can also contribute to rural employment promotion by linking up strategically with farmers' unions, cooperative organizations and other member-based organizations in rural areas. In countries where agricultural commodity production is a major sector of the economy, national employers' organizations often have affiliated crop associations that engage in sector-wide bargaining, reaching agreements with agricultural trade unions on the terms and conditions of employment that can affect wide swathes of the rural workforce. The Federation of Kenya Employers, for example, acts as a secretariat to a number of trade associations, including the Sisal Growers and Employers' Association, the Agricultural Employers' Association and the Kenya Coffee Growers' and Employers' Association and has the Kenya Tea Growers' Association as one of their affiliates. Employers' organizations can improve economic governance through the strengthening of the voice of local entrepreneurs and by building business linkages to the larger economy.

In Ghana, the Ghana Employers' Association developed, with ILO support, a training manual for strengthening small business associations. This led to a more effective participation of rural entrepreneurs in statutory local government bodies set up to stimulate and coordinate local economic development programmes in rural areas.

In Viet Nam, the Chamber of Commerce and Industry has assisted a large cashew farmers' organization to provide members with market price information updated through radio bulletins. The Chamber also introduced potential business partners to their provincial counterparts (such as the Fair Trade Organization) in order to establish sustainable market linkages.

Representative organizations can also help members through bulk buying, sharing of facilities, training, credit access or marketing, as in the case of the Federation of Agricultural Associations in Armenia, whose aim is "to support the development of member agricultural organizations and assist them to solve their common legal, managerial, technical and social problems". Local member associations and cooperatives provide representation and advocacy for their members and function to support and defend their members' common interests in legal, business and agricultural matters. At the national level, the Federation provides a platform to advocate on behalf of its member organizations with other organizations, including judicial bodies and government.

Cooperatives in many countries are significant employers, particularly in rural areas. They provide jobs in agriculture – production, processing, marketing and sales – as well as in other sectors, such as financial services, health, electricity and water, housing and tourism to name only a few. Cooperatives tend to be stable employers, especially in rural areas, as their members live in the community where the cooperative is located. The International Cooperative Alliance has estimated that cooperatives contribute to the livelihoods of some 750 million members and their families. Cooperatives are also direct providers of jobs and stimulate further employment by providing goods and services that enable other enterprises to thrive and thus keep money circulating within the community. Indeed, the decisions taken by cooperatives tend to balance the need for profitability with the needs of their members and the wider interests of the community. As a result, cooperatives often respond to community development opportunities and challenges. For example, where savings and credit cooperatives exist in rural communities, they tend to be the sole provider of secure financial services and an important conduit for remittances from migrants. So, too, with rural electricity cooperatives or biofuel cooperatives, that supply energy to local communities and family farms, where commercial companies might find it too costly or insufficiently profitable to invest.

Aside from economic benefits, cooperatives can empower individuals and communities. Often referred to as "schools for democracy", cooperatives offer members the opportunity to more fully develop their knowledge of economic issues and democratic procedures and to hone their leadership and negotiation skills. Cooperative values and principles are especially important in the rural context – self-help, self-responsibility, democracy, equality, equity and solidarity, and the ethical values of honesty, openness, social responsibility and the principle of caring for their members and their communities.

Most agricultural production is in the hands of family-owned farms, making agriculture a highly fragmented economic sector. One of the fundamental objectives of an economic producer organization (EPO) is to group farms so that agricultural producers are able to enter or enhance their position in the market, for example by improving access to credit, purchase of inputs, reduction of production costs, logistics, marketing, merchandizing, processing, or distribution. The creation of an EPO is only possible when farmers have gone beyond subsistence farming and have the capacity to develop a medium- or long-term vision for their collective project, based on values such as solidarity. Providing technical support to farmers – in the form of training, technical advice, sanitary controls, or information exchange – is one of the primary tasks of an EPO, although not all EPOs have either the interest or capacity to provide a wide range of services to their members.

According to the International Federation of Agricultural Producers, EPOs can only appear and expand where the rule of law allows for the emergence of civil society organizations, where the freedom to do business is recognized and where economic regulation, security and justice mechanisms are in place. Because they are not enterprises "like any other", EPOs must have the benefit of specific legal measures as well as legal recognition and status in order to operate. In addition, a satisfactory level of general services is needed in rural areas for EPOs to function successfully, since agricultural producers rely on access to water and energy for their storage and processing operations and communication channels between production zones and consumer catchment areas in order to market their goods. Given the important role EPOs can play in the rural economy, their representation and participation in governance bodies on agriculture and rural development are considered vital.

References

Casale G. et al. . (2006), *Re-engineering labour administration to promote decent work,* Geneva, ILO.

DFID. (2006), *Making governance work for the poor*, p. 20; USAID: Democracy and Governance: A Conceptual Framework.

ILO. (2002), *Conclusions concerning decent work and the informal economy*, International Labour Conference, 90th Session, Geneva.

ODI. (2007), *Governance assessment: Overview of governance assessment frameworks and results from the 2006 World Governance Assessment*, report from ODI Learning Workshop.

Bibliography

Ahluwalia, M. S.. "Rural Poverty and Agricultural Performances in India" *Journal of Development Studies,* Vol. 14, No. 3, April.

Anriquez G. & Stloukal L. (2008). *Rural Population change in developing countries: nlessons for Policymaking.* Rome. FAO

Barrientos A. and Lloyd-Sherlock P. : *Non-contributory pensions and poverty prevention – A comparative study of Brazil and South Africa,* IDPM and HelpAge International: 19.

Basant, R., B. L. Kumar and R. Parthasarathy. (edited). *Non-Agricultural Employment in Rural India: The Case of Gujarat,* Rawat Publications, Jaipur, India.

Black, R., (2004) 'Migration and pro-poor policy in Africa', Development Research Centre on Migration, Globalisation and Poverty, University of Sussex, Working Paper C6, 28 p.

Brue, Mcconnel, (2007) *Essentials of Economics,* Tata McGraw Hill Publishing Company, New Delhi.

Casale G. et al. . (2006), *Re-engineering labour administration to promote decent work,* Geneva, ILO.

Chadha, G.K. (2001). "Impact of Economic Reforms on Rural Employment: No Smooth Sailing Anticipated." *Indian Jl. of Agricultural Economics, V*ol. 56, No.3, pp. 491-97.

David Macarov, (2003). *What the Market Does to the People: Privatisation, Globalization and Poverty,* Clarity Press Inc. Atlanta and ZED Books, London.

Deepak Nayar (Ed.) 2002. *Governing Globalization: Issues and Institutions,* Oxford University Press, New Delhi.

Deshingkar, P., (2004) 'Understanding the Implications of Migration for Pro-poor Agricultural Growth' Paper prepared for the DAC POVNET Agriculture Task Group Meeting, Helsinki, 17 – 18 June.

DFID. (2006), *Making governance work for the poor,* p. 20; USAID: Democracy and Governance: A Conceptual Framework.

Edward J Blakely & Ted K Bradshaw, (2003). P*lanning Local Economic Development: Theory and Practice,* Vistaar Publications, New Delhi.

European Commission, (2008).*Report on the EU contribution to the promotion of decent work in the world,* Staff working paper.

Foster A.D and Rosenzweig M.R. (2004). "Agricultural productivity growth, rural economic diversity and, economic reforms: India 1970–2000", in *Economic Development and Cultural Change,* Vol. 52, No. 3.

García M. and Paiewonsky A. (2006). *Gender, Migration, Remittances and Development.* Santo Domingo.INSTRAW.

Guest, P., (2003) 'Bridging the gap: internal migration in Asia' Paper prepared for the Conference on African Migration in Comparative Perspective, Johannesburg, South Africa, 4-7 June.

Hirschman, Albert O. (1958). *The Strategy of Economic Development*, Yale University Press, New Haven, Connecticut.

Hurst P. et al. (2005). *Agricultural workers and their contribution to sustainable agriculture and rural development* (FAO–ILO–IUF).

IFAD and FAO. (2008). *International migration, remittances and rural development.* Rome.

ILO, (2009).*Protecting people, promoting jobs: A survey of country employment and social protection policy responses to the global economic crisis*, Report to the G20 Leaders' Summit, Pittsburgh.

____. (2002), Conclusions concerning decent work and the informal economy, International Labour Conference, 90th Session, Geneva.

____: (2005). "Why agriculture still matters" in *World Employment Report 2004–05*, Ch. 3. Geneva.

International Labour Office (2004) 'Towards a fair deal for migrant workers in the global economy', International Labour Conference, 92nd Session, Geneva.

Jagdish Bhagwati, (2004). *In Defence of Globalization*, Oxford University Press, New Delhi.

Jha, B.. Rural Non-farm Employment in India, A coordinated and consolidated unpublished report, submitted to Ministry of Agriculture, GOI, New Delhi.

Katar Singh, (2009). *Rural Development: Principles, Policies and Management,* (3rd Edition) Sage Publications, New Delhi.

Lanjouw J. and Lanjouw P. (2001). "The rural non-farm sector: Issues and evidence from developing countries", in *Agricultural Economics*, Vol. 26, No. 1.

Meenakshisundaram S S, (1994). *Decentralization in Developing Countries,* Concept Publishing Company, New Delhi

Mellor, J. W. *The New Economics of Growth – A Strategy for India and the Developing World,* A Twentieth Century Fund Study, Ithaca : Cornell University Press.

____. and Lele U. (1973). "Growth linkages of the new food grain technologies", in *Indian Journal of Agricultural Economics*, Vol. 28, No. 1, pp. 35–55.

Mizunoya S. et al. (2006). "Costing of basic social protection benefits for selected Asian countries: First results of a modelling exercise" in *Issues in Social Protection*: Discussion Paper 17, Social Security Department, Geneva, ILO.

ODI. (2007), *Governance assessment: Overview of governance assessment frameworks and results from the 2006 World Governance Assessment*, report from ODI Learning Workshop.

OECD DAC, (2009).*The Role of Employment and Social Protection: Making Economic Growth More Pro-Poor*, Policy Statement of High-Level DAC meeting.

Pal K. et al. (2006). "Can low income countries afford basic social protection? First results of a modelling exercise" in *Issues in Social Protection*: Discussion Paper 13, Social Security Department, Geneva, ILO.

Panda B. et al.(2007). *Some issues in rural labor markets,* Rome, FAO, mimeo.

Papola, T. S. (2007).*Employment in the development agenda: Economic and social policies,* International Institute for Labour Studies.

Perroux, Francois (1950), "Economic Space: Theory and Applications," *Quarterly Journal of Economics* 64: 89-104

Porter, Michael E. (2000). "Location, Competition, and Economic Development: Local Clusters in a Global Economy," *Economic Development Quarterly*, 14(1): 15-34.

Reardon, Thomas, Kostas G. Stamoulis and Prabhu Pingali (2007), "Rural Nonfarm Employment in Developing Countries in the Era of Globalization", *Agricultural Economics.*

Rémi Bazillier, 'Core Labour Standards and Development: Impact on Long-Term Income', *World Development* 36(1), 17-38.

Saith, A. (1991). "Development Strategies and the Rural Poor", *Journal of Peasant Studies* 17(2): 171-243.

Sen, Abhijit (2003). "Globalisation Growth and Inequality in South Asia- The Evidence from Rural India", in Jayati Ghosh and C. P. Chandrasekhar (eds), *Work and Well being in the Age of Finance*, New Delhi : Tulika Books.

Shah, Mihir (2004). "National Rural Employment Guarantee Act: A Historic Opportunity", *Economic and Political Weekly*, Vol. 39, No.49 (December 11): 5287-5290.

Sjoblom D. and Farrington J. (2007). "The India National Rural Employment Guarantee Act in relation to Agricultural Growth and Social Protection", in *ODI Social Protection Project Briefing Note 1.* London, Overseas Development Institute.

Stan Burkey, (1993). People First: *A Guide to Self-reliant, Participatory Rural Development*, ZED Books, London & New York.

Stuart Bell and Steve Gibbons, (2007).*Decent Work: Implications for DFID and for the Labour Standards and Poverty Reduction Forum.*

Tolstokorova, A. (2009). Multiple Marginalities: Gender dimension of rural poverty, unemployment and labour migration in Ukraine. Paper presented at the FAO-IFAD-ILO Workshop op.cit. Rome.

Uma Rani and Jeemol Unni (2004). "Unorganised and Organised Manufacturing in India-Potential for Employment Generating Growth" *Economic and Political Weekly*, Vol. 49, (October 9): 4568-4580.

UN DESA. (2008). *Rural Women in a Changing World: Opportunities and Challenges,* Division for the Advancement of Women, October, pp. 20-23.

UNDP. (2009). *The National Rural Employment Guarantee Act (NREGA) Design, Process and Impact,* Nreganet Series from UNDP, New Delhi.

____. (2005). *The Potential Role of Remittances in Achieving the Millennium Development Goals – An Exploration.* Background Note, Roundtable on Remittances and the MDGs, September. New York.

Vyas, V. S. and G. Mathai "Farm and Non-Farm Employment in Rural Areas: A Perspective for Planning" *Economic and Political Weekly*, Vol.13, No. 6 and 7, (February annual number): 333-347.

World Bank (1997), *Rural Development: From Vision to Action*, ESD Studies and Monographs Series. Washington DC.

____, (2007). *More and better investment in agriculture, World Development Report 2008 Policy Brief,* Washington, DC.

Index